Jewish Science Fiction and Fantasy through 1945

Jewish Science Fiction and Fantasy

Series Editor: Valerie Estelle Frankel

Jewish science fiction is a monumental literary genre worldwide, with hundreds of novels and short stories along with an enormous canon of films, plays, television shows, and graphic novels. It's also strikingly popular. Not only have works of this category just won the Hugo and World Fantasy Award while dominating bestseller lists, but talks on the subject are standing room only. The Own Voices movement has led to a renaissance of Jewish fantasy, even as its authors create imaginary worlds reflecting their unique cultures. This series seeks subtopics of exploration within the massive canon, defining aspects of Jewish genre fiction and its unique qualities. It features both monographs and anthologies focused on trends, tropes, individual authors, beloved franchises, and so on. Scholars of all disciplines are welcome, especially those in Jewish Studies, Literature, and Media Studies, while interdisciplinary and international perspectives are particularly encouraged.

Title in the Series

Jewish Science Fiction and Fantasy through 1945: Immigrants in the Golden Age,
   Valerie Estelle Frankel

Jewish Science Fiction and Fantasy through 1945

Immigrants in the Golden Age

Valerie Estelle Frankel

LEXINGTON BOOKS
Lanham • Boulder • New York • London

Published by Lexington Books
An imprint of The Rowman & Littlefield Publishing Group, Inc.
4501 Forbes Boulevard, Suite 200, Lanham, Maryland 20706
www.rowman.com

6 Tinworth Street, London SE11 5AL, United Kingdom

British Library Cataloguing in Publication Information Available

Library of Congress Cataloging-in-Publication Data

Names: Frankel, Valerie Estelle, 1980- author.
Title: Jewish science fiction and fantasy through 1945 : immigrants in the golden age / Valerie Estelle Frankel.
Description: Lanham : Lexington Books, 2021. | Series: Jewish science fiction and fantasy | Includes bibliographical references and index.
Identifiers: LCCN 2021014951 (print) | LCCN 2021014952 (ebook) | ISBN 9781793637123 (cloth) | ISBN 9781793637130 (epub)
Subjects: LCSH: Science fiction—History and criticism. | Science fiction—Religious aspects—Judaism. | Science fiction—Jewish authors. | Fantasy fiction—Jewish authors. | Jews—Fiction.
Classification: LCC PN3433.8 .F73 2021 (print) | LCC PN3433.8 (ebook) | DDC 808.83/98924—dc23
LC record available at https://lccn.loc.gov/2021014951
LC ebook record available at https://lccn.loc.gov/2021014952

To my brother Kevin and sister-in-law Tai, keeping the Jewish spirit alive with all they do for the world and with their precious new baby Elliot Avishai.

Contents

Introduction   ix

1 Roots of Fantasy: The Monsters of Jewish Folklore   1

2 Speculative Fiction in the New World   13

3 The Golden Age: American Science Fiction Begins   39

4 Stereotypes Proliferate: A Darkening Western Europe   61

5 Eastern Europe's Social Science Fiction   89

6 Kafka's Great Legacy   117

7 The Old-New Land: From Zionism to Israeli Literature   135

8 Fighting Hitler Onscreen: Marxes, Stooges, and More   149

9 More Golden Ages: Superman, Captain America, Dr. Seuss   167

Conclusion   189

Works Cited   191

Index   209

About the Author   217

Introduction

Science has always been linked with Judaism. In the Bible, God calls on Abraham to "Look now toward heaven, and count the stars, if thou be able to count them" (Gen. 15:5). As God ties the Jewish people's survival to the heavens, he launches a historic fascination with astronomy. In fact, a Stonehenge-like megalithic circle and observatory built in 3000 BCE at Rujm-el-Hiri in the Golan may have inspired the Biblical legends of giants (Neman 2012, 32).

Since the Babylonian captivity (597–538 BC), the Jews showed an interest in astronomy, connecting especially to synchronizing their calendars. As science spread through the Byzantine Empire under Persian then Islamic rule, Jewish contribution swelled in four areas: medicine; geography and cosmology; measuring instruments, cartography, and navigation; and translation of scientific works.

The first important center for medieval Jewish scientific activity was eighth- and ninth-century Baghdad. However, it was in Muslim Spain that Jewish science prospered. Jews translated books from Arabic to European languages and soon added Jewish texts. The "Toledo Tables" were compiled by twelve Jewish astronomers led by the Cordovan Arab astronomer Ibn Arzarkali ("Azarchel"). Astronomers like Abraham bar Hiyya of Barcelona and his student, Abraham Ibn Ezra, wrote several groundbreaking mathematics texts. Rambam, meanwhile, was the first to separate the pure science of astronomy from the superstitions of astrology, setting up today's scientific approach. Finally, Moses de León wrote the Zohar in thirteenth-century Spain, which anticipates Copernicus by stating that "the whole earth spins in a circle like a ball; the one part is up when the other part is down; the one part is light when the other is dark; it is day in the one part and night in the other" (quoted in Neman 2012, 32).

Jewish science tended to be motivated by a search to know God, rather than as an end unto itself. Most scientific scholars were also Bible experts. For instance, one of the most celebrated medieval Jewish scientists, Gersonides, was widely known for his Biblical commentaries, Talmudic works, and liturgical compositions but also contributed astronomical models, tables for solar and lunar motion, and theories concerning the *camera obscura*, and improved models for astronomical instruments including the astrolabe and the Jacob Staff.

The flip side of science was irrationality. The Talmud tells stories of golems, wonder-rabbis, demons, and curse breakers. Even as medieval European Jews pursued medicine, they also hung evil eye charms to ward Lilith off their babies. In the latter half of the sixteenth century, after the massacre of half the Jews in the Ukraine, superstition and kabbalistic fervor swept through the communities. The Baal Shem Tov and Shabbtai Zvi each promised enlightenment and redemption, gaining masses of ecstatic followers—the former founded Hassidism, while the latter proved a false messiah when he converted to Islam to save his life. Poverty and cruelty tormented the Jews of Europe, and in despair, they spread tales of demons and curses as well as the immanent Messiah. As Saul B. Troen (1994) explains in his dissertation on this strange balance, speculative fiction emerged in between these beliefs:

> Jewish mythology and folklore are replete with spiritual creatures, succubi, ghosts, demons, dybbuks and golems. Science fiction is a mirror image of the world of the supernatural, perhaps in a clarified, rationalized context. Jewish writers of fiction adapt the traditional historically Judaic themes, using supernatural creatures and the games they play with human souls, to teach important lessons in religious faith and the enduring nature of reality no matter in what clothing or guise this reality may be wrapped. (9)

While the Jewish roots of learning and folklore are significant, this history must surge forward to the Haskalah, or Jewish Enlightenment of 1770–1890 Europe. Science fiction as a formal genre dates to this period, connected with the Scientific Revolution.

Many call Mary Shelley's *Frankenstein* (1818) the first science fiction novel—in itself believed to have been influenced by Jewish folklore of the golem (Bertman 46-47). In the genre's early days, gothic novels, ghost stories, and other "weird fiction" developed, as did adventures on airships and journeys to other planets. One must give enormous credit to Jules Verne (1828–1905). At the same time, a nod must go to his publisher, Pierre-Jules Hetzel, who "discovered" Verne in 1860, helped him tidy *20 Thousand Leagues under the Sea* for publication, coached him, and helped publicize the provincial dreamy writer. From the first, science fiction has been aided by Jewish thought.

In Western Europe, much of the literature, like the culture, was casually antisemitic, and top science fiction authors continued the pattern. Some Jews, however, battled the stereotypes through satire and dystopia or telling their own experiences to increase sympathy. Franz Kafka's magical realism explored being cast as a mouse or cockroach in a suddenly hostile Prague while Bruno Schulz wove fanciful stories of his vanishing Jewish Poland. Russian fiction was largely realistic, but Jews there protested their treatment using imagery from the Bible, the supernatural realm, and Greek myth. Fictional golems fought for the people in books and even onscreen, even as many Jews felt themselves transformed into the monsters of fairytales. Even as Europe fell into real-life dystopias, writers protested however they could. Czechoslovakian non-Jews Karl and Josef Čapek satirized fascism in their science fiction while evoking sympathy for their Jewish characters. Meanwhile, the father of modern fantasy, J. R. R. Tolkien, studied Judaism more thoroughly, not only basing his dwarves on the Jews seeking a homeland but incorporating Hebrew and stories from the oral Torah. Certainly, all Jewish cultures of the world have distinct folklore, but it's the European Jews who can be followed through their influence on Western European and American science fiction as a formal genre.

As Europe grew increasingly dangerous, Jews set their sights on the land of promise. Some 250,000 German-speaking Jews came to America between 1825 and 1890. Between 1880 and 1924, a much larger influx of Yiddish speakers arrived from Russia—raising the Jewish population of the United States from 229,000 in small societies to 4,228,000 centered in major cities, especially New York's Lower East Side (Erens 1984, 3). These immigrants filled the garment factories and service industries, working their way up into management positions and sometimes entertainment. Yiddish theater and Jewish comedy boomed. Of course, this mass immigration was met by anti-Semitism, especially during the rising Fascism, scapegoating, and anti-immigrant movements of the twenties and thirties, with immigration quotas created in 1924.

Other Ashkenazim (Eastern European Jews) found additional destinations. Some reached South America, blending their family sagas with local folklore to create a new style of fantasy. Many locals like Jorge Luis Borges wrote about the Jewish experience in turn. On the other side of the globe, Israel was not yet a state, but Jews came to the land, creating a country that was actually based on a utopian fantasy—Theodor Herzl's *Altneuland* (Old New Land) of 1902. European immigrants like S. Y. Agnon wrote gothic stories immersed in folklore, even as they strove to create a new culture—one of tough, independent farmers who evolved a new kind of magical realism. Adventure pulps and Tarzan stories spread too, as the locals shaped themselves to be pioneers like their heroes.

In America, pulps likewise surged in the 1910s and 1920s. In 1926, Hugo Gernsback, a Jew, introduced America to science fiction short stories through his magazine, *Amazing Stories*. Many competitors followed, with Jewish writers contributing stories as well as forming fan clubs and early conventions. The golden age of science fiction was born, firmly launching the genre in America. This was also the golden age of comic book superheroes: Superman, Batman, Captain America, Green Lantern, The Spirit—all created by Jews and channeling some portion of the Jewish sensibility. In fact, science fiction magazines, comic books and the new film industry were uniquely willing to hire Jews, unlike many established trades. In this era, science fiction films were rare, and overtly Jewish characters even rarer, but the Marx Brothers, Three Stooges, and Fleisher Studios excelled at satirizing new immigrants, sometimes through fantasy and dystopia. A final memorable genre of the time is the picture book, from *Curious George*, written by Jewish French refugees, to Dr. Seuss's anti-Fascism fantasies.

While the Allies fought and finally triumphed over the Nazis, European Jewish culture—the Yiddish newspapers, publishing houses, and rising film industry—were wiped out. Survivors in the Soviet Union were barred from their religion, and the Sephardic cultures of Europe were destroyed as well—though some Middle Eastern communities survived a short time longer. The largest Jewish culture was now in America.

The history of Jewish science fiction and fantasy (that written by Jews and sometimes that written about Jews in this formative time of the genre) must conclude here, as this first era has created an already full-length book. More are planned, exploring post-Holocaust speculative fiction and then later multicultural eras through the present day, as well as tangential subjects in a wide series on the topic. This book considers the folkloric roots of Jewish fantasy, and then centers on the popular authors of the Enlightenment through the Golden Age—occasionally drifting postwar in order to keep an author's works together if the author mostly established himself earlier. Quite a spectrum of works and depictions appear—some quintessentially Jewish creators like Kafka and the Marx Brothers avoided specifying that their characters were Jewish, while some non-Jewish creators like Borges and Dr. Seuss were specifically celebrated for their sensitive depiction of Jewish themes. Jewish fiction as a genre was also in early stages at this point, as authors experimented with new forms in order to share their struggle, even as disaster approached.

Chapter 1

Roots of Fantasy

The Monsters of Jewish Folklore

FANTASY'S TRACES IN FOLKLORE

While science fiction and fantasy as formal concepts don't predate the modern era, their elements can be found in the oldest Jewish literature. Dragons are described in Job (26:13) and Isaiah (27:1). Many books on divination mention Saul's excursion into forbidden necromancy but also bibliomancy (Dead Sea Scrolls), shooting arrows (II Kings), and the patterns of oil on water (Sefer Ha Razim). Alternate history stretches back to the apocryphal Book of Judith, which depicts a thought experiment of the Babylonian conquest ending with the people returning to Zion.

Moreover, extraterrestrial visitors in early Christian and Jewish writings are not aliens, but angels. Within this context, the Greco-Roman tradition offers several fantastic voyages into outer space, most famously Lucian's *True History*. Possibly influenced by such sources, Jews wrote first-century spaceflight stories in the *Testament of Abraham, Apocalypse of Abraham, 3 Baruch, The Book of Enoch*, and the *History of the Rechabites* (Charles [1913] 2004). In all of these, God breaks natural law (thus asserting divine power), lifts the heroes into the heavens, and takes them on mystical journeys through the cosmos while the angels answer deep philosophical questions. As such, they were highly speculative fiction emphasizing the philosophical and religious over plausibility.

Fantastical beliefs were an active part of the religion. The *midrashim* (folklore filling in the gaps between Bible stories) told of demons, angels, and the supernatural. There were also *mashal* (parables and fables), rabbinic legends of heroism and exorcism, and medieval apocalyptic literature such as *Sefer Zerubbabel*. A famous work is Abraham ibn Ezra's twelfth-century *Ḥai ben Mekiẓ*, echoing the first-century texts and describing a journey to the other

1

planets to meet their inhabitants. More earth-based travelogues, inspired by stories of Jews in Africa, India, and eastern lands, reported discovering the ten biblical Lost Tribes surrounded by a magical river that refused to flow on Shabbat.

Medieval Jews wrote spellbooks and attempted magic—though only through invoking God and his angels rather than crossing a line into sorcery, which the Bible forbade. Twelfth- to fifteenth-century mystic kabbalists associated magic with the highest level of wisdom and spiritual purity (Horwitz 2016, 301). Rabbinic magic is protective—drawing circles of immunity or raising the dead only to correct a great wrong. In fact, protective spells were used widely for centuries, especially in the amulets that protected newborns from the demoness Lilith. Adult Jews in Biblical, Talmudic, and medieval times were also known to wear amulets, from the Middle Eastern *hamsa* to seals of Solomon to red threads, to, arguably, tefillin. Jews up through today have driven out demons by concealing festive occasions with diversions—shofars, salt, names changed, chickens shaken, bread discarded, and most memorably, the smashed glass at weddings. Modern traditions still insist on not counting people for fear of inviting demons, and of protectively veiling the bride while she walks around the groom in a magic circle. Some Jews still say "*Keynahora!*" (no evil eye), avoid boasting of good fortune, and spit to avert evil.

Lilith exists as a folkloric trope from medieval times, with her story first recorded in *The Alphabet of Ben Sira* (written between 700 and 1000 CE). She is Adam's demonic first wife, similar to a succubus. Two different types of Lilith plots were prevalent: killing infants and seducing men. In the latter, she is thus a projection of the sexist fears and desires of the rabbis who invented the tales and viewed her as the threatening pagan female influence. Her stories spread widely, usually with the heroic rabbi banishing her and thus protecting the community. As introduction to the folklore collection *Lilith's Cave* explains, "These fantasies and nightmares, where danger is often overcome in a supernatural fashion, helped the oppressed Jews to find an outlet for their fears. For it is well known that hearing or reading even the most frightening tales can bring about a catharsis and release from fear" (H. Schwartz 2004a, 1).

"Lilith's Cave," itself a Tunisian folktale, is an early portal fantasy—a story like Oz or Narnia in which the hero travels from the real world to a magical one. In this story, a house in Tunis is rumored to be haunted by demons. In the cellar, where demons are reputed to live, the new owners find gorgeous furniture, including an ornate mirror in a golden frame, which they carry home with them. Of course, the wife takes all the traditional blame here for her greed. Continuing the sexist bent, she gives the mirror to her beautiful, dark-haired daughter, "who glanced at herself in the mirror all the time, and in this way, she was drawn into Lilith's web" (H. Schwartz 2004b, 128).

For this mirror had hung in the den of demons, and a daughter of Lilith had made her home in it. Even though the mirror was removed from its original place, still all mirrors are gateways to Lilith's cave, the cave in which she lived after she left Adam in the Garden of Eden, the cave where she sported with her demon lovers. There she bred armies of demons, who went out into the world, and always returned through mirrors. That it is why it is said that Lilith makes her home in every mirror. (128)

Nine months after this, the mother dies, choking on a feather from the silk pillow she's greedily claimed, but the daughter claims the mirror, which she grows to love as much as herself. The demon enters her and takes over her mind. Now driven by Lilith's desires, she runs around with men, and brings shame upon her father, "for he knew that once her reputation had been ruined, no worthy young man would marry her" (H. Schwartz 2004b, 129). At last, the disgusted father curses his daughter to become a bat, flitting from man to man in the night. With this, the girl is lost. Of course, this story warns against sexuality even as it blames the young woman for external forces.

The most famous of the Eastern European minor spirits is the dybbuk, a ghost who possesses the living. Related is the gilgul, a reincarnated soul. As with other cultures, Jewish tradition also tells of ghosts who return with unfinished business or broken promises to be rectified. Beyond these, folklore compiler Beatrice Silverman Weinreich (1988e) lists additional spirits, like the shretele, the lantekh, and the kapelyushnikl (hat maker).

The kindly shretele may well have been brought along by Jews from Alsace and southern Germany, where an elf with the same name has been popular among non-Jews for centuries, and may also bear some relation to the skrzat, the house elf. . . . The naughty bridge hobgoblin, lantekh, appears to be none other than the French lutin, who was brought to Eastern Europe by Jews in the course of their migration. The teasing kapelyushnikel, who likes to pester horses, on the other hand, is apparently native to Slavic soil and may be an original Eastern European Jewish creation. (326)

Conflating two of these, beloved folklorist Isaac Bashevis Singer (1996) sees the lantuch as the Yiddish house brownie. As Singer's Aunt Yentl tells, "Yes, there is such a spirit as a lantuch. These days people don't believe in such things, but in my time, they knew that everything can't be explained away with reason. . . . A lantuch is an imp, but he's not malicious. He causes no harm. On the contrary, he tries to help the members of the household all he can" (232). After the lantuch in this story accidentally frightens a daughter of the house, he brings her her favorite dessert, "an almond cake warm from the oven" to make amends (233). Singer's adult story "The Lantuch" features a darker spirit that not only protects the household women (perhaps as their lover) but makes them increasingly insular until the house catches fire and they all perish. As Singer's narrator concludes, "If things go well, these imps hide in the cellar or between the stove and the woodshed, but when people loosen their grip, they take the upper hand. Perhaps he wasn't a lantuch but a hobgoblin or a mooncalf" ([1970] 1973, 100).

Shretele stories feature helpful household spirits that make the family's goose fat or brandy perpetually refill itself, usually in return for a gift of food or other kindness. The more dangerous creatures, including a Slavic zmore that drains people's vitality in their sleep, could generally be banished by a miracle-working rabbi or tzaddik (righteous person). Tricky shapeshifting demons are sometimes identified as jesters—letzim or letzonim, who give people a fright but cause no lasting damage in humorous tales. Generic demons also fill the stories, similar to their German counterparts but vulnerable to Jewish prayer and ritual objects. All of these creatures began in fireside tales but migrated to modern short stories and novels.

Of course, there are other Jewish monsters besides demons. The Bible describes Leviathan, the Ziz, the Re'em, the Lilith bird, the Behemoth, and so on, with Talmudic legends about them all. Beyond all these, the most popular Talmudic magical creature is the golem, which has become a hallmark of modern Jewish fantasy.

THE GOLEM

The most centrally Jewish contribution to speculative fiction is the golem, today appearing in numerous fantasy worlds including D&D, Pokémon, and Marvel. The word "golem" occurs once in the Bible with the line "Thine eyes did see mine unformed substance" (Psalm 139:16), referencing the clay that fashioned Adam. Inspired by this concept, golem legends date back to the eleventh century and tell of persecuted Jews building mythical clay people to come to life and protect them.

The golem is not mentioned specifically in *Sefer Yezirah* (The Book of Creation), a tenth-century discourse on cosmology and cosmogony, though it is from here that most of the elements of creating the golem come. The thirteenth-century commentaries by Rabbi Abraham ibn Ezra and Rabbi Yehudah he-Hasid suggest the possibilities, revealed in more detail by Rabbi Eleazar of Worms and Rabbi Abraham Abulafia.

Eleazar of Worms was reputed to have created his golem from virgin soil and reciting the incantation of "the alphabets of the 221 gates" over every single organ individually. One breathes into the figure and infuses a *nefesh*, or motor soul (rather than a *neshama,* spirit) by carving a Hebrew word or inserting a parchment with the divine name under the tongue. It then will perform domestic tasks (Burton 2013, 63). Eleazar inscribed one of God's names, *emet* ("truth") on the forehead and destroyed the creature by erasing the initial letter of *emet*, leaving *met* ("dead"), as Joshua Trachtenberg records in his *Jewish Magic and Superstition* (1939, 85–86). The concept of erasing the silent first letter of the word comes from the thirteenth-century *Sefer ha-Gematri'ot* (Book of Geometry/Writing Knowledge) (Idel 1990, 64).

Talmudic scholars were said to wield magic through the Laws of Creation, an oral collection of symbolic traditions relating to the creation of the universe. There was a deeper symbolism in the power of the devout to transform the world: "The vitality of the story of a tzadik, or holy man, forming a supernaturally strong being from clay represents the continuing tension in Judaism between passivity and action, acceptance and resistance, earthly physical force and cerebral evasion, Esau and Jacob. The legend metonymically symbolizes and emerges from the diasporic persecutions of the Jews, from the destruction of the temple to the real and imagined persecutions of the present" (Rosenberg 2001, 71). Preconditions for working cabbalistic magic were strict: "First, an untrained religious spirit, and this, according to the Judaic tradition, is a requirement which can be fulfilled only by virtue of God's immeasurable grace and by a chosen person who, at the same time, lives his world life in the ways of God." Second, a perfect intellectual disposition with great learning and discernment, third, full understanding of the Torah and Talmud (Urzidil 1980, 65–66).

Rabbi Samuel, father of Judah the Pious, was said to have constructed a homunculus which accompanied him on his travels and served him, but which could not speak. In this tradition, Elijah of Chelm (middle sixteenth century) was reputed to have created a *golem* from clay by means of the *Sefer Yezirah*, with the name of God inscribed upon its forehead. When the creature attained giant size and strength, the rabbi, fearing its destructive potentialities, tore the name from its forehead and it crumbled into dust. In eighteenth-century stories, these legends were transferred to the philosopher and scholar Rabbi Judah Loew (c. 1520–1609). Folklore collected in *Lilith's Cave* sees Rabbi Loew invoking the Jewish patriarchs and praying to understand the cause of a plague—a prayer that is speedily granted. Other legends had Loew entertaining aristocrats by transporting the contents of a palace into his home and conjuring visions that revealed the nobility's guilty secrets (Goldsmith 1981, 32–33). The historical Loew, Chief Rabbi of Prague from 1594 to his death, has a tomb in the Jewish graveyard of Prague widely visited today. Nearby still stands the Old-New Synagogue where, according to legend, his golem sleeps on, awaiting resuscitation.

Of course, the Jews were suffering under pogroms and other mass-murders, explaining why the story was invented and then why it was retold. A physically powerful hero was needed to save the people. Even the fictional version worked as inspiration for listeners. In the retold folklore and longer adaptations, the golem often succeeds, guarding the ghetto from attacks as well as acts of scapegoating.

Austrian author Gustav Meyrink's novel *The Golem* ([1915] 2017) was incredibly popular, read by soldiers on the front lines, who could see a parallel between the mythic character and the wondrous new war technology like tanks and machine guns that could kill entire armies with no compassion or human judgement. Echoing this surge, Yiddish theater embraced the golem legend with musicals and lavish spectacles in a variety of plays, musicals, and operettas.

As non-Jews adapted the folklore, Paul Wegener's 1915 German silent film *The Golem* (the first of three golem films he would make), influenced the creepy Frankenstein movies that followed. "The redeemer was a solidly packed hunk of clay—played by Wegener—who moved his massive frame through town inch by inch, disallowing anyone or anything from getting in his way, his square, stone-faced visage glaring at the Jewish populace he was created to avenge" (Samberg 2000, 144). Though it's slow-paced, the film is a fascinating example of the silent movie. The monster turns increasingly destructive, inviting reprisals. "If you have brought the dead to life through magic, beware of that life," the rabbi is warned. "The lifeless clay will scorn its master and turn to destroy him and all it meets." Joel Samberg in *Reel Jewish: A Century of Jewish Movies* (2000, 145) observes: "There are moments of great visual impact, such as an overhead shot of Jewish men praying, during which their fervor is quite clear, and special effects showing an exodus of people in a way that convincingly portrays their panic." In a twist ending, a curious five-year-old girl pulls off the amulet animating the golem, reverting it to lifelessness just in time.

It should be noted that the prequel, *The Golem: How He Came into the World* (1920) inserts a more antisemitic flavor. The rabbi who creates it is a glory seeker, unable to handle the consequences of his act. Florian, a heroic Christian who transgresses by loving a Jewish woman, dies, in the story's judgement on mixed marriage. He perishes in a Christlike pose, casting him as the martyr and the Jews, suggestively, as his killers. Further, at story's end, the golem menaces a group of blond children (suggesting a Jewish threat against Christians). The blond child who succeeds in destroying the golem is thus an image of the holy warrior saving her people from the Jews. The rabbi orders the golem to save Emperor Rudolph II and his court from a collapsing ceiling. However, his demands that the Emperor repeal his expulsion order makes this a moment of self-interest rather than altruism. Despite the problematic images, overall, the film's emphasis on marginalization functions as a plea for tolerance.

In another interwar adaptation that blended fantasy with social commentary, Russian Jewish writer H. Leivick's poem *The Golem* (1921) follows the traditional story, though this golem actually starts slaughtering the Jews, before the rabbi sorrowfully sends him to eternal sleep. Here, the Maharal laments that in his haste and eagerness for violence, he has defied the Jewish tradition of patience and killed those he sought to save. In addition, the wonder rabbi is forced to drive off the Messiah as his time has not yet come. The poem, with its consideration of the Messiah, individual power, and the responsibilities of creation, made a huge impact in Yiddish literature. Meanwhile, the destructive golem suggests the Russian Revolution "which Leivick feared as much as he desired" (Madison 1968, 357) as well as a Jewish resistance. In 1922, Yiddish writer Israel Joshua Singer reviewed the work and wrote that World War I was a "gigantic global golem . . . that has risen on clay feet and set out on its path, knocking down everything that stands in its way" (quoted in Barzilai 2016, 74). Everyone, he added, was a tiny piece of clay caught up in the unstoppable violent mass. Leivick ended with *The Salvation Comedy—The Golem Dreams*. The golem, revived after centuries, ventures into the wilderness to find the Messiah and unchain him at last. The final war comes, with false messiahs and credulous followers as Leivick stresses that all must choose sides for the world to be reborn.

The golem also influenced seminal non-Jewish works. Many call *Frankenstein* the first science fiction novel, with an artificial man animated through electricity. What's interesting is that it's rooted in the folktale of the golem (Bertman 46–47). "The cabbalists believed that the person with the right qualifications could animate not only golems, but also a human corpse" (Urzidil 1980, 65). Losing control of one's monster is a central theme. The creature's poignant pleas for love and acceptance certainly echoes minorities' struggles through the history of Europe. A further metaphor appears as Adam (which author Mary Shelley envisioned as her creature's name) feels abandoned by his Creator as in the Eden story. Both versions also consider whether there are barriers man is not meant to cross and what the consequences can be when man takes on the power of creation.

Similarly, Czech writer Karel Čapek wrote the play *R.U.R.* (short for *Rostrum's Universal Robots*). In it, an island factory makes artificial people called "robots" in a play on the Czech noun *robota*, meaning "labor." Of course, this play famously introduced the term. "Čapek is said to have retrospectively come to conclusion, after he had finished the play, that he had written a version of the Jewish legend of the golem," explains critic Harry Brod (49).

Much later, author Isaac Asimov built on Čapek's concept. Asimov points out in *The Rest of the Robots* that the golem inspired all these artificial beings (Gunn 1982, 56). In fact, Asimov's laws offered protection from the golems running amok. Today, the concept of the golem—that a righteous man may create artificial life—is still relevant: it's used as a moral basis in philosophical texts when questioning genetic engineering, cloning, and more.

THE DYBBUK

The concept of the soul and rebirth was also heavily tied into Jewish fantasy. "The life of the soul was transformed into part of a complex system of reward and punishment that broke through the bounds of the terrestrial world and became tied to the supernatural world, extending between the poles of holiness and impurity," writes Daniel M. Horwitz in *A Kabalah and Jewish Mysticism Reader* (2016, 303). In this tradition, a dybbuk is an unsatisfied ghost who returns to possess the living. This ghost would take over the victim's body and speak through him or her. Historically, this called for an exorcism, in a practice first documented in the 1540s, as Agnieszka Legutko (2010) explains in "Feminist Dybbuks: Spirit Possession Motif in Post-Second Wave Jewish Women's Fiction":

> The term "dybbuk" comes from the Hebrew *lidbok* to "cling," "cleave," "adhere" and was first used in a Yiddish text from Volhynia in 1680. It refers to a soul of a dead person (usually a sinner) who, having been refused entrance to Gehenna, enters a living body of a person who may or may not be guilty of a slight religious misconduct, thus seeking redemption. The root . . . (daled-bet-kuf) refers to the sexual union between a man and a woman, as is stated in Bereshit, the first book of the Torah: "Al-ken ya'azov-ish et-aviv ve'et imo vedavak be'ishto vehayu levasar echad. A man shall therefore leave his father and mother and be united with/cleave unto his wife, and they shall become one flesh" (Gen 2:24). (Legutko 2010)

Spirit possession was a common myth, affecting everyday practice like the Ashkenazi tradition of not naming a child for a living person: "The desire to bless a child with a richly endowed name was balanced by the fear that the soul of its previous owner would be transported into the body of the infant—a fear which stood in the way of naming children after living parents or after any living persons, and thus robbing them of their soul and their life" (Trachtenberg 1939, 78). This tied into kabbalistic beliefs, which raised the possibility of passageways between the revealed world and the hidden, as they ruminated on transmigration and spirits, demons, and angels. This concept quickly turned on one gender in particular. Trachtenberg (1939, 50–51) explains that women were considered less evolved than men, so demons could more easily inhabit them. Echoing this gender hierarchy, in Yoram

Bilu's analysis of sixty-three literary and non-literary documented dybbuk possession cases, 65 percent of the possessed were women and 92 percent of the possessing spirits were male—there was no record of a female spirit possessing a man (Legutko 2010).

Certainly, medieval beliefs in possession and witchcraft are described by psychologists today as repressed young women acting out in the few ways allowed by their society. Dybbuk possession included symptoms of fainting, experiencing epileptic fits, speaking in tongues, performing seemingly impossible mental or physical feats and exhibiting subsequent amnesia (Dauber 2010, 176). Modern observers, on viewing dybbuk possession, tend to conclude "the possessed are physically ill; they are mentally ill, in a thousand ways, they are poisoned; they are in an altered state induced by drugs; they are taking a culturally sanctioned opportunity to express 'bad' feelings about the family, the church, and sex" (Dauber 211).

However, in medieval culture, demons were the standard diagnosis. "Demons who have taken possession of a human body exercise such complete control over it that the personality and the will of the victim are extinguished. They can be expelled only by the most powerful exorcisms," writes Trachtenberg (1939, 51). The story of "The Dybbuk," retold by Ber Horovitz and collected in Neugroschel's *Yenne Velt: The Great Works of Jewish Fantasy & Occult,* describes a possessed boy whose mother was lax enough to allow a dybbuk to take him over before birth. Once again, the blame goes to the woman. In Singer's "The Dead Fiddler," a teenage girl's increasing neurosis transforms into a dybbuk possession, which can be read as a genuine haunting or as her only possible strike back from her repression. In many dybbuk stories, the storytellers—often male rabbis telling stories of their successful exorcisms—tended to blame the young women for small transgressions that made them spiritually vulnerable. The young women in turn were painted as reveling in immorality as expressed through the dybbuk. The early artistic representations of the possessed women, created mostly by male authors, appear to be a projection of men's darkest fears of female sexuality, which they associated with evil.

S. Ansky (a pseudonym for Russian author Shloyme Zanvl Rappoport) adapted folktales into his 1914 Yiddish play *The Dybbuk*, which became a model for much of the writing that followed. In his "Supernatural Horror in Literature" essay ([1927] 2009), famed author H. P. Lovecraft complimented this play in particular, adding, "Jewish folklore has preserved much of the terror and mystery of the past, and when more thoroughly studied is likely to exert considerable influence on weird fiction."

As the play explains, "There are vagrant souls which, finding neither rest nor harbor, pass into the bodies of the living, in the form of a Dybbuk, until they have attained purity" (Ansky [1926] 1971, 82). However, unlike the shtetl folklore that inspired it, the play emphasizes the possessed woman, making her problematic marriage the center of the story, not the heroic exorcist. When Leah meets Khonen, her intended, they fall in love, but because he is poor, her father forbids the match and arranges a richer husband, Menashe. In the meantime, Khonen dies of despair and poverty. At Leah's wedding, she rips off her veil, shrieking that Menashe is not her husband. In fact, she is possessed by her destined groom, in place of the earthly one. "Ansky, however, reveals the complexity of the encounter between worlds by describing it from the unexpected perspective of soulmates whose loving desire for each other undermines a coerced match—the perspective of a bride and groom denied the opportunity to marry but ultimately joining in death beyond the bounds of time and space," Rachel Elior explains in *Dybbuks and Jewish Women* (2008, 116). The plotline can be read as a woman resisting her arranged earthly marriage in favor of a fantasy love, or as something spiritually deeper: In this moment of early feminism, Leah "challenges the religious, parental, patriarchal and societal authority-wielding power over her. She refuses to become an object of transaction between men—her father and the groom's father—in an arranged marriage" (Legutko 2010).

Taken over by her male lover, she also crosses gender boundaries, suggesting her female form is as discardable as a piece of clothing. In her new hybrid form she takes control of the story, demanding a different relationship with it. It's subversive, assertive. It's also a gateway to freedom: through madness, the spirit transfers the bride and groom to the world of the dead, "thereby liberating the bride from a union she does not want and allowing her to unite with her longed-for mate who entered paradise or engaged in the ecstatic life of *devekut*" (Elior 2008, 116).

The story hints at an additional ghostly presence, as the bride is told to cry at her mother's grave and beseech her spirit to attend the wedding. Much is also made of a grave where a couple were killed in a pogrom moments before they could be wed. The bride, Leah, asserts how this culture affects them all, insisting, "It isn't evil spirits that surround us, but souls of those who died before their time, and come back again to see all that we do and hear all that we say" (77). In this culture of sadness and loss, with pogroms rising in Europe, she's literally and metaphorically haunted.

Reframing this story, the film *Der Dybbuk* was made in Poland in 1937, adapted by Alter Kacyzna and Marek Arenstein and directed by Michael Waszynski (*The Dybbuck*, 1938 in America). Its film location encourages an exploration of the tension of assimilation versus tradition:

> The film's handling of Hasidism is not unsympathetic; Leah and Khonnon first meet over a traditional Shabbat (Sabbath) meal. However, shtetl culture appears unfavorably in scenes highlighting divisions between rich and poor; and in

Der Dibek's closing moments, the figure of the wise but weary tzaddik, who lacks his predecessors' abilities to command the spirits of the dead, suggests an embattled, declining tradition—reflecting the ambivalent attitudes of assimilated Jews like Ansky and Waszynski. (Wright 2010)

As a pre-Holocaust film starring Polish Jews, it remains a monument to a lost culture, as well as the vanished actors. Joel Samberg (2000), author of *Reel Jewish: A Century of Jewish Movies*, writes, "That adds a chilling postscript to the story. If only their own dispirited souls could have sought justice" (146). A new tragic air thus blends with the narrative. The film, in Yiddish with subtitles, is set within a book like many Disney fairytales, giving it the air of a story many times retold. As people's frailties and sins have doomed the star-crossed couple to misery and torment, the film is strikingly serious and poignant in its tragedy.

Chapter 2

Speculative Fiction in the New World

THE FIRST IMMIGRANTS

Famously, the Sephardic community, masters of art and science during Muslim Spain, were expelled in 1492. Some settled in Europe, remaining culturally distinct from the Ashkenazi Jews, while some traveled to more distant lands. In Colonial America, the majority of Jewish immigrants, settling in port cities and universally supporting the Revolution, were Sephardim, such as the 1654 Jews who fled the Dutch colony of Recife, Brazil, for New Amsterdam. (One was an ancestor of Emma Lazarus, who wrote the poem on the Statue of Liberty.) Twentieth-century authors Robert Nathan and Primo Levi were Sephardic, as were Mordechai Manuel Noah, Penina Mo'ise, Elizabeth Cardozo, Nancy Cardozo, and Annie Nathan Meyer. From the eastern Mediterranean Sephardim came the ancestors of Leon Sciaky, Stanley Sultan, Stephen Levy, and David Raphael.

In fact, American synagogues through the eighteenth century conducted their business in Portuguese. Only the nineteenth-century German immigration changed the landscape, with the arrival of 250,000 Yiddish-speaking Ashkenazim. At the same time, a significant number of Sephardic Jews immigrated to the United States from Turkey, Greece, and the Balkans from 1880 through the 1920s, echoed in a smaller number of Mizrahi Jews arriving from Arab lands.

Overwhelming the balance, two million Eastern European Jews arrived between 1880 and 1924, eager for American freedom of religion. Ida Maze's autobiographical novel *Dina* ([1970] 1994) is set in White Russia during the 1905 Revolution. Her story of immigration to America uses lenses of fantasy. About to board the ship, she and her friends speculate about how flying like birds or an airship would be safer than ocean travel. On the train, she imagines,

"She had been pried from the earth and was now being carried away on thousands of monstrously wild wings to the accompaniment of grotesque noises" (143). Malka Lee's autobiographical journey from Galicia, *Through the Eyes of Childhood* ([1955] 1994), does the same. As she writes poems in her childhood, her father decides this means she has "demons in her heart" (160). Indeed, finding her father has burned the poems, she turns into a "wild thing," no longer human, while her mother shrieks "in an alien voice" (161). She decides to travel to America where she will be free to create. There, she gets a job as a draper and fantasizes about the mannequin coming to life and dancing around joyously, even as her supervisor judges her with "wolf-like eyes" (179). For both young women, America is the land of possibility and imagination, where they can fulfill their dreams of creativity as well as success.

Magic was part of the everyday after arrival as well. Science fiction author William Tenn ([1966] 1991) tells an autobiographical story of his mother's epic cursing. The narrator describes all the shawled women as witches, glowering at children playing boisterously. They utter curses like "May you never live to grow up. . . . But if you do grow up, may it be like a radish, with your head in the ground and your feet in the air" while his mother spits at bedtime to ward off the evil eye (216). As he adds, "My mother was a Yiddish witch, conducting her operations in that compote of German, Hebrew, and Slavic" (216). He describes the byplay of curses and blessings that feature in daily superstition, with an impromptu competition the women of the neighborhood held on the street. All this was blended into ordinary life in a way that was all-too-believable.

Accustomed to living in insular Yiddish-speaking villages, "east European Jews found that their main challenge was how to Americanize without losing their Jewish identity, whether defined in religious or in secular terms" (Bernardi et al. 2012, 3). Their language offered a bridge to the old country, while allowing the immigrants to continue moving forward. One Yiddish story that shows such a bridge is Moyshe Nadir's "The Man Who Slept through the End of the World" ([1924] 2001). Using the patterns of folklore, it describes a man who enjoys sleep so much that he wakes in "a strange void" (231), without his wife or bed. Puzzled and lost "he bethought himself: I'll go to sleep. He saw, however, that there was no longer any earth on which to sleep" (232). He takes the end of the world in stride, but soon falls into depression, not knowing where to find food or a job. Without the comforts of the ordinary world, like movies and malted milk, he despairs. This story pushes the ludicrous to extremes, even as it meditates on the world's modern comforts. Has he assimilated too far, grown too reliant on urbanization, the story wonders.

Another folklore-based Yiddish story is closer to portal fantasy. Nadir's "In the Land of Happy Tears" ([1936] 2018) describes the River Ampsel.

"Once in 666 years, when the Sabbath falls on a Wednesday, you can approach the river backward so it thinks you're walking away" (3). The listener should throw an onion, recite a rhyme, and so fly to Tearania. There, the earth is baked bread and the cow meat regenerates. It rains wine and the mountains are soft as cotton balls. The only thing they don't have is salt—so the families must make themselves cry on the food to salt it. This seems a particularly Jewish fantasy world, as even in all this luxury, the families dwell on their pain, at least momentarily.

Yhyoyesh (Yehoyesh-Shloyme Blumgartn) was born in Lithuania and emigrated to America, where he published many poems in Yiddish. Notable is his ballad "Shloymes ring" (Solomon's Ring, 1916), "a love story of exotic charms and dramatic tenseness" with "moral overtones" (Madison 1968, 174). Solomon wields the ring majestically, ordering demons to build him a palace and ruling with a thousand sages to his left and a thousand demons to his right. However, Amadeus lays a trap with an astoundingly beautiful queen. Solomon woos her and when he agrees that she can worship her own gods, Solomon's divine favor leaves him. His corruption has caused his tragic downfall. This too suggests a threat from assimilation, in this case intermarriage. Such fiction revealed immigrants' fears even as they settled in the new country.

Dr. Stephen J. Whitfield of Brandeis argues that Jews and popular culture of the time were tightly intertwined. "What's odd is that Jews and mass culture come to the United States at about the same time. Mass culture offered economic and cultural opportunities that were basically unavailable in the Old World" (quoted in Davin 2006, 166). With a democratic ethos that valued skill over parentage, the new immigrants thrived. Those part of the Yiddishkite culture of 1880 to 1914 crowded in cafes of the Lower East Side to argue about the Old World while struggling with the new. "There, in the same locale as the offices of the SF magazine empire from the late twenties onward, the boundaries of immigrant imagination emerged. These boundaries were the space of imagining new contours of Americanization through the articulation of ritual and public discourse," explains Batya Weinbaum, writing about the era (1998, 184).

This cultural concentration led to a small renaissance. "The Yiddish press and the Yiddish theater attained high points during the 1920s that would be viewed, decades later, as the Golden Age of American Yiddishkayt" (Kitchen and Buhle 2009, 3). In its midst, Israel Zangwill invented the popular "melting pot" metaphor to describe American absorption of immigrants and popularized it in his 1909 tour of his play by that name. Further, his *The Big Bow Mystery* was the first locked-room mystery novel. At the same time, Jewish women's charitable associations altered their activities between 1879 and 1919, shifting to Jewish education and current affairs of specific concern to women. The National Council of Jewish Women (NCJW), created in 1893, fought for Jewish education and greater synagogue roles as well as social reform (Lacoue-Labarthe 2016).

Yiddish fiction and nonfiction soared in the New World. From the thirties to the fifties, there were Yiddish radio stations with regular programs— realistic dramas, poetry, humor, advice shows, game shows, and talent shows. Culture soared in all the mediums available. "Via serialized novels, sketches, short stories, and essays, the Yiddish newspaper served as a major vehicle of integration, as did Yiddish books and pamphlets and, most of all, the Yiddish theater. Still, most Jewish immigrants remained committed to moving toward the English language and saw little wisdom in preserving the autonomy of Yiddish at the expense of their efforts at Americanization" (Bernardi et al. 2012, 4). In this multifaceted advance in culture, Yiddish films explored the shtetl or the lives of new immigrants and sometimes added a bit of folklore. The now-lost Yiddish play *Der Lamedvovnik* (One of the Thirty-Six, Jenryk Szaro, 1923) was made into a film in 1925. It adapted the Talmudic legend of thirty-six altruists that keep the world running to tell of a shtetl attacked by Russians in the 1830s and the humble hero who sacrifices himself to save it. Other Yiddish fantasy plays include the operetta *Di Kishefmakherin* (The Sorceress, 1878) written by Avrom Goldfaden, the father of modern Yiddish theater. The evil stepmother Basye, partnering with the neighborhood witch, Bobe Yakhne, frames the maiden Mirele and sells her into slavery in Istanbul, until all is put right. Eschewing the mysticism of golem and dybbuk tales, this show clearly derives from mainstream European fairytale tropes, though with familiar themes of false accusations and injustice from those in power. The melodrama was also popular, and quickly incorporated into Jewish writing. Yiddish melodramas included Joseph Lateiner's *Ezra oder der Ewige Jude* (Ezra or The Eternal Jew) and *Sotn in dem gortn fun eden* (Satan in the Garden of Eden). In Jacob Gordin's *Got, mentsh un tayvl* (God, Man, and Devil, 1900), Satan bets God that an American Torah scholar can be corrupted by money, and a Faustian plot follows. These fantasies all blended old and new cultures while cautioning about the price of change.

Peretz Hirschbein's *Tkias kaf* (The Contract, 1907), echoes *The Dybbuk*, as the heroine is claimed by her dead betrothed. After arriving in America, Hirschbein crafted the plays *Die puste kretshme* (The Haunted Inn), and *A farvorfen vinkel* (A Forsaken Corner) which shared elements of lore from his native Russia. *Di moyz mitn glekl* (The Mouse with the Bell, 1924) offered more mythic symbolism. In this dramatic poem, a man is pushed into a foundry and emerges alive, as he forces his boss and fellow workers to confront their anti-Semitism. Many of these works weighed the effects of superstition and ties to the past even as characters embraced a modern sensibility.

There was puppet theater too, offered by Yosl Cutler and Zuni Maud. This included a full-length Purim play, *Akhashveyrosh,* in rhyming couplets with nicknames and language styles pointedly placing Mordechai as lower-class like the audience. American pushcarts and modern songs help update the story. There was also a famous puppet parody of Ansky's *The Dybbuk,* as the directors of rival theaters attempt to drive out the ghost, even while joking about the playwrights who were modernizing their works into English. After the Depression, puppet newspaper editors and President Herbert Hoover adapted the Dybbuk parody to further comment on issues of the time.

The rise in Yiddish literature in New York was second only to that of Warsaw, and immigrants felt free to blend traditions. Inspired by the new culture, early Yiddish sscience fiction novels include A. Tanenboym's *Tsvishen himel un vaser: A visenshaftlikher roman* (Between Sky and Water: A Scientific Romance, 1896), *Doktor und tsoyberer* (Doctor and Magician, 1899) and *Di shvartse kunst: A vissenshaftlikher roman* (The Black Art: A Scientific Novel, 1899); Moses Seiffert's *Baym tir fun ganeydn, oder A puster holem mit a groysen emes: A Fantastisher Roman* (At the Paradise Gates or A Dream of the Greater Truth: A Fantastic Novel, 1917); Solomon Bogin's *Der ferter internatsyonal, Fantastishe dertseylung* (The Fourth International, Fantasy Story, 1929); Leon Kussman's *Narnbund, Fantastishe trilogye* (Union of Fools, Fantasy Trilogy 1931); Y. L. Goldshtayn's *Tsuzamenbrukh oder iberboy: Fantastisher roman in fir teyln* (Breakdown or Construction: A Fantastic Tale in Four Parts, 1934). Even postwar, a few significant ones followed this tradition with Velvl Tshernovetski's *Erev der ferter velt-milk- home, Hines-di kenign fun Mars* (On the Eve of World War IV: The Martian Queen, 1959) and Leybl Botvinik's *Di geheyme shlihes: Fantastishe dert- seylung* (The Secret Mission, A Fantasy Story 1980). (Encyclopedia 2018).

Today, the Yiddish Book Center has these and others like the short story collection by Eda Glasser (1940) *A rayze tsu der levone* (A Journey to the Moon) and Aleph Katz's short story *Dos telerl fun himl* (The Saucer from Heaven, 1934). Children's fantasies of giants, unicorns, and werewolves include the novels *Moyshele's kinderyorn* (Moyshele's Childhood, 1921) by David Kassel; *Yingele ringele* (The Boy with the Ring, 1929) by Leon Elbe; and *Dos kluge shnayderl* (The Clever Little Tailor, 1933) by Solomon Simon.

More Yiddish novels were based in realism, with Ansky and Isaac Bashevis Singer standing out for their integration of fantasy tropes. Singer in particular is one of the central transmitters of shtetl culture, with his folklore still popular today. He continued transmitting this culture post-Holocaust, and received the Nobel Prize in Literature in 1978. Many of his stories, whether set in Eastern Europe, in New York, or on the boat in-between, focus on messy human life and its relationships, all against a heavy Jewish back- ground. They also document a culture that would soon be lost: "Removed by time and distance Singer's survivors recall, in disconnected fragments, the terrible events of their European pasts," writes Lewis Fried (1988, 428) in the *Handbook of American-Jewish Literature.*

Even in his contemporary tales, ghosts and dream visitations sometimes appear to guide the characters. Dybbuks invade the helpless while other more benevolent souls return to care for family. Several stories take place in the afterlife, with souls there speculating on their pasts and futures. A variety of demons appear. In fact, a number of his stories are told from an imp or devil's point of view, gleefully detailing how he seduces ordinary people into sin and abandons them. The results, divorce or unmarriageability in the condemning eyes of the townsfolk, reveal much about their lifestyle and religious ethics.

Feminist stories were appearing too. Esther Singer Kreitman (Isaac Bashevis Singer's sister and the inspiration for Yentl) wrote the auto-biographical *Der Sheydim Tanz* (The Dance of the Demons, [1936] 2009). Within her family, Esther, nicknamed Hinde, was considered to be inhab-ited by a dybbuk, so rebellious was she against her arranged marriage. She became a Yiddish writer and a radical to her family's surprise. In the novel, Deborah grows up the educated daughter of a rabbi, frustrated when told she is to grow up to be "nothing." At her wedding, she performs the dance of the demons, a Polish countryside dance that suggests a magical origin for herself, now stifled in conventionality. In the morning, she lies limply, overwhelmed by the foreign feeling of her ring and wig. Her new family is terrible—the three-hundred-ruble earrings the groom's family promised her are made of paste and her new family disapprove of her "freethinker" reading materials about the Haskalah (81). In Antwerp, her husband lies around all day and lives off his father's allowance—when it disappears, the couple must pawn Deborah's jewelry. He doesn't care that she's in love with a radical she met in her youth.

The magical imagery continues as metaphor—in her head, she calls the landlady a witch and her husband notes that she shrinks from him as if from a monster. As time goes on, she succumbs to the madness of many feminist characters and frustrated women of the time: "no sooner did she set eyes on a book, than a cloud of specks, like a swarm of troubled insects, began to dart about all over the printed page" and "she looked more dead than alive" (91). She finally flees back to her parents on the train. She finds herself traveling with a hag and a skeletal child who reflect her own desperation and arrives to find her parents have vanished . . . only to be woken by her husband and discover her running away was a dream.

Isaac Bashevis Singer's "The Jew from Babylon" ([1932] 1988) features a devout Jew from the Far East who "maintained that he had learned the arts of clairvoyance and healing in Babylon. He can cure insomnia and madness, exorcise dybbuks, and help bridegrooms who suffered from impotence or from spells brought about by the Evil Eye" (4). Here is much of the Jewish ancestral fantasy—ghosts and curses and their expulsion. However, even Kaddish's own people distrust him and forbid him to live among them. Thus ostracized, he keeps struggling toward goodness, even as succubae torment and tease him at night. After the rabbi banishes him, leaving Kaddish so stunned he's unable to describe all the lives he's saved, the demons carry him off. As they parody a wedding around him, with all inverted and defiled, "Kaddish closed his eyes and knew for the first and last time that he was one of them, married to Lilith, the Queen of the Abyss" (13). The tale reflects people's intolerance and willingness to turn on the stranger among them . . . though it also hints that Kaddish's lifestyle may have led him down this path. Thus, it ends ambiguously, unwilling to take sides in the story of the man who flouts the edges of propriety until the demons take him. It's easy to see this as a metaphor for being shunned by the community, who are quick to leap to conclusions.

Singer's serialized novel from the thirties *Satan in Goray* ([1955] 1996) is more metaphoric, set in Poland after a great massacre. The survivors rebuild, though historically, "the tragically haphazard condition of the Jews stimulated fantastic messianic hopes" (Madison 1968, 480). The rabbi tries to quash these, but news of the Messiah keeps arriving. This hope also leaves the villagers open to darker beliefs. On the night of Kol Nidre, the air is "full of those ghosts that could find no resting place" (65). When a young man insists Shabbtai Zevi is not the Messiah, the townspeople beat him up, using words of Kapparot, the Yom Kippur scapegoat ritual. The sheltered Rekhele falls for a faith healer, and the town's morals disintegrate until she's certain she's pregnant with a demon. She has hair "like a witch's" and insists only Satan would marry her (76). This licentiousness reflects an era of nearly insane hope and desperation for belief: With this, Singer "presents the epic of Shabbtai Zevi in its extreme superstitious grotesqueness: its depression of reason and exaltation of unreality, its asceticism and eroticism" (Madison 1968, 48).

Singer's midrashic "The Death of Methuselah," only translated and published in 1988, features the title character as a terrible sinner who cavorts with demons. On his deathbed, Naamah comes to him. She is the daughter of fallen angels, who has now joined them in their camp among the daughters of Lilith and children of Cain. Luring him to her land of pleasure, where sin and lust are virtues, she offers the provocative comment that God "had only one wife, the Shekinah, and for countless years they have been separated because of his impotence and her frigidity" (241). Among the fallen angels, demons, and hobgoblins, Methuselah finds a place of eternal pleasure and joy. Meanwhile, across the world, Noah readies his ark, all too aware that the world is full of sin. The story contrasts two paths—God's or Lilith and

Cain's, lavishly exploring the latter before reminding readers it was all wiped from the earth at God's command. It's a biblical parable, one that ends by popping like a soap bubble.

Turning to science fiction as a means of social criticism, Singer wrote a story in which deniers of the Big Bang founded Chelm, a town of silly people beloved in Polish folklore. Post Big Bang, "Slowly Chelm cooled and was covered by a crust, like a pot of porridge that has been left standing. The first Chelmites, the scholars say, were not people but microbes, amoebas, and other such creatures. Later a river formed in Chelm. It contained many fish, and these were the ancestors of the Chelmites. This may be the reason why the Chelmites love fish, especially gefilte fish" (Singer 1973, 4). It's unclear how long it took to cool since there wasn't a calendar there, or a watch. Following this comes Marxism, war, and everything else Singer chose to satirize. As soon as the Chelmites become civilized and literate, they invent words like crisis and realize they have one. Struck by their poverty, they make war on their neighbors to prove they are the cleverer ones. When they lose, the people form a new government. New laws insist, "Elections will be held every forty years, on Purim. Only members of the Revolutionary Party will be eligible to vote" (14). Further, money is abolished in order to end class division. The barter system goes terribly, and the people insist on a return to a money system. Counter revolutionaries seize the town and lead the people back to war. On and on it goes until the Chelmites finally proclaim that they have the wisdom to choose not to war on their neighbors and to be paid for their labors.

The beloved Chelm stories spread through America mostly from Singer, Vekhiel Yeshaye Trunk, and Aaron Zeitlin. Trunk's Chelm is visited by Og, last of the ancient giants, but also Einstein, setting it in an ambiguous time. As such, it leans into its fantasy qualities and universality. It also exists aware of older folkloric traditions. In one story, Chelmites travel to Prussia where they're bewildered by the language. They decide they've crossed the mythic river Sambatyon into the land of the Red Jews, and beg for money on the streets, gleefully fooling the locals by pretending to be blind "not humbled but, as true Chelmites, proud and excited to be mocking the foolish world" (Von Bernuth 2016, 27). They are not just fools but successful tricksters, getting the better of the conventional world.

Zeitlin's play *Khelemer khakhomim* (The Wise Men of Chelm) launched in 1933 New York. In this adaptation of the traditional stories, the Angel of Death decides to become human. The blend of Chelm tales with the supernatural plot is unusual, presumably written to give the play a more epic nature. While the people of Chelm have their famously silly adventures, the angel masquerades as a rich secular German Jew, while a frantic hobgoblin called Yekum Purkan labors to make him resume his burden. After the angel weds, the hobgoblin sends imps to torment the couple at night. The angel sadly returns to heaven, while his bride marries according to her religious duty and life resumes. Fantasy takes over the world of the old country, but only briefly. Chelm stories as well as Singer stories of shtetl culture never went out of fashion and continued being told and retold by storytellers and jokesters throughout Jewish life.

SOUTH AMERICA AND BORGES

The Jewish presence in Latin America dates back to the Spanish expulsion of 1492. Though Jews were forbidden from traveling to the New World, many "New Christians" did so, while concealing their faith, at least for a time. The nineteenth century offered Jewish texts that adapted Bible stories, including Mexican writer Justo Sierra O'Reilly's *La hija del judío*, which follows a New Christian's persecution by the Inquisition. There's also Brazilian poet Castro Alves's "Hebraia" and novelist Machado de Assis's *A crista nova*, in which Jews stood for other marginalized groups or marginalization in general. Of course, Jews of South and Central America had basically all become Catholic by this point. Jorge Isaacs's novel *Maria* (Colombia, 1867), stands out, as his father converted to Judaism and the novel explores the author's pull in contradictory directions.

Meanwhile, the late nineteenth century brought a wave of Ashkenazi immigration, which received varying acceptance and hostility. Jewish immigrant fiction blended folklore of the old country and the new to create a distinctively innovative sensibility. Nadia Grosser Nagarajan's *Pomegranate Seeds: Latin American Jewish Tales* (2005) collects oral stories of this time. In one, Malvina grows up in Warsaw reading *Tzenah Urenah,* with its Yiddish wonder tales. In 1929, sailing to Argentina, she reads about Jonah even as the sailors discuss sea monsters. At last, she sees a creature, like a huge snake with "a large head, shaggy mane, and many arms" (2005c, 102). She reaches the New World safely and marries, but the sea monster, like her childhood stories, remains as a reminder of Polish Judaism, soon destroyed forever. As another story describes, Jewish newcomers to South America integrated local traditions or merged them with their own in Curacao. Umbilical cords are buried with local trees to tie the people to the land, even as they guard their children from both sets of demons. "When a baby is born, one has to watch it for eight days to prevent the African spirit, Eze, from snatching the child. The color blue is considered effective in keeping away Eze as well as other vicious spirits. A chalky substance (called *blous* in the commonly used Papiamentu language) is smeared on the crown of the babies' heads and the soles of their feet. This is a custom reminiscent of the precautions taken by Jews to prevent

the wicked Lilith from kidnapping the newborn" (2005d, 158). Through tod-
dlerhood, the child wears a cultural blend—a hamsa amulet, local beads, or a
blue-dyed pattern on the back of the clothes to ward off evil.

"The House on Back Street" (Nagarajan 2005a), a story of St. Thomas
island collected in *Pomegranate Seeds: Latin American Jewish Tales*, has a
traveler visiting the synagogue, oldest in the Western Hemisphere, where his
great-grandfather worshipped. Afterward he discovers hazy images from the
titular house and realizes he's discovered ghosts. A woman tells him a Jewish
family has died there, killed by the angry ghosts of a former Catholic rectory
on the site. A Mocko Jumbie, or African stilt dancer and healer gives the man
blue and red crystals of the goddess Yemeya, which he refuses, though he
keeps the ghostly picture. The cultural mash is too much for him, even as he
acknowledges its power.

In another blend of magic from the same collection, "The Rabbi's Tomb"
tells of a holy place in Manaus in the heart of the Amazon visited by Jews
and non-Jews alike. The Moroccan Jews who settled there told stories of
their wonder rabbi as well as another treasure—a 400-year-old Torah from
Portugal. "The people believe that the scroll has no magical powers; it is,
nevertheless, a talisman they guard with great love and pride, an additional
legacy they carry in their hearts" (2005b, 88). The rabbi's heroic servant
Florzinha has legends as well, as the rabbi's blessing has left her able to heal
through touch.

Simkhe Gelman emigrated from Poland to Buenos Aires in 1924. His
plays—*Akht in suke* (Eight in the Sukkah), *Bal-shem* (The Bal-Shem-Tov),
and *Rambam*—were staged in Argentina for many weeks. He was the country's most beloved Yiddish feature writer under the penname Freylikh and a
children's author under the penname Litman. His whimsical story "The Girl
in the Mailbox" ([1936] 2020b) gleefully explores new technology as a father
accidentally mails his daughter. The girl, surrounded by mail happy and sad,
travels to Europe and back to Argentina, where her father hurriedly buys her.
The story is notable because Europe is not yet presented as dangerous (at
least not to the young readers) and the massive Jewish emigration is treated
as a lighthearted adventure. In a more allegorical story, "The Birds Go on
Strike" ([1936] 2020a), all the birds refuse to sing until they're granted better
conditions by the humans: no more catching them, locking them in cages, or
looting their nests. The humans agree. "And when the birds burst into song,
many great musicians laid down their instruments and said, 'We've never
heard birds sing like *that* before!'" If the birds are mistreated workers, or
even the minority Jews, a little consideration enriches the entire community.

Albert Van Der Naillen, a Belgian occultist, wrote several books linking different practices. His *The Great Message* (1925) celebrates Kabbalah,
Jewish mysticism, which he describes as coming to Mexico with the Spanish.

Such a theory is possible, though unlikely. As he explains, "Cabála with the accent on the middle syllable, is the word used by the Caziques when they speak of what is known among them as heaven: home of mystical science and the laws, forces and powers of this science. The same word, Cábala, but with the accent on the first syllable, means just the reverse. It means evil forces, evil influence, intrigue, and the lowest plane of man's spiritual development" (9). In the book, a professor meets with the Miracle Man in Mexico, learning his methods. However, the school of masters and apprentices in different robes doesn't sound Jewish at all—the story is closer to universal mysticism than Jewish lore.

This was an intriguing trend at the time for many authors, Jewish and not. Viewing Kabbalah as a pathway to the mystical in fiction, celebrated horror writer H. P. Lovecraft ([1927] 2009) writes:

> A very flourishing, though till recently quite hidden, branch of weird literature is that of the Jews, kept alive and nourished in obscurity by the sombre heritage of early Eastern magic, apocalyptic literature, and cabbalism. The Semitic mind, like the Celtic and Teutonic, seems to possess marked mystical inclinations; and the wealth of underground horror-lore surviving in ghettoes and synagogues must be much more considerable than is generally imagined. Cabbalism itself, so prominent during the Middle Ages, is a system of philosophy explaining the universe as emanations of the Deity, and involving the existence of strange spiritual realms and beings apart from the visible world, of which dark glimpses may be obtained through certain secret incantations. Its ritual is bound up with mystical interpretations of the Old Testament, and attributes an esoteric significance to each letter of the Hebrew alphabet—a circumstance which has imparted to Hebrew letters a sort of spectral glamour and potency in the popular literature of magic.

Some Latin American authors addressed Jewish topics specifically. At the same time, Latin American fantasy is subtler than European-American fantasy, so it's much less distinct as a genre. There is a notable exception from a man who particularly defines magical realism.

Borges

Jorge Luis Borges famously adored many Jewish practices, especially Kabbalah. He was not Jewish but felt open to being so. In his essay, "I, a Jew?" he explains, "Who has not, at one point or another, played with thoughts of his ancestors, with the prehistory of his flesh and blood? I have done so many times, and many times it has not displeased me to think of myself as Jewish" (quoted in Stavans 2016b, 4).

He continued to allude later in life to his probable Portuguese Jewish ancestry on his mother's side, and in "La muerte y la brújula," he gives one of the
Jewish victims of the murders a last name (Azevedo) effectively identical to his
mother's family name (Acevedo). Meanwhile, Borges refers at numerous points
in his writings to Jews as practicing in an exemplary form the prerogatives of a
peripheral culture, which, he claims, may borrow at will from more dominant
cultures without feeling fully invested in them—prerogatives he believes that
Argentine and Latin American writers may also enjoy. (Shullenberger 2013, 65)

As he considers both Jews and Latin Americans as people torn between
cultures and capable of multiple affiliations, he admiringly explores how
Jews confront identity. Borges particularly appropriates the doubling of
Jewish culture, seeing how well it fits into his Argentinian life. He seems to
appreciate the intellectual Jewish life. Professor Ilan Stavans (2016a) notes
that he dissects Judaism through short stories "The Secret Miracle," "Baruch
Spinoza," "The Golem," and "Death and the Compass," among others.
"True, his view tends toward the allegorical. Jews, for Borges, are vessels of
memory. They are at once insiders and outsiders in culture, at once witnesses
and participants. Their devotion to languages and the intellectual is the result
of a transient journey through a labyrinthine diaspora."

Borges wrote admiring pieces on Kafka and Spinoza. "He spoke against
Nazism during the World War II, when few in Argentina dared to; he visited Israel and eulogized the small desert nation; he was a friend of Alberto
Gerchunoff and other figures in his country's Jewish community," Stavans
adds (2016a). He also enjoyed S. Y. Agnon's writings, including *Days of
Awe* and *Tales of the Ba'al Shem Tov* but especially the *Contes de Jerusalem*
(Stavans 2016b, 67). In response to this last, Borges wrote of Israel as a
nation "made of the accumulated memory of successive generations" (quoted
in Stavans 2016b, 68). Borges sees such memory becoming embedded in
its authors and concludes of Agnon, "Somehow he knew he was the living
memory of that admirable people to which, beyond the vicissitudes of blood,
we all belong: the people of Israel" (quoted in Stavans 2016b. 70).

To Borges, Jews' constant questioning was an immense draw. Borges
described himself as a non-believer for whom God was at best an unknowable entity. His often-quoted opinion that religion is a branch of the literature
of the fantastic emphasizes the value he places on imagination and creativity
over dogma. In this tradition, Borges's "The Aleph" ([1949] 1967) introduces
a magical world, contained in a trunk in a mysterious cellar. It is "The place
where, without any possible confusion, all the places in the world are found,
seen from every angle" (147). The narrator descends, discovers the infinite,
and utterly lacks the words to share it: "All language is an alphabet of symbols whose use presupposes a past shared by all the other interlocutors. How,

then, transmit to others the infinite Aleph, which my fearful mind scarcely encompasses?" he asks (149). He notes that of course Aleph is the first letter of God's sacred language, which in Kabbalah "signifies the Ein-Sof, the limitless and pure divinity" and speaks of man's inferior world beside God's divine one (153). This story adapts the kabbalistic view of an original, perfect hidden world only God can see, linked with a more accessible world of attributes through which one can know God.

> The narrator is invited by his rival to contemplate the mystical Aleph in its transcendent glory, and the passage describing his extraordinary Experience ranks among Borges's most poetic writing. But the majesty of the Vision is disturbed on a number of counts: first, it takes place in grotesque surroundings and includes sordid details of lust and betrayal; secondly, it has no spiritually uplifting effect, as shown in the "Borges" character's pettily vindictive reaction in denying the experience, and thirdly, the uniqueness implied in the name of the microcosmic disk is severely compromised by a long list of other universal mirrors and finally when another more genuine Aleph is suggested. (Fishburn 2013, 59)

Even man's vision of the divine is imperfect, and its appearance in the squalid basement does not just give the narrator a sight of transcendence but becomes a tool for petty cruelty as he suggests his rival demolish the house. This emphasizes that while God and Kabbalah may be pure, man will see them imperfectly and put them to an even more imperfect use.

"It should be borne in mind that for Borges, the literature of the fantastic is not one of escape, but a means of approaching and expressing the mysterious character of the universe. This explains, in part, the widespread presence of religious motifs in his writings, particularly his fiction" (Fishburn 2013, 56). Borges writes several stories on the sacred search for God's holy name. This connects to the kabbalistic deeper significance of letters, which in turn connects not only to the creative process but to the concept of crafting fiction. In his essay on the Kabbalah, Borges explains how the sacred text is eternal and perfect, every one of its words purposefully chosen. While the original details must not be changed, the writing can be interpreted in contradictory ways. With all this, Borges admires the Kabbalists' method of dealing with a changing world.

His story "The Library of Babel" ([1941] 2007) explains, "The mystics claim that their ecstasy reveals to them a circular chamber containing a great circular book, whose spine is continuous and which follows the complete circle of the walls . . . this cyclical book is God" (52). Borges carries the reader to the circular library containing such a book, where scholars go seeking the mysteries of the universe, in languages that cannot be separated. His fascination with numbers, codes, and universal truth, a distilled form of the Kabbalah's worldview, appears through the imagery here. As with "The Aleph," man cannot bear the Divine and must cheapen it with squabbles: "These pilgrims squabbled in the narrow corridors, muttered dark imprecations, strangled one another on the divine staircases, threw deceiving volumes down ventilation shafts, were themselves hurled to their deaths by men of distant regions" (55).

"The God's Script" ([1949] 2007) places the priest Tzinacan in a stone cell, preparing for his sacrifice on a pyramid. There he recollects a sentence God wrote on the first day of creation. The priest wonders whether he is the chosen one appointed to read it. However, once he discovers it, through meditating on the beauty of the jaguar in the next cell, he finds, as with the narrator of "The Aleph," that he lacks the words to fully own the name, and refuses to say it, though its devastating power could save his life. The priest's fervent belief in the universe's inherent textuality (suggested in the title) adapts kabbalistic belief yet again. Moreover, his belief in this lost secret message, which he can only recover through mysticism, echoes the tradition that Adam was born with total wisdom, which humanity today still struggles to reach. Beyond this, the story blends many cultures' belief systems, emphasizing the universality of the quest to understand God, even (or perhaps especially) in the face of death.

> In asserting a typology of identities uniting Argentines and Jews, Borges's "Jewish uncanny" reiterates the anti-Semitic allegations of liminality and mimicry, but converts them into a trope of Argentine self-affirmation. Borges, in other words, attributes the same qualities to Jews and Judaism that his erstwhile political nemeses do, but subjects these qualities to a kind of Nietzschean "transvaluation": alleged Jewish liminality, mimicry, and simultaneous capacity for similarity and difference all become traits that the Argentine writer should embrace. (Shullenberger 2013, 65)

"The Secret Miracle" ([1943] 2007) similarly echoes some of these elements. Arrested by the Nazis for translating the mystical Book of Creation, the Jewish protagonist Jaromir Hladik of Prague is sentenced to execution. Like the priest, he spends the night contemplating his death, as well as the sacred letters that comprise God's name. However, as the soldiers prepare to fire, the universe stops—Hladik has found what Tzinacan dared not attempt—he has frozen time in a secret miracle. "He had asked God for a whole year to finish his work; His omnipotence had granted it" (93). While he cannot share his findings with the world, God grants him this private transcendence—a chance to finish his spiritual exploration.

Finally, "Death and the Compass" ([1942] 2007) works the search for the holy name into a murder mystery. Three murders occur, at points that make an equilateral triangle, while a written message at each insists one of the letters of the sacred name has been uttered. The latest victim is the delegate from Podolsk to the Third Talmudic Congress, Doctor Marcel Yarmolinsky, who has already undergone "three thousand years of oppression and pogroms," as Borges notes. The clever detective Erik Lönnrot and the more oblivious one investigate and Lönnrot points out the rabbi's published works: "A Vindication of the Cabala; An Examination of the Philosophy of Robert Fludd; a literal translation of the Sepher Yezirah; a Biography of the Baal Shem; a History of the Sect of the Hasidim; a monograph (in German) on the Tetragrammaton; another, on the divine nomenclature of the Pentateuch." Here, Borges gets in a fan's salute to topics he admires, while also showing off his knowledge. The police commissioner dismisses them as "Jewish superstitions," but Lönnrot identifies them as motive. Further, the Jewish editor of the *Yiddische Zeitung* is allowed his own zinger as he points out that Christianity is really no different. Lönnrot's certainty that everything is connected makes him a stand-in for Borges and his philosophy. Using his observations of a repetition of the number four (suggesting God's name), Lönnrot anticipates the fourth murder and awaits the murderer there. Thus, "Death and the Compass" transcends the ordinary detective story with numerical and biblical allusions saluting a deeper reality.

Borges has other mystery thrillers such as "Unworthy" and "Emma Zunz"—the latter story has the Jewish heroine enact a gruesome revenge on an enemy. While the story is straightforward, critics like Professor Edna Aizenberg see her as embodying the Shekhina, "the feminine hypostasis of the divine—who is separated from her heavenly progenitor and falls into an unclean physical-sexual world as a result of sin" (quoted in Stavans 2016b, 30). "Deutsches Requiem" features a psychological drama between concentration camp director and prisoner, with the usual twist of the prisoner penetrating his tormentor's conscience. These stories idealize the Jewish characters, regarding them as the Christians' guides and advisers, more allegory than human. Of course, this is often the case when stories of Jews are told by outsiders.

Borges also experiments with the legend of the golem. He writes in "The Circular Ruins" ([1940] 1967): "In the Gnostic cosmologies, demiurges fashion a red Adam who never manages to get to his feet: as clumsy and crude and elemental as this dust Adam was the dream Adam forged by the nights of the wizard" (71). The wizard teaches his creation the mysteries of the universe. He creates a son and reluctantly leaves him to carry on . . . however, in the final line the wizard realizes he too is someone's dream. Arguably, this retells the golem legend, as the wizard builds and tutors his creation. The reference to Adam emphasizes it as a reimagining of the creation story as well. Borges also combines these two stories in his poem "The Golem." It focuses on the name of God, which, as the poem remarks, Adam knew in the Garden. Further, the book offers a level of understanding above the wizard, as God looks down and contemplates the creator of the golem. However, more than on creation, the poem obsesses over the mystery of God's lost name: "which essence / Ciphers as God and Omnipotence / Preserves in consummate letters and symbols." In the final stanza, "Borges lays bare the core of his skepticism, as he imagines God's possible disappointment in the imperfection of his creation, the scholarly mystic Judah Loew, and, by a logical extension, in man" (Goldsmith 1981, 164). The poem uses similar word choice to the story, casting Rabbi Loew as a "wizard" and the golem as the "son" he teaches. Indeed, Loew was called the Maharal (acronym for most venerated teacher and rabbi) and was a philosopher, astronomer, astrologer, and natural scientist—a renaissance man for his era. Borges is exploring his connection with mysticism while also tying it to modern fantasy, providing a bridge between the secular modern and historic Jewish. Borges's background may be outside the faith, but as a dreamer and reimaginer, his fantasy transmits and updates the mystical into the tangible and transcendent.

NEW WORLD LITERARY FANTASY

Abraham Moses Klein was one of Canada's most celebrated Jewish writers. Born in the Ukraine in 1909, he moved to Montreal as a small child. Klein served as editor of *The Judaean, The Canadian Zionist,* and the *Canadian Jewish Chronicle*. He's best known for his 1940 essay "Hath Not a Jew." Klein also translated and reviewed many Jewish works, helping to spread scholarship and awareness even as his essays directly defended his people. During World War II, he published a poetry collection filled with elegies to those lost in the Holocaust.

Myth and fantasy often appear in mainstream literature, as do ghosts, the afterlife, prophecy, and reincarnation. Bible story adaptations generally go in this category as well. Most often, of course, this is a marketing decision, as mostly mainstream authors' subtle forays into the uncanny will be shelved alongside their completely realistic stories. One could call this "social fantasy"—stories that focus on characters and symbolism rather than the fantasy elements themselves. Of course, during this time period, fantasy was rare outside children's literature, so marketing as literature was preferable to labeling works as the sensationalized monster-battling pulp adventures. At the same time, this blend of myth and upscale literature allowed new opportunities to share one's message.

Klein's *The Hitleriad* ([1944] 1974) was a satirical mock epic, though critics found it more bitter than funny. Using the conventions of the epic but flipped, Klein imagines apocalypse—a heavenly war against God and his commandments. He asserts, "The Madman named the Lord his personal foe/and chained the bearers of his sacred word" (205). With this, Hitler leads pagan hordes in a savage charge that echoes imagery of Wagner and Ragnarök. Barbarity triumphs and God is silenced. At the same time, Klein uses mythological allusions to de-mythologize Hitler. He is total ugliness as Helen of Troy is the apex of beauty, clumsy and simplistic compared with the artistry of Michelangelo. With all this, he demonstrates "The total bigness of / All little men" (188). While emphasizing his reign as a de-evolution, the epic highlights the need to restore society. Klein's final vision of redemption insists the world must let the dead "speak out" and thus find a voice, if not justice (207).

His one novel, *The Second Scroll* ([1951] 1985) explores whether the Messiah is coming and whether he will be recognized if he does. The novel blends poetry, drama and prayer in a metafictional form, divided into sections named for the books of the Bible. It is very modernist, often compared to Joyce's *Ulysses* for its artistic symbolism. Numeric symbols include a list of thirty-six people and a camp tattoo, which, in gematria, translates to "He has come" (Edel 1975, 27). The protagonist journeys to Israel on an epic quest to find his uncle Melech Davidson (King, son of David), a messianic figure and miraculous survivor of the Holocaust and other genocides. This scene is deeply thematic: "The task of the modern Jew was to escape not only the German lime pits but the ideologies that enslaved him before and after Nazism came to power, beginning with Communism" (Wisse 2000, 261).

Melech is also faceless thanks to a gasoline attack (a skewed anointing as Klein explains) (Edel 1975, 25). This gives him a supernatural stature and allegorical presence—he is the Wandering Jew, the Messiah, the faceless image of God, even—a martyr and eternal survivor in one. Through the Holocaust and the founding of Israel, many believed they had reached messianic times, so extreme were the destruction and also the rare miracles. During the journey, the narrator believes he sees his uncle in everyone he meets. As Klein explains, "Our tale intends to suggest that the Messiah is, or is of, or is in, the ubiquitous anonymity of universal Jewry's all-inclusive generation, he is the resurgent creativity of the incognitos of the folk" (quoted in Edel 1975, 25). Thus the narrator indeed sees the Messiah everywhere—he is the crowd itself. However, his uncle had already perished as Israel was formed: the Messiah will not complete his mission now, at least not in the flesh, though he has inspired Jews by restoring their ancient land.

Short stories celebrate the miraculous in the everyday. The local "Simeon the half-wit," unemployed and constantly dozing, shows up for Passover in Klein's "Prophet in Our Midst: A Story for Passover" ([1930] 1983c). The family invite him in and the father, joking, names him Elijah and gives him

Elijah's cup of wine. Simeon is tickled by this label. "And truth to tell, since that night, he has changed his name to Elijah, and as the spirit moves him, he indulges in petty prophecies" (17). When the young narrator peers outside, he sees Elijah walking, establishing that helping another in his name is as righteous a deed as hosting Elijah himself.

The elves of *A Midsummer's Night Dream* appear in Klein's "Once upon a Time" ([1932] 1983b) to consider why mankind has left them behind. Among them is "Elijah, the only Hebrew elf known in history" (87). Tipsy from all the wine, he advises the others to wait out the modern era, as the people will return to their faith in the supernatural someday. Further, Elijah finishes the discussion by suggesting they find the Jewish fairies who have become assimilated. As the story adds, "He was not the only Hebrew sprite. He was only, so to speak, the last of the Mohicohens. His smile apologized for the atrocious pun" (88). With a proclamation from one of the fauns: "Next meeting in Jerusalem" they part ways, having inducted Jewish fairies among the more traditional ones (88). Continuing the fantasy tropes beyond the obligatory golem story, "The Chanukah Dreidel" ([1930] 1983a) has Satan come by and play dreidel for the owner's soul, while in "The Lost Twins" ([1930] 1983b), two children on a mission to the rabbi meet a helpful dwarf in the fairytale forest. Other stories travel to heaven and explore the world beyond our own. Amid several on fairy tale themes, his poem "The Shechinah of Shadows" ([1926] 1990) blends imagery of Greek myth with that of God's mystical feminine presence to celebrate the magic of nature.

Finally, "Master of the Horn" ([1932] 1983a). blends a biblical power with European folklore as the shofar is blown at synagogue only to emit "battalions of dwarfed witches, legions of imps" and all the "discord of Gehenna" (67). With this, the ancient power of the shofar as a demon-fighting tool, though one that can be corrupted, presents this as a blend of Jewish fantasy in truth.

Sephardic American author Robert Nathan wrote forty novels, two children's books, two nonfiction books and ten books of poetry in his lifetime. His *Portrait of Jennie*, *The Clock*, and *The Bishop's Wife* were made into films.

His work was also published in an anthology of early literary science fiction called *Edges of Reality*, with stories by F. Scott Fitzgerald, Oscar Wilde, Henry James, Jr., H. G. Wells, and Leo B. Kneer. His contribution to this anthology was the soulful and loving *Portrait of Jennie* (1949). Eben, the narrator, paints landscapes, but he's floundering. As the beginning of the story explains, "There is another kind of suffering for the artist which is worse than anything a winter or poverty can do; it is more like a winter of the mind, in which the life of his genius, the living sap of his work, seems frozen and motionless, caught—perhaps forever—in a season of death; and who knows if spring will ever come again to set it free?" (3–4). However, the hero's art starts selling much better when he draws Jennie, a little girl he meets in the park. Her moroseness and references to dead friends and family finally reveal, of course, that she is a ghost. References to God and being chosen suggest Jewishness while the narrator struggles with the concept of what it means to be an artist.

> Many of Nathan's novels contain Jewish minor characters, such as Gus the taxi driver in *Portrait of Jennie* and Rosenberg the violinist in *One More String*, who comment ironically on the agonies that are part of the general human condition. The novels *Jonah* and *Road of Ages* refer more specifically to the Jewish exile, but they make clear that the possibilities for humans to reveal their spirituality and morality rest in a Judeo-Christian tradition, not just a Jewish one. Nathan wrote all of these works prior to 1940. It is in *A Star in the Wind* (1962) and in some of his poetry, especially *A Winter Tide* (1941), that we find full exploration of his personal relationship to Jewishness. For Nathan, Jewish history is sacred and compelling, and Jewish survival depends on memory of this history. (Matza 1992, 394–395)

He wrote *There Is Another Heaven* in 1929. It's a quiet and contemplative book in which several characters journey across the River Jordan and into the afterlife. George Herman Wutheridge, a one-time professor of Semitic languages, travels with Sammy Lewis, born Levy. They consider how benevolent they were before death. Dr. Crisp thinks of Lewis as he narrates, "And here was this Jew, with his talk of angels and other theological phenomena; as though that could make any difference. Wasn't it enough to be saved, to be in a state of bliss, to be comfortable and at peace? But Jews were like that—they always made a nuisance" (105). When they arrive, the angels aren't present, and neither is Jesus. The professor says of the angels, "They were beings of another world, which perished long before this city was ever dreamed of" (112), as few later mythological systems have them. As he adds, Jesus would not be in the Jewish or Christian heaven as he and the Jews chose different paths and then Christianity diverged massively from his vision (113). Lewis reveals that he converted to be more accepted on earth, which he was, but now in this empty heaven, he doesn't entirely see the point. He goes on an arc through the story, finally accepting that differentiations of this type are meaningless. All this makes an interesting philosophical commentary on religious conflict and what comes after death.

Nathan continues introspection of this sort. Sophia the angel and Buckthorne the demon are sent to investigate the violence on earth in *Heaven and Hell and the Megas Factor* (1975). The book is not strictly Jewish, thanks to the dualistic afterlife. Nonetheless, Sophia in her lacy blouse first stops by a synagogue, inspiring the rabbi to lead the congregation in a happy song of praise. Buckthorne, by contrast, makes everyone feel less satisfied. The human hero, Michael George, loved a Jewish woman and tells Sophia of the origin of angels in the Jewish Bible. Up in heaven, speaking through the author's snarky commentary, Saint Patrick and Saint Teresa agree that God chose the Jews but did not necessarily love them, as proven by all the suffering on earth (110). Buckthorne also attests that witches lived East of Eden and married Cain, in a spinoff of the Lilith legend (44). As they quest and fall in love, Sophia and Buckthorne actually discover the disease that causes human megalomania, and so save the world. It's a highly philosophical text that enjoys contrasting religious practices.

"Nathan did not see the Jew, as the Eastern Europeans did, as the quintessentially modern alienated victim; instead, in his poems and novels, he emphasized the Jew's singular position as reviled and suffering but still chosen and surviving. From this foundation springs his concern with a larger humanity and belief in the regeneration of the spirit" (Matza 1992, 394). Continuing to explore these themes, his *The Innocent Eve* has Lucifer and his sultry female assistant Samantha crash a Halloween party in Manhattan while seeking control of atomic technology. There, Lucifer is immediately charmed by the purity of a Midwestern farm girl named Mary Ann. Likewise, *The Devil with Love* (1963) is a Faust tale updated to modern times with a flustered Mephistopheles. In *The Bishop's Wife* (1928) the archangel Michael falls for the wife of a corrupted bishop, though he is unable to consummate their relationship. Robert Nathan also has a Bible story adaptation called *Jonah*, giving the character family and a romance as he struggles with God's commandment. All of these weigh reward and punishment, considering Jews' position in this world and the next.

"It was on the second of May, in the morning, that Robert Whittle, professor of History at Caraway College, decided that the world was coming to an end," begins *Mr. Whittle and the Morning Star* (1947, 3). Because humanity has learned to explode the atom but not to live peacefully, they are ruined. When he lectures at the church that people will doom themselves, separate from God's influence, he enrages the audience. After his wife betrays him, he demands answers from God and to his surprise, God comes down and speaks with him. God says, "You worry too much about what is going to happen" (142). He equates the atom bomb with humanity's corruption from the Garden of Eden but also insists that tiny human struggles still have meaning. In a second conversation later, God offers more philosophy about the imperfect world that He nonetheless loves and relies on mankind to improve. Once more, Nathan uses theology to share his thoughts on how people are meant to live in the world.

Road of Ages (1935) begins with the Jews going into exile. Western and Eastern Europeans and Americans too, all the Jews of the world, unite down the long, slow road. They are all refugees from the Nazi attacks. A few million have survived, though many more have died. As one man insists:

> There are many thousands on the roads from here to the border. There are great numbers of French and English, Americans, Germans, Hungarians; and armies of ragged saints and beggars. It's like going through the world, to travel twenty miles. . . . I'm told that the Jews from Syria and Morocco are going by ship across the Black Sea to Azov—how many, I don't know. Every day our numbers increase. (58)

The story zooms in on individual families, speculating that they will end up in Mongolia. They celebrate holidays together, from Yom Kippur to Passover. Mr. Neiman, a flawed leader in whom the people have imperfect trust, leads them as well as all the chief rabbis. As they walk, some dream of a better world and others quote the Bible to reassure themselves. Many show kindness, though a few pick fights, especially over others' observance. "How shall we sing the Lord's song in a strange land," one asks plaintively, quoting the Bible (94).

On the road, robbers attack, insisting that all Jews are rich and that they kill little children. After, their victim sadly asks, "Why are all men's hands raised against us? Is it because we are the chosen people and out of envy? I have a nose, eyes, mouth; I am like anybody else. But I arouse only dislike in the world" (106). The book is a dystopia of suffering but also a plea for tolerance that humanizes all the refugees on the road. The book ends with their finally reaching the destination, though the future remains uncertain. The author, of course, was speculating on what a mass expulsion might resemble, though with only knowledge of the thirties, he could not guess at the European Jews' final fate. While many have died before the story begins, the image of all the Jews in the world uniting and walking to their homeland together is powerful and inspiring.

THE PULPS:
SEEKING LOST TRIBES AND ANCIENT ARTIFACTS

Beloved science fiction author Isaac Asimov notes in his 1994 autobiography that pulp fiction flourished before World War II. "And in those days, racism and racial stereotypes were an ingrained part of the American scene. It was not till World War II and the fight against Adolf Hitler's racism that it became unfashionable for Americans to express racist views" (41). Pulp magazines, named for their cheap paper, offered sensational fiction from 1896 to the late fifties. Characters like Flash Gordon, Tarzan, Conan the Barbarian, John

Carter of Mars, and The Shadow flourished here, soon giving way to more formal science fiction and fantasy as well as inspiring the superhero comics. Jacob Hennenberger launched *Weird Tales*, the first all-fantasy magazine, in 1923. It published early horror author H. P. Lovecraft and sword and sorcery creator Robert E. Howard as well as some science fiction. Still, there were problems inherent to the genre besides unlikely scenarios: "Jews were comic characters when they were money-mad" and all the other minorities appeared in equally unflattering stereotypes (41).

In the pulps, many non-Jewish authors tackled Jewish themes or characters, often quite problematically. H. Rider Haggard launched the lost world genre with *King Solomon's Mines* (1885), with a biblical setting but no actual Jews. In this tradition, Lewis Grassic Gibbon wrote *The Lost Trumpet* ([1932] 2001), a search for the shofar that brought down Jericho. This adventure through Egypt has a distinctly Indiana Jones feel, this time with a Jewish character joining the ragtag team. There's also an anti-Semite among them, giving the protagonist the opportunity to angrily silence him in a model for readers. At the same time, the Jewish character, Huebsch, is identified over and over as "the Jew," emphasizing difference. Huebsch is, as the story tells it, "in every detail of appearance the Jew of caricature and controversy: with a large head, an ovoid head, whence outbranched a great, curving beak of a nose" (28). The archaeologist who discovered Jericho, he now dreams of restoring Jerusalem. The end echoes Indiana Jones as well, since the shofar proves itself divinely deadly, but those who survive have transformative revelations and all set out to fulfill their greatest dreams. This Jewish quest, appropriated by the troupe of characters, nonetheless offers readers a path to mutual respect and enlightenment, though with some unfortunate description.

Edgar Rice Burroughs, beloved author of Tarzan and John Carter, included a few overblown Jewish villains, like the heavily accented Adolph Bluber, who quests to steal gold in *Tarzan and the Golden Lion* (though the character is not particularly worse than other villains). It should be noted that Burroughs's antagonists use a variety of ethnic slurs, but Tarzan, the model hero, never does. In a contrasting portrayal, Burroughs's *The Moon Men* ([1925] 2015) has the Moon Men in fact take over earth in a communist metaphor. Moses Samuels, a friend to the protagonist Julian, appears as a fully formed, sympathetic figure who addresses anti-Semitism, noting the pure Kalkars "do not hate a Jew more than they hate other Earthmen." While religion is forbidden in this future dystopia, Samuels gives his friend an ancient carving of Jesus (linking him to the old ways and spirituality of all types), and he dies saving Julian. As Julian thinks at the end, "He had been a gentle character, loyal to his friends, and inclined to be a little too forgiving to his enemies—even the Kalkars. That he was courageous his death proved."

S. P. (Sterner St. Paul) Meek crafted *The Drums of Tapajos*, serialized in *Astounding* and *Amazing Stories* in 1930–1931. The questing heroes find a lost advanced city founded by Atlanteans in the wilds of Brazil. The people there serve a mysterious monotheistic group who are either Hebrew-speaking Trojans (hence the city is named "Troyana"), or the ten Lost Tribes. The Atlanteans even worship a golden calf and practice human sacrifice. As is common in these stories, a clash of cultures ensues, and the explorers stumble back to civilization with wild tales to share. The sequel, *Troyana*, returns to this world. This time, the rebels and their leader Amos destroy the golden calf and form a new government. This stereotypical depiction of the Brazilians is hardly stellar, but it's meant as a fun romp for readers.

Meek's "Giants on the Earth" (*Astounding*, December 1931–January 1932) has the Jovians, or biblical "sons of God," conquer the earth. "The newcomer stood five inches over six feet in his flat sandals, but it was only in his unusual height and his enormous strength that he showed the blood of his Jovian father," the story narrates. At last, in an alien twist, these immensely strong giants can only be destroyed with the help of giant caterpillars from Mars. Like many pulps, the story brings in biblical tales but is more action-orientated than introspective.

The thirties also offered A. Hyatt Verrill's lost world adventures, broken into sections and published in *Amazing*. His "Beyond the Green Prism" (1930) journeys to a hidden South American tribe reduced to microscopic size, whose god statue Wira Kocha has "Hebraic features." On seeing the statue, the narrator describes them as "European" but also "distinctly, indisputably Semitic." As he adds, "But if there had been any question, there were the garments. Upon the head was a tight-fitting skull-cap with tabs or ears, a cape or shawl was over the shoulders, and a toga-like robe covered the body." All this describes an Ashkenazi Jew like those the author has seen. The image is jarring, not just for the stereotype but on considering the ancient timeline involved:

Wira Kocha, most revered of the ancient Peruvian divinities, the Bearded One, as he had been called, had actually existed, and he had been a European, a white man, and that ages, centuries before Columbus, a Semite, a Hebrew—or more likely many of the race—had reached the shores of the New World and had visited Peru. . . . Wira Kocha, the Semite, had come from the east, he had been revered as a divinity; he had taught the people their arts, their religion, their civilization. . . . All were descendants—or partial descendants—of those wandering Jews, who, no one could say how long before, had reached America, had settled in the land, and had left their indelible imprint upon the people, the civilizations, the mythology of the ancient American races.

A preColumbian Jew would not dress as a Hassid, and evidence suggests they didn't find the New World. Of course, it's a fantasy, and the character in question is long dead and mummified.

Verrill returns to his lost tribes in "Through the Andes" (1934) when the explorers find ancient writing that may be Hebrew. At last, they read a carved record of the Jewish explorers who, directed on their journey by the Prophet Elijah, taught the locals to worship, dress, and speak like them. It adds, "It is a goodly land and the people are like unto the Sons of Israel. Yea, verily do I believe that they be of our race . . . but gone astray to become idolators. . . . So we have spread the Faith and have won them back to become the Chosen Ones of God, and have taught unto them our arts and our wisdom that when our lives be spent they may forever follow in our footsteps." The explorer, reading it, finally realizes: "Wira Kocha, the Creator! Why had it never occurred to me that it was but a slightly garbled and corrupted form of Jehovah." The place names, too, come from Bible terms. With this, the lost history is revealed, though there are no present-day Jews complicating the romanticized and rather garbled narrative.

By contrast, a few authors demonstrated what the lost world genre would look like from a Jewish perspective. Lazar Borodulin is said to have written the first Yiddish science fiction novel, *Af yener zayt Sambatyon* (On the Other Side of Sambatyon River, 1929), in which a journalist encounters a mad scientist in the land of the Red Jews (one of the Lost Tribes). In fact, the river of the story comes from Jewish lore as the place where the Lost Tribes were exiled, and the story builds heavily on Talmudic lore. At the same time, the scientist's ray gun and the lost land's encapsulation by geysers give it a more science-based setting. Once again, the story is told of the adventure, discovery, and return to civilization.

In this vein, Ben Aronin's *The Lost Tribe: Being the Strange Adventures of Raphael Drale in Search of the Lost Tribes of Israel* (1934) has a Jewish teenage hero growing up in Connecticut after his rabbi father died rescuing the Torah in a Russian pogrom. As such, he reflects many immigrants fleeing violence in recent memory. Raphael begins reading Eldad Hadoni (Eldad the Danite) "a fantastic tale of a man's adventures in search of the lost tribes of Israel" (17). He soon becomes obsessed, discovering that Eldad was his ancestor, and that the book contains a coded map. After a long pirate adventure on the open seas, Raphael reaches the lost tribe of Dan, isolated Hebrew-speakers hidden in the Arctic who don't realize the Temple was destroyed. They are pledged to remain there, secretly, until the Messiah returns. Moreover, the People of Dan have ancient mystical understandings of the heartbeat of the world, powered by the life force breathed into it at creation. Raphael is quite surprised at their teachings. He also falls in love with Miriam, a young woman of their tribe. Of course, the story has a traditional end, with Raphael returning to the ordinary world to tell of his fabulous adventures. Still, the Jewish lore is presented honestly, adding a pleasing authenticity to the writing,

After this, Aronin's *Cavern of Destiny* (1943) quests for the ancient Breastplate of Judgement used in the First Temple. Echoing the conflict over the Temple Mount in realistic social commentary, all the different faiths revere this treasure. The hero thus understands it must be sacrificed to have peace. He drops it out of his plane into the Mediterranean and explains: "The only Caverns of Destiny for my people are the furrows of the earth. Out of them will come the most precious of all treasures—the golden grain, the bread of man. All of Palestine is our third Temple and every man and woman who labors here a Kohen—a priest." Both stories emphasize how well the pulp genre blends with Bible-inspired stories, already filled with discovery, adventure, and artifacts of power. An author who knows Jewish culture can add the spiritual dimension often missing and explore all the deep understanding available from the ancient world.

Other authors inserted the Jewish experience more subtly. Henry George Weiss (writing as Francis Flagg) created "The Synthetic Monster" (*Wonder Stories,* March 1921). Edwards, the narrator, moves to Arizona and begin working for the mysterious Dr. Jacobs, a biologist. With his suggestively Jewish name, the character gets to step into Victor Frankenstein's shoes. A horrible creature prowls the area, emitting strange blubbering noises from his strange flat face. Eventually, Edwards finds his employer's notes and discovers he has been building an artificial man. However, much like the classic golem that may have inspired this tale, his creation has no power of speech and little thought. The end comes with a shocking twist as the police arrive to discover that the monster has swallowed Jacobs's head. No one is identified as Jewish, but monster and scientist share Jewish imagery. "Thus the SF pulps were part of a unique contribution to American culture as the Jewish influence spread out into the mainstream disguised, like Popeye and Betty Boop" (Weinbaum 1998, 185).

Jewish characters between 1858 and 1960 have several patterns. Often, they're stereotyped as Shylock, the Wandering Jew, the master manipulator. "The main characters are never the dashing, action-oriented adventurer types that one so often finds in other science fiction or fantasy stories" (Jaret 1985, 129). When positive, they're mad scientists, rabbis, occult advisers—bookish characters who offer little violence. "The fascination and charm of these stories and their characters lies in the narrative in conversation, wit, and atmosphere" (129).

A rare sympathetic depiction that flips this is William Wirt's Jimmie Cordie stories, which ran in *Frontier Stories, Argosy,* and *Short Stories* in the twenties and thirties. It stars a group of soldiers of fortune: Jimmie, Red

Dolan, George Grisby, and Putney, joined in its spinoff series by The Boston Bean (John Cabot Winthrop) and The Fighting Yid (Abraham Cohen). The Jewish character, included for multiculturalism, is presented as a respected member of the team, countering stereotypes of the bookish pacifist Jew.

In another stand-out offering, George S Viereck and Paul Eldridge's Wandering Jew trilogy was shockingly erotic for thirties readers, arcing through *My First Two Thousand Years: The Autobiography of the Wandering Jew; Salome: The Wandering Jewess;* and *The Invincible Adam* (1932), in which much is made of the lost "rib." The protagonist Cartaphilus is not miserably suffering in this version but embraces the opportunity to live forever. Here, the Jewish hero is cast as a sympathetic and universal figure rather than a stereotype. Further, he discovers other miracle workers post-Jesus, and thus decides that Jesus's powers were a natural phenomenon. Eventually, he meets his perfect mate in the likewise immortal Salome. At the same time, his quest to topple oppressive Christianity leads to his inspiring Mohammad, Attila the Hun, and Martin Luther and subversively revels in alternate paths to understanding. The trilogy ends in modern times, suggesting that the rise of Lenin and Mussolini are Cartaphilus's final attempt to reshape humanity. As the hero and Salome finally retreat to the Garden of Eden, she attempts to create an artificial being, more female homuncula than golem, who is destined to usher in a better future for humanity. This reimagines Eden on several levels, including with a female creator and creation. Seriousness and comedy alternate through this subversive world history tour that considers the effect of religion on humanity's evolution. It has more of a Jewish critical sensibility than most stories of the time, reflected in its Jewish protagonists.

Pulps were far from Jewish. Still, some authors embraced them. "Pulps may also be read as icons expressing the cultural sacrifices of assimilation made by Jewish writers of the time" (Weinbaum 1998, 180). Accordingly, Catherine "C. L." Moore, who wrote the extremely popular Jirel of Joiry sword and sorcery tales, and married Henry Kuttner, added a suggestively Jewish character to her other pulp adventure "Tryst in Time" (*Astounding Stories*, December 1936). In it, Eric Rosner, former soldier of fortune, is the action hero and time traveler. On all his journeys, from Roman times to Medieval France and Elizabethan England, he meets the same woman, until they finally find a path to be together. True, it's more romantic than science- or even logic-based, but the time travel signifies an early look toward science fiction, with one of the first Jewish adventure heroes.

Chapter 3

The Golden Age

American Science Fiction Begins

FIRST FANDOM

Isaac Asimov (1975) said: "Science fiction can be defined as that branch of literature which deals with the reaction of human beings to changes in science and technology." While some Roman and medieval stories could be classified as science fiction (though highly unrealistic and generally unexplained), the genre as it's known today begins in the Industrial Revolution as technology began changing society. In this era, Jules Verne and H. G. Wells invented many of the popular concepts and heavily influenced the authors that followed. For instance, after becoming editor of *Galaxy*, H. L. Gold (1951) wrote that as a "dazzled boy" he "discovered science fiction in 1927, at the age of 13." *Amazing Stories* had been out for a year, but he first found Wells's *War of the Worlds*. "The personal impact was that of an explosive harpoon, and when I belatedly discovered those beautifully garish Paul covers, decorated with heroically paralyzed men in jodhpurs and simperingly paralyzed women in blowy veils, among giant insects and plants with leering heads, I was hooked."

As Hitler turned on the Jews, 300,000 German Jews—including many scientists, scholars, and artists—escaped to America (Erens 1984, 5). Still, American Jews in the thirties were mostly second-generation working-class citizens. They were starting to settle in and explore new opportunities but were horrified by the plight of their cousins in Europe, even as an echoing Fascism was rising in America. Asimov explains a general feeling of unease: "We were not safe even in the United States. The undercurrent of genteel anti-Semitism was always there. The occasional violence of the more ignorant street gangs always existed. But there was also the pull of Nazism"

(1994, 20). These anxieties about the future and liberal leanings found a home in imaginative fiction.

During the Golden Age of Science Fiction (generally specified as beginning with John W. Campbell Jr.'s assumption of the editorship of *Astounding* in October 1937 and ending with World War II), Jews found themselves writing and editing it. It was an excellent match: "The disproportionately high involvement of Jews performing such writing might have resulted from the sense of existing in two cultures that was part of most Jewish households of the era . . . early as pulp texts might exemplify struggles of changing modalities of Jewish immigrants trying to make contact with Americans, the latter perceived at times as even an alien species" (Weinbaum 1998, 180). Saul B. Troen (1994, 2) adds in his dissertation on the topic that it was a place to voice their concerns in a shifting world: "It was not difficult to adapt and modify the imagistic and impressionist flights of prior storytellers to address the pressing needs of concerns of contemporary Jewish life in its multitudes of countries and guises." Jews, already writing cross-cultural ethnic fiction of the immigrants' struggle, began projecting cross-species experiences of arriving on other planets. With this, they adapted traditional Yeshiva wrangling about the nature of the universe into a secular form. As the Yiddish café culture faded, science fiction magazines in English took its place: Metaphors addressed the Jewish demonization in Europe while invoking "the spirited nature of the arguments of quasi-religious nature in the readers' columns about the nature of the cosmos and the limitless horizons of the scientific and stellar universe, the juxtaposition of Jewish sense of outsiderness onto other planets, the identification of the Jewish alienated sense of self and other" (Weinbaum 1998, 184). At a time when the media wanted to sideline these social topics, science fiction tackled them directly.

Further, it was one of the few professions not shut to Jews. Comic book writer Will Eisner explains of his field, "This business was brand new. It was the bottom of the social ladder, and it was wide open to anybody. Consequently, the Jewish boys who were trying to get into the field of illustration found it very easy to come aboard" (quoted in Davin 2006, 175). The same was true of science fiction, with both Jewish-run industries open to hiring. Eisner adds:

> Early science fiction fandom was overwhelmingly Jewish. Indeed, observed Fredrick Pohl, "most of the science fiction fans and writers I grew up with were Jews. For example, the world's very first science fiction fan club, the Scienceers, launched in New York City in either 1929 or 1930, was composed mostly of Jewish teenagers like Mort Weisinger, Allen (Aaron) Glasser, and (joining in 1931) Julius Schwartz, all of whom would later become professionals in the field. Some of the thirteen members who did not go on to professional status

included Jewish fans Isidore Manson, Arthur J Berkowitz, Lester Blum, Leo Schubert, and Philip Rosenblatt." (Davin 2006, 176)

Hugo Gernsback (1884–1967), a Jewish Belgian immigrant sometimes called the "Father of Science Fiction," invented a dry-cell battery and began selling the first mail-order radio set. Working in this mindset, he wrote an electronics-based short story called "Ralph 124C 41+," impressive for predicting microfilm, vending machines, tape recorders, synthetic fibers, the jukebox, the television, satellites, and spaceflight. Further, a blueprint for radar, years before its invention, casually appears within the text. As Gernsback continued writing futuristic short stories based on real science and technology, he sought a home for them all.

He created the first science fiction magazine, *Amazing Stories*, in 1926. This ninety-six-page magazine slowly climbed to sales of 100,000 copies. It was devoted to "scientification," a term Gernsback coined. Rebelling against the simplified girl-and-monster pulps, he preferred a more literary and thoughtful story. He cultivated many authors, and a new genre was born. Some identify this as the "Age of Wonder"—the beginning of American science fiction.

In 1929, Gernsback founded *Science Wonder Stories* which finally described its content as "science fiction." Gernsback hired David Lasser, the son of Russian Jewish immigrants, to edit, making him the world's second Jewish science fiction editor. Third Jewish publisher Ned Pines changed the name to *Thrilling Wonder Stories* and had Mort Weisinger edit it. Pines, meanwhile, went on to publish *Startling Stories*, *Captain Future*, *Fantastic Story Magazine*, and *Strange Stories*. More Jewish editors joined the lineup as Louis Silberkleit published *Science Fiction, Future Fiction, Dynamic Science Fiction and Science Fiction Quarterly.* Bernard Ziff published *Amazing Stories* after 1938 and *Fantastic Adventures* after 1939. Publishers Sol Cohen, Joseph Ferman, Leo Margulies, Irwin Stein, Abraham Goodman, and Arnold E. Abramson join the list, along with magazine editors Horace L. Gold, Samuel Mines, Norman Lobsenz, Cele Lolli, and Judy Lynn del Rey (Moskowitz 1976, 44–45).

Meanwhile, Mort Weisinger and Julius Schwartz launched one of the first sci-fi fanzines, *The Time Traveller* (January 1932), edited by Allen Glasser. The first issue shared the history of science fiction. "What we did not realize at the time," Schwartz recalled later "was that its history was actually about to begin" (Davin 2006, 176). Next, Weisinger and Schwartz founded the first science fiction literary agency, Solar Sales Service, and represented many of the pros like Weinbaum, Kuttner, Bester, Lovecraft, and Bradbury. First Fandom, as it's sometimes known, from 1933–1936, emphasized serious science. In 1934, Gernsback founded the Science Fiction League for the promotion of this attitude. *Fantasy Magazine* was the central fanzine, alerting everyone to new magazines and opportunities.

Other Jews made massive contributions to the genre. For indeed, many short story authors of this era were Jewish: Henry Kuttner, Forrest J. Ackerman, Stanley G. Weinbaum, Avram Davidson, Horace L. Gold, William Tenn (born Philip Klass), John Christopher (Christopher Samuel Youd), Curt Siodmak, Howard Fast, Robert Sheckley, Nat Schachner, Gertrude Friedberg, Herbert Kastle, Ward Moore, David V. Reed, Robert Bloch, Cyril Kornbluth, Raymond Z. Gallun, Arthur Leo Zagat, Isaac R. Nathanson, Judith Merril, and of course Isaac Asimov.

In late 1936, as *Fantasy Magazine* declined, fans became more interested in science fiction for its own sake. John Campbell took over Gernsback's magazines in 1936, discouraging ethnic and women's author names as well as stories on cultural difference. While many Jewish authors appeared then and a generation later, there were limited numbers of Jewish characters. The genre was solidifying, and characters were growing homogenized. Jewish editor Donald A. Wollheim's printed fanzine *The Phantagraph* took *Fantasy Magazine*'s place until Wollheim, along with John B. Michel, started the Fantasy Amateur Press Association in August 1937. Wollheim also edited two of the earliest science fiction periodicals, *Cosmic Stories* and *Stirring Science Stories*, starting in February 1941. Two years later, Wollheim edited the first mass-market science fiction anthology *The Pocket Book of Science Fiction*. For twenty years, he published Ace Books, launching many new writers including Philip K. Dick, Samuel R. Delany, Ursula K. Le Guin, Leigh Brackett, and John Brunner. During this time, he and coeditor Terry Carr began the annual anthology series, *The World's Best Science Fiction*. He and his wife, Elsie Balter Wollheim, would go on to launch the influential Daw Books, still publishing today.

Meanwhile, early fandom was splitting into two camps: political and less so. Teenage Sam Moskowitz's side sought out conventions and professional speakers. "The other group gathered around Wollheim and his friend John Michel, whose views were expressed in a leftist manifesto, 'Mutation or Death,' that argued that fans should strive for the kind of social change that they saw within their favorite stories," writes Alec Nevala-Lee in *Astounding: John W. Campbell, Isaac Asimov, Robert A. Heinlein, L. Ron Hubbard, and the Golden Age of Science Fiction* (2018, 101). This, of course, was a very Jewish concept, encouraging readers to consider the texts' messages and become repairers of the world.

In May 1938, Sam Moskowitz and William Sykora chaired the Newark Convention, officially the First National SF Convention. When Campbell showed up with writers John Clark and L. Sprague de Camp, they discovered fifteen people in attendance. Looking out at the gathering, the editor remarked dryly, "Better than I expected" (Nevala-Lee 2018, 101). However, the gathering quickly swelled to a 100 people, larger than any of the previous regional science fiction meetings. Plans for a WorldCon the following year were announced, though here the political split caused sparks: "Wollheim would be in charge. Moskowitz responded by founding a rival organization. New Fandom, to wrest back control. The situation became so rancorous that Margulies was forced to dissolve the Greater New York Science Fiction League, and Wollheim and Michel responded by starting the group that became known as the Futurians" (Nevala-Lee 2018, 102).

The Futurians included Wollheim, Michel, Asimov, Kornbluth, Merril, Fredrick Pohl, Jack Rubinson, Herman Leventman, James Blish, Chester Cohen, Rosalind Cohen, Larry Shaw, Doë "Leslie Perri" Baumgardt, Daemon Knight, Jack Gillespie, Dick Wilson, and Robert A. W. Lowndes. Asimov recalls, "They consisted of a group of brilliant teenagers who, as nearly as I could tell, all came from broken homes and had led miserable, or, at the least, insecure childhoods. Once again, I was an outsider, for I had a tightly knit family and a happy childhood, but in other respects, I was charmed by all of them and felt that I had found a spiritual home" (1994, 61).

In his book about the group, Damon Knight described them as "a group of hungry young science fiction fans and would-be writers which evolved into a sort of subculture: the Futurians had their own communal dwellings, their folklore, songs and games, even their own mock religion" (Liptak 2013). Further, Knight described himself and Lowndes as the only non-Jewish core members (Davin 2006, 176). "Many were Jewish, and most were fervent communists, more out of the excitement of being part of a movement than from any deep ideological conviction." Amid the depression, with many of the members scarred from childhood illnesses, they saw science fiction as a gateway to possibility. The politics were off-putting for some, however. Asimov was especially interested in their fanzine, of which he wrote in his diary, "I intend to write for [the magazine], but hesitate to put my name to violently radical and probably atheistical articles, so I am wondering if they will allow me to write under a pseudonym" (quoted in Nevala-Lee 2018, 102).

The years 1938–1946 offered astonishing activity. The pulps were giving way to more scientific trope-defining stories. Reaching a peak in 1953, science fiction magazines published 37 different titles with 176 individual issues. (A year later, however, many of these were closing from oversaturation.) Paperback science fiction lines like Avon and Bantam began appearing, publishing works by the Futurians and others.

From 1939–1941, Horace L. Gold was an assistant editor on a trio of science fiction magazines—*Captain Future, Thrilling Wonder Stories,* and *Startling Stories.* In the early forties, Gold freelanced as a writer for DC

Comics. He launched *Galaxy Science Fiction* in 1950, which was soon followed by its companion fantasy magazine, *Beyond Fantasy Fiction* (1953–55). All these targeted young male readers with stories of adventure and wonder tied to the beloved pulps. Notably, he insisted on offering three cents a word (in contrast with many competitors' one cent) and let authors retain reprint rights for anthologies. In 1953, Gold shared the first Hugo Award for best professional magazine with Campbell.

WorldCon (still held today) premiered July 2, 1939. It was held in conjunction with the New York World's Fair, with a fitting theme: "The World of Tomorrow." However, the schism among fans continued. In fact, six members of the Futurians weren't allowed through the doors. Moskowitz asked Wollheim to promise that he would do nothing to disrupt the event. Wollheim refused. Pohl later recounted in his memoir: "When we came to Bahai Hall, Don Wollheim, Jonny Michel, Bob Lowndes, Jack Gillespie and I were turned away. Other Futurians were let in and ran courier between us excludees and the action inside, but we were Out" (Liptak 2013). The Futurians gathered in a nearby cafeteria, where they spent time with other convention goers, such as Forrest Ackerman (the first cosplayer), Ray Bradbury, and others. After, there was fallout, but most members made up and continued to work as peers in the science fiction industry. From the first through today, the genre struggled with how much of the political to incorporate and how to get along peaceably.

ASIMOV AND HIS FOUNDATION

Isaac Asimov was born in a Russian shtetl near Smolensk and emigrated to Brooklyn with his parents at age three. He comments, "My mother is Jewish and my father's mother was Jewish and that makes both my father and myself Jewish by definition," though he didn't have a Bar Mitzvah or attend synagogue regularly (Asimov 1974, 1). In his autobiography, *I, Asimov*, he describes growing up quite secular: "I remained without religion simply because no one made any effort to teach me religion—any religion" (1994, 12). He did attend some Hebrew school and read the Bible. He called himself a Humanist, though he regarded the world with a particularly minority-based lens, even without many direct Jewish references.

He also describes a childhood in which he wasn't beaten up for being Jewish though he remained conscious of difference: "I was taunted often enough, sometimes openly by young yahoos and more often subtly by the more educated" (1994, 19). During the war, Asimov became a mechanical engineer for the Navy. He recalls experiencing "an atmosphere of mild anti-Semitism" there (Nevala-Lee 2018, 164). When all the Jews petitioned to take Yom Kippur off instead of Christmas, he was secular enough that he worked on Yom Kippur, but signed the petition to help the others.

Presumably, this time inspired the silly story "My Son, the Physicist" ([1962] 1969) with its very recognizable Jewish mother. Her son Gerard is shocked at her arrival at his military base, where he's been distracted by alien radio signals from Pluto. She, meanwhile, offers a sweet smile that "made something shrieking out of the confusion that enfolded her in the huge government building" (329). As he dashes through the building, explaining the circumstances to the visiting general, his mother offers around oranges and suddenly solves their conundrum—instead of sending a message and awaiting a response, they should keep transmitting until they receive one. She adds that all women understand how to spread news. As Gerard and the general depart, she muses, "Such a fine man, her son, the physicist. Big as he was and important as he was, he still knew that a boy should always listen to his mother" (322).

In 1942, Asimov established the three laws of robotics in his short story "Runaround." This set of ethics was used as the basis for many robot-based stories by other authors, including *Terminator*, *TRON*, and *Forbidden Planet*: A robot may not injure a human being or allow one to come to harm. Beyond this, a robot must obey orders and then preserve itself as long as this does not contradict the prior laws. Asimov's concept of robots echoes the premise of the golem, which, since it could only be created by a worthy man, tended to only be given ethical orders. Further, this hierarchy of altruism is compared by some to the Ten Commandments or Talmudic precepts, which lay out the guidelines for ethical conduct with preserving life as the central concern. These ethical guidelines ensure that Asimov's robots are trustworthy. In many stories, they become a persecuted class. Like a fictional anti-Semite, "a human being who fears or mistrusts robots is either a villain who must be defeated or a skeptic who must be convinced (and given Asimov's views, the two often coincide)" (Portelli 1980, 151).

His *Pebble in the Sky* ([1950] 2017) also deals with prejudice and its results. This, Asimov's first novel, stars the retired tailor Joseph Schwartz, who is suddenly whisked thousands of years into the future. The author comments, "I didn't come right out and say he was Jewish, but I've never found anyone who thought he wasn't" (1974, 3). He seems a wish-fulfillment character, not only in his grand adventure but in his new telepathic powers.

The novel was partly based on Robert Browning's poem "Rabbi ben Ezra," which suggests transcending difference as life on Earth is but one step of the soul's experience. At the same time, Asimov adds, "Some people thought they saw a resemblance to Judea and the Roman Empire of the first century there, and, who knows, maybe they were right" (Asimov 1974, 3). Asimov's biographer James Gunn concurs, explaining that in this work, "Earth is a

Judea with special characteristics; it is a Judea with radiation poisoning and institutionalized euthanasia, and it is a Judea given an opportunity to right its wrongs and regain its freedom" (Gunn 1982, 147).

Certainly, *Pebble* has a metaphor of time-travel as emigration. Meanwhile, the futuristic world is replaying old prejudices, to the point at which a new Holocaust is rising. With this, the hated earthborn clearly parallel the Jews of Europe. Physicist Affret Shekt, of earth, complains that people limit contact with them because of propaganda created, as he says, "by the stupidity of your own bigots" (51). Shekt fights back with intellect, inventing a device that improves brainpower, which he uses successfully on Schwartz. Shekt's daughter Pola falls for someone whose race hate earth humans, and they face the remarks on their mixed marriage together. Lord Ennius, the Imperial Procurator for the Earth, complains later, "Yes, I can blame them. . . . Let them turn from their dreams and fight for assimilation. They don't deny they are different. They simply wish to replace 'worse' by 'better,' and you can't expect the rest of the Galaxy to let them do that" (74). The high minister of Earth adds, "My people are an obstinate and stiff-necked race, who over centuries have withdrawn into themselves because of the—uh—lamentable attitudes toward them in parts of the Galaxy. They have certain taboos, certain fixed Customs—which even I could not afford to violate" (158). Obviously, the word choice in all the dialogue evokes the Jews.

However, in a flip on the Holocaust, the citizens of earth are not to be the victims but the attackers. Shekt blames "a handful of leaders, perverted by the gigantic pressure that excluded them from the Galaxy, hating those who keep them outside, wanting to strike back at any cost, and with insane intensity" (183). The centuries of prejudice have finally pushed them to revenge. As Shekt protests, "As long as we of earth are treated as pariahs, you are going to find in us the characteristics to which you object. If you push us intolerably, is it to be wondered at that we push back?" (51). Of course, this philosophy is more in keeping with the words of Shylock than of the actions in the Holocaust, but post-Holocaust Americans and certainly Israelis were heading toward this sentiment. "The novel is, in the end, a plea for ethnic assimilation and its marked gradualism opposes 'extreme' demands for immediate equality" (Portelli 1980, 151–152).

If the Empire surrenders all they have to the people of earth, they may offer the antidote to their genetic warfare. However, Schwartz, revolted by the genocide, uses his earth knowledge to bomb their temple and thus save the galaxy. The author thus concludes his tale with the ascension of civilization and sanity, destined to heal the earth from the insanities of the tiny groups obsessed with racial superiority.

Asimov has other stories in which he considers the minorities' plight, presumably from an insider perspective. "Evidence" (1946) tells of a robot who is elected mayor, even in an anti-robot community. In "Strikebreaker" (1957), the protagonist processes human waste and is thus shunned in society. When he attempts a revolution, the other people of his artificial world prefer death to supporting him, and he discovers society isn't ready for him to become their equal. Obviously, in the days of racial segregation, this story clearly reflects many cultures. In *The Bicentennial Man*, likewise, the robot struggles for equal rights in a world biased against him. At last, this robot truly assimilates, to the point of becoming organic and even dying in order to be accepted. Only by giving up his gifts and distinctiveness is he welcomed. In this vein, R. Daneel Olivaw, in Asimov's *Robot* and *Foundation* series, is the first robot created who appears identical to man. Through him, Asimov speculates about "passing" in a world of prejudice. "He knows he cannot be accepted as an equal among humans but cannot understand why, since he feels in no way their inferior" (Portelli 1980, 152). Around his human colleague, who fanatically hates robots, Olivaw takes a special pleasure in blending in and thus proving his humanity.

Asimov's Foundation Trilogy, set in a future galactic empire, consists of *Foundation* (1951), *Foundation and Empire* (1952), and *Second Foundation* (1953). It received a Hugo in 1966 as Best All-Time Science Fiction Series. Meanwhile, it uses Yiddishisms to create a simplistic underdog character. This is Preem Palver, who appears only a rustic farmer. However, the stereotype is subverted, as far from being unintelligent or countrified, Palver is the first speaker of the Second Foundation. As Asimov explains:

Sometimes . . . it was necessary for me to have a character whom, for various nefarious purpose of my own, I wanted the reader to underestimate. The easiest trick was to give him a substandard version of English, for then he would be dismissed as a comic character with at most a certain limited folk wisdom. Since the only substandard version of English I can handle faultlessly is the Yiddish dialect, some of the characters in *The Foundation Trilogy* speak it. (Quoted in Brod 2012, 51)

Still, there's more. In the far future are wise, far-seeing people of the book—literally a tribe of encyclopediaists who have been sequestered on a planet at the far end of the galaxy. Some see the specter of the Holocaust or other dark times in this philosophy (for instance, the oral Torah was written down because so many scholars were being killed in the days of Atilla the Hun). Rabbi Gil Student writes: "Over the centuries of widespread pagan and barbaric beliefs and practices, we Jews kept to ourselves as much as possible and maintained our ancient truths and attitudes. We served as outposts of culture and literacy throughout the Dark Ages, maintaining God's truths" (quoted in Price 2013).

These futuristic "people of the book," surrounded by hostile planets, use their smarts to develop increasingly advanced technologies, open clandestine trade routes, and eventually subsume their enemies through simple endurance. They reach out to readers through pure intellect: "The reader's engagement with the story requires only faith in reason, not the suspension of disbelief required by fantasy. The combination of Jewish commitment to rationality, embodied for modern consciousness in science, the Jewish idea of meaning unfolding in history, and Judaism's messianism make futuristic science fiction a natural avenue of exploration for the Jewish imagination" (Brod 2012, 51). Mayor Hardin's rant against the dead scholarship that has replaced science in the Empire appears to be Asimov's reaction to a certain strain of Rabbinic Jewish thought.

The encyclopediaists are the followers of social scientist Hari Seldon, who has applied mathematical equations to behavioral patterns of large groups. He anticipates the fall of the Empire and is devoted to guarding the last remnants of human knowledge and cultural values during the dark age to combat the encroachment of "feudalism," or fascism he predicts is coming. It's notable that one Hebrew word for foundation is *mossad*, the name of Israel's national intelligence agency. "And what about Hari Seldon's name? Perhaps we should ask using the barely concealed Hebrew version, Ari Elyon, Lion Most High," notes critic Roger Price in "Isaac Asimov, Two Foundations and the Jews" (2013). His name is not only suggestively Jewish but offers a symbolic warrior angel association.

As a safeguard, Seldon made sure that a Second Foundation would be placed "at the other end of the Galaxy," should the First Foundation fall—a parallel to the division of biblical Judea and Israel. Moreover, in Seldon's philosophy, there's the kabbalistic theme of a trajectory to the universe that only the most informed can see. As the book *Foundation and Empire* reveals, the foundation has secrets. "They have books, old books—so old that the language they are in is only known to a few of the top men. But the secrets are shrouded in ritual and religion and none may use them" (Asimov [1952] 2008, 58).

The public face of the Second Foundation, Preem Palver and his wife, are very Jewish, based on their dialogue. Characters include the archetypal Jewish mother who can say, "So shut your mouth, Pappa. Into you anybody could bump." Of course, the characters are not specifically identified as Jewish, but the elements are present, as Brod observes, including "Jewish commitment to rationality, embodied for modern consciousness in science, the Jewish idea of meaning unfolding in history, and Judaism's messianism" (51). Bayta and her husband Toran arrive at Haven in *Foundation and Empire*. She has dark hair, close-set eyebrows, and warm brown eyes, hinting at stereotypical Jewish features. "And behind a very sturdily built and staunchly defended façade of practical, unromantic hard-headedness toward life, there was just that little pool of softness that would never show if you poked for it, but could be reached if you just knew how—and never let on that you were looking for it" (90). The pair jokes together not just like an old married couple but a Jewish married couple. All these characters are quite recognizable for readers. By transmitting his culture as well as his ideals in this celebrated series, Asimov made the genre more Jewish from the beginning.

Asimov is also famous for short works, often with Jewish characters or allegory. "Unto the Fourth Generation" ([1959] 1969) is what Asimov calls "the only Jewish story it occurred to me to write" (299). It has a highly assimilated Jew, Sam Levkowich, wander New York only to have old-world Levkowiches appear everywhere around him. Puzzled, he goes through his day believing he's losing his mind, until at last he meets his Russian ancestor, who reveals he was granted only two hours to return and see his great-great-grandson. He addresses Sam by the old world name "Schmu-el," reconnecting him with his ancient heritage. Meeting him, Sam feels the love of all he once left behind. He kneels before his ancestor and begs a blessing "that it may be well with me all the days of my life" and afterward feels a new confidence in his modern culture (306). The title, beyond a Bible quote, stresses the distance assimilation creates and the yearning to connect with the culture left behind.

Asimov's famous "Nightfall" ([1941] 2003) posits a world that rarely experiences night. The humanlike civilization there greets it with panic and claustrophobia bordering on madness and anarchy. The previous darkness, it's said, is described in the Book of Revelations. "The Cultists said that every two thousand and fifty years, Lagash entered a huge cave, so that all the suns disappeared, and there came total darkness over the world!" (119). Meanwhile, the names (Aton, Sheerin, Beenay, Yimot) are very Hebraic. Even as people prophesize in the streets, the darkness comes and with it a great revelation—not a handful of stars but countless thousands, in a divine vision for all that also echoes Abraham's blessing. The story is very biblical and deeply religious, expressing awe and the beauty and wonder of the universe, even while transposed to another planet. Here is the epitome of Jewish science fiction, finding spirituality in the larger universe.

HUMOR AND SATIRE

In some of his short works, Asimov is more direct, often writing little quirky joke pieces. His "The Last Question" ([1956] 2000) marries science fiction with the Bible, connecting the future and the ancient past. It begins in 2061, when Alexander Adell and Bertram Lupov ask the new Multivac computer the deepest question of their existence—what will humanity do when all the stars blink out? After entropy runs its course in a trillion years, can it be reversed? Multivac replies that there is insufficient data to answer. Over the centuries, different people inquire, but the answer remains the same. After ten trillion years, the last human asks, and still the answer remains. However, the computer continues working and working. When all the collected data from the death of the universe has been compiled, "It came to pass that AC learned how to reverse the direction of entropy" (223). Since there is no human to tell, it arranges a demonstration and writes a program in the dark chaos. And AC says, "LET THERE BE LIGHT!" (223). It restores civilization through the power of creation and the words of the Bible. Playing with the concept again in "Darwinian Pool Room" (1979), Asimov insists the concept of Genesis is incorrect. He uses pool as a metaphor for how far-fetched this plan would have to be, even as he insists on questioning the basic premises of civilization. This, of course, is a recognizably Jewish approach.

Asimov also offers the light "The Two-Centimeter Demon" (1988), in which a man keeps the biblical demon Azazel in his pocket. A classic story of imprecise wishing follows, as the demon, asked to make a girl's fiancé a great basketball star, is happy to help but knows little about the game. He makes the young man score over and over but fails to realize the difference between the home basket and the visitor's basket. So ends the attempt to prosper through demonic advantage. Azazel himself is friendly, with a subtle nod to his biblical origins. "He says that his country is kindly, decent, and highly civilized, and he speaks with enormous respect of his ruler whom he won't name but whom he calls merely the All-in-All" (4). Beyond this, the story only gives the classic genie adventure a Jewish coating. Over time, Asimov wrote an entire series of stories about Azazel, finally giving them a science fiction explanation to bring them nuance beyond the fantasy genre.

Asimov also enjoyed puns. The goofy "A Loint of Paw" ([1957] 1978) has Montie Stein, a character given a pointedly Jewish name, arrested for theft. However, "It was his manner of avoiding arrest during that interval that brought on this epoch-making case of the *State of New York* vs *Montgomery Harlow Stein*, with all its consequences. It introduced law to the fourth dimension" (1). To avoid arrest, Stein entered a time machine and sped seven years into the future, thus invoking the statute of limitations. Lawyers argue on both sides even as the character, like so many loveable underdogs, dodges the consequences of his actions. At last, the judge releases him, saying, in a pithy phrase, "A niche in time saves Stein" (20).

Other authors stood out for their Jewish humor during the formative years of science fiction. After publication in *Astounding*, especially of his story "Child's Play" (1947), William Tenn was hailed as the field's reigning humorist. The author explains, "Now, looking back on it, I now know I was trying to write humor, and tell a moral tale at the same time—and now, if you ask me what I was writing, I would say I was writing moral fables" (Rich 2009, 380). In this story, set in 2353, the protagonist receives a Build-A-Man Set #3, ages eleven to thirteen, for Christmas. As the instructions explain, the equipment "will enable the child of this age-group to build and assemble complete adult humans in perfect working order." One's mind must immediately leap to the golem, though there are also reflections of the Jewish perception of angels as the instructions continue:

> "Never forget that mannikins are constructed for one purpose and one purpose only." I won't, Sam promised. "Whether they are sanitary mannikins, tailoring mannikins, printing mannikins or even sunevviarry mannikins, they are each constructed with one operation of a given process in view. When you make a mannikin that is capable of more than one function, you are committing a crime so serious as to be punishable by public admonition." (257–258)

In Judaism, angels are divine messengers, each likewise sent with a single task. Later on, the story goes more directly allegorical, explaining, "Sam wished he had anything—even a fig leaf—to cover his nakedness. He felt like a character in the Garden of Eden trying to build up a logical case for apple-eating" (270).

The protagonist, a stereotypical nice guy whose romantic interest has chosen someone else, decides to duplicate her (even as she insists on keeping Sam as her sensitive friend since her fiancé is too businesslike). Instead, a copy of himself appears and immediately starts judging him: "I'm unstable?" his image demands. "Look who's talking! The guy who's been mooning his way through his adult life, who wants to marry an overdressed, conceited collection of biological impulses that would come crawling on her knees to any man sensible enough to push the right buttons" (268). After this literal self-assessment, the hero must prove that he is human and more worthy of life than the copy, but eventually comes up short. The author reveals that he wrote the story while purser on a cargo ship, early in 1946, after an episode where his shipmates got him drunk and he had no hangover, all amid mild anti-Semitic hazing (Rich 2009, 380). With all this, his efforts to explain pen-names, Jewish resilience, and others' expectations combined into a massive metaphor and led to this story's creation.

Clifford Simak offers a different metaphor in "The World of the Red Sun" (1931). Harl Swanson and Bill Kressman travel to the future only to find a reddish wasteland. Primitive men take them captive and force them to fight to entertain the Golan-Kirt, a thought monster, who is in fact a giant brain. The men realize that ridicule weakens it and taunt the creature, saving society. The brain controlling the thoughts of the mob, of course, is hard to ignore as a Hitler allegory. The solution, Simak suggests, is mocking it and dismissing all it offers.

Jews (or Jewishly named characters) in adventures like this one were rare but not unheard of. Stanley G. Weinbaum (1902–1935) died early from lung cancer, robbing the world of a writer whom Asimov named the world's best and many called the first modern science fiction writer thanks to his fully formed alien characters. His "A Martian Odyssey" ([1934] 2003) sends his team to explore pyramids on Mars. The team consists of Leroy the biologist, Harrison the astronomer and captain, Dick Jarvis the chemist, and Putz, the engineer. When Harrison insists a crew member "spill it," Putz puns on the request, suggesting a "spiel" is a story, and otherwise drops Yiddishisms and silliness on the adventure (2). While identifiably Jewish heroes were rare, a few continued to slip in as the authors determinedly wrote in an increasingly hostile world.

Humor has always tied into many Jewish works, and the new genre was no exception. Horace L. Gold's beloved "Trouble with Water" ([1939] 1974) has a Jewish concessions seller snub a water gnome while he's out fishing. In response, the creature curses him with repelling water. He can't shave, he can't serve sodas, he can't drink anything but beer. Worse, he frightens off his daughter's suitor. At last, an Irishman who understands the ways of gnomes helps him apologize. Through the story runs the taint of the schlemiel—the man who's guaranteed to screw up anything and blow any lucky break he gets. Thus, this story ostensibly about the Irish supernatural offers a particularly Jewish flavor even as a cross-cultural solution appears.

Kuttner and his wife C. L. Moore's "Nothing but Gingerbread Left" (1943) also played with humor, this time in an anti-Nazi satire typical of the war years. The story introduces a compulsive jingle that will damage the German war effort and drive Hitler mad. The fictional gingerbread marching song is so terribly catchy and distracting that it slowly sabotages morale and efficiency. Its writer, Professor Rutherford, works out the "perfect sematic formula." Anyone who tries to reason, including a creepy Nazi doctor, immediately has his mind drift to gingerbread. All these authors invoked Mel Brooks's later philosophy, disarming the enemy and then their memory with humor—through in this case, their own lives were on the line.

FEMINISM

Jewish women, heavily involved in progressive and labor movements, marched for equal rights in Eastern Europe and carried these sensibilities to America. In New York, they accounted for 17 percent of the founding members of the Woman Suffrage Party (Lacoue-Labarthe 2016). As well as engaging in politics, they pushed their philosophies through their writing. Judith Merril (born Zissman), a Futurian, wrote *Shadow on the Hearth* (1950), which depicts a nuclear World War III. This story, seen from the quiet, understated perspective of a suburban New York housewife, was eventually televised as *Atomic Attack*. She wrote other stories of small characters caught up in great wars, presumably reflecting her own experiences. This brought a female perspective into the many post-apocalyptic stories of the age. Many of her other works were subversively feminist as she, like a small group of other female writers, embarked into this new genre.

Non-Jewish author Catherine "C. L." Moore married Henry Kuttner and wrote with him jointly (sometimes as Lewis Padgett and Laurence O'Donnell), though she also had impressive solo credits. Her "Fruit of Knowledge" ([1940] 1998) follows Lilith as she creates herself within the Garden of Eden. "I have secrets of my own," she says, "and power not even God can control" (56). To her shock and horror, after she and Adam fall in love, God punishes her defiance by shaping her discarded form into Eve, Adam's new love. "There was a roundness and an appealing softness to her that was new in Eden, but the shape she wore was Lilith's and none other" (58). Lilith realizes that this is God's punishment for her tampering with his plans. Not only is she a fully developed character, but she's not entirely the villain of the narrative. Subversively, this Eve is shrewish, childish, and manipulative. "Lilith may be representative of evil, but Eve is not representative of good. Instead, the differences between the two fall along the lines of intelligence versus ignorance, desire versus ambivalence" (Osherow 2000, 74). Even as Lilith pleads for Adam to return to her, Eve tempts Adam, and both are cast from the Garden. However, Lilith does find a feminist freedom. God ends the story by offering Lilith, "Make your own choice, Queen of Air and Darkness."

She responds, "Let my children and Adam's haunt hers to their graves then! . . . Mine are disinherited—let them take vengeance!" (75). Adam's betrayal after she loved him has earned him punishment eternally. With this, Adam will always remember what he has lost. More importantly, Lilith has chosen her own fate. "This revisionist work moves Lilith into a place where she may be viewed as vital, powerful, and sacred. Lilith remains active at the end of Moore's story, present in all her awesome mystery" (Osherow 2000, 74).

Moore's "Tree of Life" ([1936] 1975) appeared in *Weird Tales* in 1936. Despite its biblical title, this story offers a dryad-like alien encounter with another touch of Lilith. A questing man hears a crying woman in a Martian temple and seeks her out. She is "huddled against an angle of fallen walls and veiled in a fabulous show of long dark hair" with "something uncannily odd about her" (319). He can barely focus on her features, seeing instead a "luminous blot of whiteness in the gloom" (319). She pleads with him to guide her back to the Tree of Life, and he succumbs. When they arrive, however, the tree people reveal that he is intended as a sacrifice. The tree itself is powerful yet horrific, as danger breathes from it "so strongly that Smith felt the hair lifting on his neck as he stared" (332). This encounter between ordinary man and the ancient, unknowable power of woman and tree hints at the numinous Edenic power forbidden to man.

Leslie F. Stone (a pseudonym of Leslie F. Silberberg, born Rubenstein) published eighteen stories between 1929 and 1940. Daughter of celebrated poet Lillian Spellman, she offered many female protagonists and characters of color. In "The Conquest of Gola" ([1931] 2018), Earth invades Venus and plans to terraform for profit, though the planet is already inhabited. The story presents the female aliens there as sympathetic and beautiful in their telepathy, explaining from their perspective, "How envious they must have been of our beautiful golden coats, our moveable eyes, our power to scent, hear, and touch with any part of the body, to absorb food and drink through any part of the body most convenient to us at any time. Oh yes, laugh though you may, without a doubt we were also freaks to those freakish [humans]" (101). The alien women defeat the human invaders, they rebel, and the aliens defeat them again, emphasizing humanity's warmongering ways. The wise, pacifist people who are so different and only long to live freely could be any persecuted group, from women to Jews.

While Stone gave her characters non-Jewish names, her themes included criticizing "the breeding of an Aryan superior race and the questioning of dual loyalty of members of a race that had a national identity plugged in elsewhere but took posts in American government" (Weinbaum 1998, 186). In her novel *Out of the Void*, the first astronaut to visit Mars is a woman disguised as a man: once more the metaphor of "passing" can represent multiple minorities. Still, she dreams of a utopia ruled by gentle pacifists. In her "Letter of the Twenty-fourth Century," humanity has replaced life in the cities with a utopian garden that evokes Eden.

Some compare Stone's paired stories "Men with Wings" and "Women with Wings" to the golem legend, as the second story artificially augments the women. However, there are more interesting themes in the context of Hitler's rise to power. Stone begins with the superhuman, the winged male, abducting the weaker human female to aid in breeding. However, she critiques this concept, as for decades women had been rising beyond the pedestal of the "angel of the house" and, she suggests, need not be dominated. Feminism, from the vote to jobs, threatens the patriarchal structure as shown through the story's dictator and the men who swoop down to assert dominance. "Stone also thus satirizes Nazism as a masculine movement that emphasized violence and virility. As with other writers of the times, Stone seemed intent on showing how Nazism was a virile ideology in which one could lose oneself and become part of the whole" (Weinbaum 1998, 301). In this way, the captured women lose themselves as the oceanic feeling sweeps them into a mindless community submerged beneath the state. "As did others of her period, Stone critically depicted how the individualized subject dissolved and reached sacredness, examining the heart of what was Nazism" (Weinbaum 1998, 302). She masterfully satirized sexism and Nazism at once, even as these ideologies dovetailed.

JEWISH MYSTICISM

Arnold Goldsmith in *The Golem Remembered* (1981) describes kabbalistic tales inspiring much of early science fiction: A man of light in Stone's "The Fall of Mercury" echoes Rabbi Loew's using the Torah to connect the physical and spiritual worlds. Other authors joined in, as Harl Vincent's work robots in "Energy" (*Astounding,* Jan 1935), echo the golem. Schachner's "Emissaries of Space" and Bernard Sachs's "The Memory Machine" transfer memories between people, echoing kabbalistic belief as well. Weinbaum adds, "The fantastic always played a role in Jewish literature (including in Torah or Old Testament, read daily). Thus, the polarity of rational and irrational, real and unreal, did not historically exist for Jews, allowing for ease of picking up the genre that went beyond the limitations of American realism by its very nature" (1998, 182).

The cult of the Children of Hagar meets in New York in Kornbluth's "Kazam Collects" ([1941] 1997). Its leader Kazam insists he is an "occult engineer" who can use mystic forces to accomplish wonders, though he has no religious belief. He describes finding a book written by "a small, very ancient sect of Edomites" that tells of a seer transporting rabbis to a place of wonder (368). Thus, Kazam pits himself against his archenemy Runi Sarif as each quests for a diamond big enough to transport him to paradise. Witnessing all this is a mundane New York detective, who only catches the faintest glimpse of these forces beyond his reality. This story adapts Jewish lore directly, eschewing the metaphor for once.

Asimov, in his introduction to the second Jewish science fiction anthology *More Wandering Stars* (1981) responds to his own question, "How many stories with Jewish themes are written in this field?" As he acknowledges in his answer, the roots of Jewish science fiction date back to the biblical account of Creation (13). Indeed, science fiction based on Bible stories appears in many Golden Age works. Whether these reference the Jewish Torah or Christian Old Testament is debatable, as authors often choose the stories for familiarity more than religious questions seeking answers. Most often, survivors arrive on a distant planet and finally reveal themselves to be Adam and Eve. These include A. E. van Vogt's "Ship of Darkness," Charles L Harness's "The New Reality," Nelson S. Bond's "Another World Begins," and Robert Arthur's "Evolution's End." Longer, more elaborate Adam and Eve fantasies include George MacDonald's *Lilith* (1895), Mark Twain's *Extracts from Adam's Diary* (1904) and *Eve's Diary* (1906), George Bernard Shaw's allegory *Back to Methuselah* (1921), and John Erskine's *Adam and Eve: Though He Knew Better* (1927).

Jewish author Alfred Bester's last-man-alive story "Adam and No Eve" ([1941] 1997) uses the names ironically as Adam's rocket touches off a chain reaction that destroys the planet. He is left the last man on earth and must kill himself so that his DNA, as he hopes, will someday evolve into complex organisms once more. Other stories name the first robot Adam, like Eando Binder's *Adam Link, Robot*. William C. Anderson likewise imagines a cyborg named Adam M-1, paired with Eve M-2. On the cusp of technological invention, French novelist and playwright Villiers de L'Isle-Adam imagined Edison's creation of the perfect woman in his 1886 novel, *L'Ève Future* (Tomorrow's Eve).

Weinbaum's *The New Adam* (1939), published posthumously, expresses much more of the immigrant experience. It shapes a "Jewish alien" growing up as a feral child in human society. Edmund Hall is born different with a "threeknuckled thumb" and "fourknuckled fingers" with a "yellowish gray gaze." In each scene, he feels disconnected. He even hires someone to take him to parties and explain human behavior. He's a prototype for Spock—pure, tortured intellect who can't connect with mankind. He is also Nietzsche's superman, far smarter than any normal human, but this status leaves him miserable. At last, he finds a mentor: Professor Albert Stein, who clearly evokes Einstein: "The brilliant little Jewish savant was already famous; his measurements of electrons were beginning to open up vistas looking to the unknown. Behind his nearsighted eyes and slightly accented speech, Edmond perceived a mind alert and intuitive."

Edmund invents groundbreaking technology, using radium to create energy and cure disease, and then marries his admirer Vanny, not because he's fallen in love, but to save her feelings, as marriage means little to him. She's drawn to his exoticness, which he flourishes for her when he takes her to a Russian restaurant and orders her strange dishes like borscht. Considering all the Russian Jews immigrating to America at the time, this appears a metaphor for the author's own culture, which Vanny doesn't share. Once married, he feels that he and Vanny are too different to really converse or have children. However, when he meets a woman like himself, he's captivated. Further, he sees her as even more exceptional compared with his more ordinary self: "Sarah was a great artist, Edmond admitted to himself—a worthy Eve for her generic Adam, the superwoman intrinsic."

As he struggles to understand the universe, his metaphysical observations take a particularly biblical angle. "Before there was anything, there was Something, for there was the possibility of being—an existability, without which all things were impossible. . . . Then trembling turned away and fled, for Something gibbered in the dark!" After he reads this to Sarah, she understands perfectly—the universe was formed as a creative act, beyond and yet representing the male and female united. Their relationship lacks the passion of the previous one, but is a true meeting of the minds. As Edmund talks with Sarah, he explains that "masculinity is of inceptions, and femininity of growth. The sperm is mine, but the child yours. You are right, too, in saying that there is a compulsion laid upon us, not in the sense of a duty, but as a tenet of nature. We two have received a trust, that our kind survive. We must reproduce." This imagery is not only Edenic but Kabbalistic, emphasizing the feminine and masculine sides of creation.

Chapter 13, called "Lilith and Adam," has Edmond observe, "There is a sort of Satanic majesty about Sarah." She is cold, but he's drawn to her. He's also troubled that, growing up on earth, he's drawn to Vanny as the ideal woman even though more naturally he should be with Sarah. "My love is thus sundered, so that I love one with my brain and another with my body." This may reflect a Jew's worry of assimilation, with advertisements of American skimpily-dressed blondes confusing new immigrants. Edmund continues being torn between the intellectual woman like himself and the sensual "pagan" woman, drifting from one to the other rather callously as he seeks a path to enlightenment and happiness.

ANTI-FASCISM

Asimov particularly admired Nat Schachner (1895–1955), who wrote many historical novels. His "Ancestral Voices" (1933a), introduces the Hitlerian dictator of "Mideuropa" to an accountant who is convinced of his superiority over his boss because he is Anglo-Saxon rather than Spanish. Schachner also includes a boxing match between an Aryan champion, Hans Schilling and a Jewish challenger, Max Bernstein, evoking the fight between Max Schmeling and Max Baer during that year. The main plot is one of the earliest "killing one's grandfather" time-travel paradoxes—the protagonist kills a Hun who attacks him in ancient Rome and wipes out tens of thousands of modern people—an emphasis on the ridiculous illusion of racial purity. Likewise, his "Stratosphere Towers" of 1934 is a great project conceived to benefit mankind but taken over by a dictator and destroyed. Considering the publication date, it's clearly a strike out against rising eastern Fascism.

Other American stories also tackled the European dictatorships. Schachner's "The Eternal Dictator" (1933b) has a 200-year dictator shooting down foreign ships, despite living in a utopia. When a group of scientist heroes come to restore democracy, the dictator is revealed as not truly immortal but a puffed-up demagogue. "I Am Not God" (1935) has Stephen Dodd invent a permanent suspended animation gas. Meanwhile, a European warlord (clearly Hitler) tries to manufacture the gas, then acquire it from him. Even as Dodd's loved ones succumb to the gas, he injects himself with the antidote and survives. After this, however, he begins considering whom the earth truly needs. His eugenics program is flawed as he plays favorites, and traitors revive the warlord and his legions. Dodd decides "I am not God" and revives everyone, to let them continue as they will. In this case, Schachner critiques eugenics themselves, even as the story turns prophetic for American Jews, surviving as their brethren in Europe slowly vanish.

Asimov calls C. M. Kornbluth (1924–1958) "the youngest of the Futurians and in some ways the most erratically brilliant" (1994, 65). After the war, the Jewish author, having witnessed firsthand the sufferings of newly liberated concentration camp prisoners, wrote pulps under pseudonyms as well as science fiction alone and in collaboration. He died at thirty-five of a surprising heart attack.

Kornbluth's novel *Not This August* (1955) posits an America defeated by the combined forces of Russia and China, with visions of camp prisoners like those whom he encountered in wartime Europe. "April 17, 1965, the blackest day in the history of the United States, started like any other day for Billy Justin. Thirty-seven years old, once a free-lance commercial artist, a pensioned veteran of Korea, he was now a dairy farmer, and had been during the three years of the war. It was that or be drafted to a road crew—with great luck, a factory bench," it begins. Chapter 1 is a story of deprivation and rationing—a held-back egg, a few hours of daily electricity, ration coupons, "a big, big" half-ounce imitation chocolate bar on sale, lies about winning on the radio, and other hallmarks that seem straight out of *1984*. Then the Chinese and Russians triumph. This does not end the deprivation but increases it—the farming quotas gradually rise until everyone is frantically farming all day and night. They start hauling people away—some to disappear forever, some to be tortured and then return to work. During the war, Kornbluth saw Nazi and Russian atrocities and found them both of a kind—barely able to be differentiated. Here, he explores all his political fears, leaning into allegory to examine them. In fact, this new communist takeover also turns on the Jews, including nonpracticing ones:

"I should have warned you," Gus said bitterly. "You're taking a chance being seen with me. I'm under suspicion as a dangerous conspirator—to be exact, a rootless Zionist cosmopolitan. The MVD came around last week. They searched the house. They took our Menorah, the Sabbath candlestick I haven't lit since Pop died. And in the attic they found the real evidence. A bunch of mildewed haggadas, Passover prayer-books I haven't used for twenty years. And Granpa's Talmud in forty little volumes of Hebrew and Aramaic which I can't read. That makes me a rootless-internationalist-cosmopolitan-cryptofascist-Zionist conspirator. They warned me to keep my nose clean. I guess they'll be back one of these days when they haven't got anything better to do and haul us away." He lapsed into silence.

However, in response, he and his wife begin keeping kosher and praying again: "The old phenomenon of persecution, the one that persecutors never learn, was working itself out again," the narrator explains. Presumably this is autobiographical, exploring many modern Jewish responses to the Holocaust.

At the climax, Justin discovers a hydrogen bomb project. However, the officer who completed it, perfectly following orders, has severe PTSD from the horrible crime he was ordered to commit. Justin opens the door and "starved concentration-camp corpses tumbled out into the tunnel." Justin screams in horror. The officer takes his arm and insists, rather madly, "There was no pain. I was never sure of that. Naturally I was told it would be painless, but they'd tell me that anyway. But it was true. They never knew what hit them, Justin. I feel just a little better now." He has gassed his own crew of scientists to keep the project secret, revealing a horror clearly inspired by Kornbluth's wartime experience. Justin leads a revolution, but the novel has no apologies, no redemption for the military that would commit such a crime.

Kornbluth constructs another clear Holocaust analogy in "The Marching Morons" ([1951] 1997). Barlow, a racist and repugnant contemporary man, is defrosted in the far future to discover there are now five billion people with IQs below forty-five who enslave and mistreat a small more intelligent group. The small group is determined to throw off their oppressors—except that in grisly fashion they have no idea how dispose of billions of corpses. The image of the mob is heightened by "superimposing upon them the image of an intellectually advanced minority whose abrupt surrender of responsibility signifies an equally abrupt surrender of their humanity" (Rich 2009, 164). Barlow offers to solve the problem in return for wealth, fame, and a small dictatorship. As a conman, he weaponizes human nature with knowledge of the past. He advertises that "Venus must be American!" and provokes nationalism, recruiting people to emigrate in one-way rockets. The author adds a pointed analogy directly: "Luckily, Barlow remembered that the problem had been solved once before—by Hitler. Relatives of persons incinerated in the furnaces of Lublin or Majdanek continued to get cheery postal cards" (393). Other countries, enraged by America's claiming Venus, immediately launch their own missions and the death count rises. Finally, Barlow is executed by his coconspirators, who are horrified at the savagery to which he's brought them. As the author concludes, this is always the pattern. Kornbluth's biographer explains that the story's complexity "arises from his playing with reader expectations as to who the morons actually are" (Rich 164).

The novel Kornbluth penned with Pohl, *The Space Merchants* (1953), about two enormous advertising agencies and their domination of the future world, pointedly satirizes the McCarthy era and its anticommunist stance. *Snowbound* fictionalizes Kornbluth's war experiences through a Jewish protagonist and speaks "in a frank manner that combined astonishment and understanding" about American soldiers' greed and brutality on entering Germany (Rich 2009, 121). Literary agent Virginia Kidd called Kornbluth a "strict Jewish moralist" with good reason. Many of his stories such as "The Doomsman," "The Words of Guru," and "The Last Man Left in the Bar" consider the ramifications of weapons of mass destruction.

Kornbluth's "The Mindworm" ([1950] 1976) is just as dark as his other war-influenced works, though this one takes place in a world closer to ours, reflecting the paranoia and surveillance fears of the fifties. It has an abused child attack people with his mental powers and kill them. This child, resulting from a liaison between a US Navy lieutenant and a nurse aboard ship during early atomic tests, invokes anxieties of the time. In fact, Kornbluth had been about to board a ship to invade Japan when news of the atomic bomb arrived (Rich 2009, 123). As the story continues, it, like "The Marching Morons," considers the depravity of ordinary human nature. As the protagonist journeys through America, he continues reading minds and begins to realize how much darkness hides beneath the polite exteriors. At last, as the Mindworm infiltrates an Eastern European community, they identify him as a vampire and kill him. Reworking the vampire legend, Kornbluth kills off the Mindworm not through educated doctors as in *Dracula* but through an old Polish man who stakes the vampire in the traditional method. Casimir, a political outsider located on the margins of society, emphasizes the strength in old wisdom (matching Kornbluth's own heritage), which defeats the modern technology that has wrought such horrors. Certainly, the character is a mass murderer, but arguably the darkness in others has driven him to this path. Considering that Kornbluth liberated concentration camps, he must have been struck by their savagery and desperation as well as the horrific acts concealed under friendly faces.

Chapter 4

Stereotypes Proliferate

A Darkening Western Europe

JEWISH TALES VERSUS TALES OF JEWS IN FOLKLORE

A rabbi decided to exchange places with his coachman for a day. While the rabbi waited with the horses, the coachman enjoyed a fine Shabbat dinner and afterward spoke about his interpretation of the law. Then, one of the guests asked quite a difficult question. The man was stumped. "Why," he said. "That's an easy one. I'll bet even my coachman outside can answer it." So goes a classic Jewish folktale, a very short story of everyday stock characters like a rabbi, cantor, or town beggar, which relies on a shared culture but is simple and often funny. More complex Jewish folktales include oral versions of *midrashim* or the Talmudic tales of wonder rabbis and miracles. Beyond this, Yiddish folklore, originating near places where the Brothers Grimm collected their tales, often identifiably retells the Christian stories. Many were recorded in the sixteenth-century *Mayse-bukh* (Book of Tales), compiled in an attempt to create a national culture. Later folklorists also made an effort. Just before World War I, S. Y. Ansky traveled Eastern Europe for 3 years recording nearly 2,000 tales from 66 villages (Weinreich 1988c, xxii). Tales gathered at the YIVO Institute for Jewish Research in Vilna (rescued postwar and shipped to YIVO in New York) include the Cinderella variant "Why Meat Loves Salt" (Weinreich 1998b). This time, when the third daughter is driven from the house for saying she loves her father as much as meat needs salting, the prophet Elijah (a common Jewish stand-in for the little old helper of fairytales) appears to her and directs her to a rabbi's house, where, having followed all his religious instructions, she dresses beautifully to attend a wedding. There, she charms the rabbi's son, though he must track her down with her dropped shoe.

At the same time, Isaac Bashevis Singer's Cinderella story "The Gentleman from Cracow" ([1957] 2004), with a rich man driving into the poor village and proposing a dance at which he will choose a bride, is more of a cautionary tale. The people frown on such an immodest and frivolous plan and the rabbi thunders, "Frampol is now Cracow. All we need is a ball! Heaven forbid that we bring down a plague and innocent infants be made to pay for our frivolity!" (24). Only after the villagers reassure him that all the laws will be followed does he allow it. Men and women dance separately, and the occasion seems to spark many Jewish matches. However, the rich man dramatically reveals himself as Ketev Miri, chief of the devils, and the village is burned down in punishment for the people's sinful wantonness. The clear message is not to rise above one's station by flaunting oneself to marry well but to treat such an offer with skepticism and keep to God's law.

The Tom Thumb story, "Little Bean" likewise emphasizes Jewish values as it begins with a barren couple offered a choice by an angel "to have a son who will be no bigger than a bean or a daughter who, when she is thirteen, will abandon Judaism for another faith" (Weinreich 1988d, 47). The boy is born tiny but generous, and his giving food to a beggar means that his adventure of being swallowed by a cow ends with the beggar kindly carrying him home. Here, as with other reflective tales, the local Jews found the lessons of the Christian tale aligned with their own, and they altered a few details for a stronger fit.

"Rabbi Akiva's Daughter or the Jewish Snow White" (Frankel 1989a) indeed merges these two stories. After Akiva's historically beloved wife Rachel dies, he remarries and the new wife torments his daughter Miriam. Instead of dwarves, she's taken in by a kind Jewish man who marries her. The story is actually closer to the ubiquitous fairytale "The Armless Maiden," as the stepmother's servant cuts off Miriam's hand, and she regrows it in the wilderness with the aid of Elijah. Merging this tale with the famous rabbi's is an odd choice, as his romance with his wife is legendary, but the parentage establishes the heroine's piety.

There are variants on "Toads and Diamonds" and "The Shoemaker and the Elves," with many tales of the Simpleton succeeding like a very recognizable "The Donkey, the Tablecloth, and the Stick." Howard Schwartz's collection *Tree of Souls* (2004a) tells of a demon kingdom mirroring the human one, in which the demons will try to snatch a human mate. This parallels changeling tales, though with a more malicious otherworld (230). As folktale editor Beatrice Silverman Weinreich explains, "One can postulate that only stories that felt culturally 'right' in form and content were translated into Yiddish by Jewish storytellers. But in time, and after successive retellings, they began to sound and feel like traditional Yiddish folktales" (1998e, 67). An emphasis on scholarship and wisdom for male and female heroes helped, as did the inclusion of Yiddish proverbs or rabbinic sayings proven by the events of the tale. Schwartz's collections in particular feature royalty and clever peasants in tales of far-off fantastical kingdoms more "fairytale" than "folk."

Within these obviously similar stories transmitted from culture to culture, the local Jews added a few clear agendas. The mysterious forest filled with monsters and witches (often in Christian stories metaphors for the Jews themselves) is rare. In fact, Yiddish folktales warned listeners not to go into the wood lest they be accused of snatching children. Instead, the hero travels into the big city, there to win a princess with cleverness. While the Christian fairytales sometimes have the hero-child guess riddles and sometimes slay monsters, the Jewish ones leave out violence in preference of wisdom and kindness. In one, a peasant boy cures the dying princess not with magic but with humble garlic cloves. In another, the humble shoemaker's son wins the princess by challenging the king with a riddle questioning who values her more.

There's a Grimm story in which the king, horrified to hear his daughter is destined to wed a peasant, buys the baby and throws him in the river, and then attempts to murder him again and again, only for all to turn out as was prophesized. In the Jewish adaptation, a doctor heals him (something basically unknown in *Grimm's Fairy Tales*) after the doctor's horse refuses to walk past the dying boy, in a scene that evokes the biblical Balaam and Balak. When the king's failure to change fate is revealed, he adds in the moral, "With God's will all is possible" (Frankel 1989b, 369).

The threat of anti-Semitism sometimes appears, often in metaphor. A folktale in which a clever lad wins the princess's hand by telling a story so ridiculous that she's prompted to speak goes about the same as its goyish counterpart until the boy, after winning the task, is suddenly to be executed by servants who disbelieve he's succeeded (Weinreich 1998g). Only luck saves him, teaching listeners that when the young hero beats his competitors, gentiles may be quick to take revenge. While the wolf in Red Riding Hood could be regarded as the archetypal terrifying foreigner, the Jewish version of "The Wolf and the Seven Kids" is disturbing in its own way. A bear devours a rabbi's seven children, so the parents turn to bribery, glutting him with treats until he falls asleep. With this, they cut open his stomach, free the still-living children, and sew up stones in the bear's belly. In context, the bear resembles a human predator with local authority, who must be bribed and tricked to keep the family from destruction (Weinreich 1998f).

There's also an entire subgenre in which the Jew debates a Christian leader and outwits him with articles of faith. In one, for instance, the king passes a Jewish classroom as the teacher is explaining the passage that God topples the mighty and raises the humble. Enraged, the king insists he prove this or be condemned to death. The teacher, a lamed-vavnik, prays for aid. When the king goes swimming, a demon steals his clothes, servants, and identity, leaving the real king to wander naked in the forest and turn beggar. Only after he asks the teacher for help does he learn to overcome the false king. "And from then on, and to the end of his days, that king was a friend to the Jews" (1998a, 79). Stories of a false replacement are deeply psychological, in which the protagonist lets bad behavior take over for a time and must reclaim the self (as, indeed, in dybbuk stories). Thus, the story works symbolically as a king gives into violence and then learns to repent, ending the story with the most vital issue for the Jews—that the government should show them leniency.

Of course, the Christian variants on these tales often carry a disturbing hatred for their neighbors, metaphoric or painfully overt. The Brothers Grimm included the much older "The Jew Among Thorns" in their nineteenth-century collection. In it, a young hero tortures a Jewish peddler in graphic fashion. Pat Pinsent (2000), author of "After Fagin: Jewishness and Children's Literature," wonders how many children's collections have retained the tale and thus are teaching children painfully prejudiced messages. As Pinsent adds, "This rather unpleasant little story really typifies anti-Semitism in seventeenth-century Europe, and it is interesting to note how the servant is constantly referred to as 'good' presumably not only for his years of faithful service, but also for his exposure of the Jew as a thief" (Pinsent 2000, 313). These stories emphasize the climate in which Jews were telling their own stories of hope and perseverance against injustice.

Other stories, encouraged by the church, emphasized Jews' untrustworthiness or evil. "The Jews' Stone" from Austria (Grimm no. 353) actually has the Jews buy a Christian child and kills him, on a stone that gives the story its name. The child's mother makes the father confess what he has done:

> He was about to show her the money that would free them from poverty, but it had turned into leaves. Then the father became mad and died from sorrow, but the mother went out and sought her child. She found it hanging from the tree and, with hot tears, took it down and carried it to the church at Rinn. It is lying there to this day, and the people look on it as a holy child. They also brought the Jews' Stone there. (Ashliman 2005)

The story is unambiguous: Jews are murderers, the child a saint. Further, the Jews have supernatural powers of illusion to pay in money that changes to leaves. "The Girl Who Was Killed by Jews" (Grimm no. 354) is a similar tale, with blood streaming from the dead child's wounds when Jews approach. They are executed and the dead child revered as a saint once again. This one, like the first, disturbingly ends with proof through physical evidence, as "The child's coffin, with an inscription, stands next to the bell rope near the entrance to the palace church at Pforzheim" (Ashliman 2005).

"The Expulsion of the Jews from Prussia" from the 1840 *Die Volkssagen von Pommern und Rügen* (The Folk Tales of Pomerania and Rügen) takes a different angle, blaming their expulsion (something that rulers regularly did based on religious fanaticism or financial gain) on a Jew's sacrilege of teaching a peasant to catch more fish by placing a consecrated host in his nets (Ashliman 2005). Here, once again, the Jews do magic, but this time with Christian talismans, suggesting that true power comes from the church. "The Bloody Children of the Jews" begins the same way, insisting, "Between about 1492 and 1500 in many areas of Germany, for example in Brandenburg and in Mecklenburg, the Jews were committing all kinds of godless sins, especially the desecration of the holy sacrament. For this reason, they were expelled from the country by their lords." In this story, a couple is cursed for only going through the motions of conversion, until they embrace it (Ashliman 2005). The bringing forward of folklore from previous centuries muddles the original tales—any historical fact has been replaced by fancy and rumor, yet the dark themes remain.

Sita Bell (2009) documents these and many other malicious tropes in her *Anti-Semitic Folklore Motif Index*. Alongside a long list of unpleasant physical stereotypes and reasons behind kashrut, there are motifs of Jews being changed into pigs, Jewish doctors who poison patients, and Jews in league with the devil.

Of these traditions, the Wandering Jew is the best known. The character reflects the Christian view of the Jews as a single homogenized image, doomed to wandering among nations as punishment for not being Christians. It was used as a societal metaphor for the actual migration and persecution of whole societies of Jews through history. Karen Grumberg (2019) explains in *Hebrew Gothic:* "The Wandering Jew came to represent the antithesis of the various European national identities that were coming into being. Stateless, unbound to temporal and physical laws, desiring death yet unable to attain it—the Wandering Jew compelled European readers because he embodied difference" (54). In him were both Jewish assimilation and Jewish foreignness, both of which were thought to threaten Europeans as they formed modern nations. The Wandering Jew legend is based on his rejecting Jesus (which Jews did) and thus being banished from ordinary life (which Jews often were). It's a tale to justify prejudice and abuse. Nineteenth-century British literature like *Carmilla* added a gothic vampiric impulse—that he sustained his immortality through drinking blood. The motif worked its way into fantasy as a permanent addition.

Jews and Christians alike spent the following century responding to this image that had so permeated cultural consciousness. Tragedies in the classical style included Quinet's epic *Ahasuerus*, Sue's *The Errant Jew*, and Shelley's "The Wandering Jew: A Poem." George MacDonald's *Thomas*

Wingfold, Curate (1876) recasts the Wandering Jew as an Anglican minister who is tormented by his eternal life blocking him from the woman he loves. Even as he attempts suicide, Jesus forgivingly escorts him and his beloved to Paradise. However, even as French and English literature extended sympathy, "German literature became possessed with negative and historicized version of the myth. So here we have another genetic fallacy: myth became history" (Gibson 2000, 352). As fairytale expert Jack Zipes (1980) explains in his essay on anti-Semitic tropes, "The push toward emancipation and assimilation did not contribute to greater acceptance of Jews when the German nation was founded in 1871, but to a new form of racist and political anti-Semitic segregation and definition of Jewishness" (58).

In Germany by the early nineteenth century and in England by the late eighteenth century, the medieval legend of the Wandering Jew began to be associated with the "Jewish Question" that emerged in the wake of debates about Jewish assimilation, transforming the Jew from a religious to a secular, political, racialized figure and rendering his representation increasingly sinister. The legend itself is markedly ambivalent, regarding the Wandering Jew by turns with sympathy, admiration, and scorn, and depicting him as intelligent, handsome, or tragic. His post-Enlightenment literary manifestations in both the German *Schauerroman* (terror novel) and British gothic literature, however, focused increasingly on the threat he posed. In Germany, France, and Britain, the birth pangs of national identity in the nineteenth century were accompanied by and defined against the development of the Wandering Jew from a religious outcast to a demonic vampire. (Grumberg 2019, 55)

Modern science fiction and fantasy continued to use this staple, if rarely. The best-known is Walter M. Miller Jr.'s *A Canticle for Leibowitz* followed by Wilson Tucker's *The Planet King* where he becomes earth's last survivor. There's also Brian Stableford's *Tales of the Wandering Jew: A Collection of Contemporary and Classic Stories*. C. S. Forester transfers the curse to Hitler in "The Wandering Gentile" and Susan Shwartz offers a sympathetic revision of the tale in *The Grail of Hearts*.

EARLY HORROR

Gothic stories had a late-nineteenth-century revival, giving Jews new imagery to contend with as they found themselves cast as the frightening foreigners. Oskar Panizza's German story "The Operated Jew" ([1893] 1980) is famous for its anti-Semitism. In it, a young Jewish man invests an enormous sum in doctors and scientists to transform him into a gentile in appearance and behavior. Zipes (1980) considers how Jews at the time were treated as the collective shadow of the German world. "In order to feel safe, the pathological anti-Semite must eventually kill or completely control that side of him/her, which cannot be accepted" (57). The German characters thus gladly operate on the Jew to control him and their own fears. Linguistically and physically, Itzig Faitel Stern is an outsider. He's described as small and bony, with fine suits that fit badly thanks to "Christian tailors" (63). He walks like a stork and speaks with a heavy dialect. He is "in every way an amalgamation of exaggerated stereotypes and as such he appears like an imagined collage of anti-Semitic insults" (Jacobs 2015, 59). Though the narrator describes himself as Itzig's close friend, the description is far from flattering and he even calls him a "monster" (66). The procedure stretches Itzig to be taller, shortens his neck so he stops stooping, and even breaks his legs and repairs them to fix the bow-leggedness. Gymnasts and orthopedists and beauticians help (making him a stiff-legged blond who speaks pretentiously and reveres the upper class in a satire on German society), even while debating whether he has a soul. As critic Joela Jacobs (2015) adds, the story emphasizes "the impossible demands of assimilation by means of hyperbole and the use of similar stereotypes about Germans" (59). With this, despite the painful description, it challenges categories such as race that readers may have considered clear-cut.

At the same time, Itzig's intelligence and culture suggest the author's subtle envy. Zipes (1980) notes, "Panizza attacked Jews for wanting to be a part of a philistine German society and argued that they would be better off by not giving up their peculiar faith and racial characteristics" (47). Treatments grow more outlandish, with a blood transfusion from pure Aryan virgins and proposed wedding to a blonde German woman to complete the change. At the wedding, the illusion holds for a while and then embarrassingly collapses, leaving him a puddle on the floor. At the time, baptism led to equality, but only technically, with the prejudice continuing. The character's attempts to become Christian destroy him, even while revealing the ludicrousness of German expectations. Zipes notes, "It is chilling to see how Panizza, no matter how disturbed he was, placed his finger on the sore spots of German-Jewish assimilation at the end of the 19th century and anticipated a virtual destruction of Jewish identity due to German and Jewish compliance with the operative social procedures and customs of the time" (47).

In 1922, Salomo Friedlaender published "The Operated Goy" as a direct parody. "Friedlaender's narrative reverses the outcomes of Panizza's text in order to hold a mirror up to German society and criticize its increasingly one-sided and paranoid view of assimilation more explicitly" (Jacobs 2015, 64). This time, a young count, son of one of the most anti-Semitic German families, goes to Bonn to study. His parents hope he will marry an Aryan woman called Frigga and name their children Baldur, Thor, and so on. They even give him a giant servant called Odin to protect him from the seductive wiles of Jewish women. "As soon as anything Hebrew showed itself, [his servant made] a shrill sound with a silver whistle. Of course, it would be superfluous to remark that the Count's Great Dane was carefully trained to bite any Jew who came too close. In addition, the raven Hugin would correctly chirp the well-known Borkum anti-Semitic hymn" (Zipes 1980, 77). The animals can sniff out Jews by their odor, a traditional slur from the Middle Ages. However, Rebecka Gold-Isaac hears of these plans and decides to marry the young count "out of revenge" (78). She charms him until he's willing to convert for her, and he changes his name to Moishes Moandovidwendedich Koscher (replacing the cross in his name with the Mogen David). Still, she insists he go still further and undergo surgery to make him squat, bow-legged and dark. With this, she will achieve "complete assimilation and incorporation of the enemy" (Zipes 1980, 79). His family storm the wedding but the young count perseveres. "While Faitel belonged neither here nor there after his failed assimilative endeavor, Kreuzwendedich will be fully absorbed by the Jewish community at the end of the story, so that cultural assimilation ultimately comes to mean cultural annihilation" (66). More importantly, the result of his experiment is a lessening of anti-Semitism, as "One no longer bases everything on racial differences. Racial blood has stopped being considered a special kind of vital juice. Meanwhile, Professor Friedlaender gathers it in bottles and continues to transfer it undauntedly from one vessel into another" (Zipes 1980, 85). They can all change races so much that the artificial definition of race has no meaning. The story here is exaggerated to ludicrousness, even as both versions emphasize how much race is an imaginary construct, built of stereotypes.

Jewish tales about werewolves go as far back as the biblical Benjamin, whom medieval commentator Rabbi Efraim ben Shimshon described as not just like a "ravenous wolf," but capable of turning into one. However, in a pointed example of the tradition of hiding from anti-Semitism, the rabbi explained that Benjamin's danger wasn't in attacking others but in changing among strangers and being killed by them (Sacks 2017).

Growing up in one of the oldest Sephardic families in Bulgaria, Elias Canetti moved to Vienna and then London after the Anschluss. In his works, especially his autobiographical memoirs of his childhood, he describes a childhood of fairytales about werewolves and vampires. His juxtaposing this with an autobiographical memory of speaking German in public and Ladino in private casts him as a similar hybrid and outsider. "Only especially dramatic events, murder and manslaughter so to speak, and the worst terrors have been retained by me in their Ladino wording, and very precisely and indestructibly at that. Everything else, that is, most things, and especially anything Bulgarian, like the fairy tales, I carry around in German," he explains

(80). Thus, the stories of childhood work their way into his conscious life. Other works include "Purim: The Comet" with nightmares of a werewolf coming to eat him and *Masse und Macht* (Crowds and Power), a psychological study of mob violence in an imagined world of disorder. Jews internalized these ancient tales and, when they began writing modern fantasy, often brought in these monsters of the shtetl.

In another Jewish spin on gothic tropes, S. Y. Agnon's "The Lady and the Peddler" (1943) has a Jewish peddler do odd jobs for a widow in exchange for food. He soon moves in with her as her lover and enjoys the unkosher food she serves him. However, he never sees her eat anything. At last, she smiles. "You want to know what I eat and what I drink? I drink men's blood and I eat human flesh" (206). As she reveals she has had many husbands, he begins to grow terrified. Still, he is so drawn to her he cannot leave. (This may reflect the plight of so many European Jews, knowing they are courting death and should flee, yet unwilling to do so.) The peddler, meanwhile, says the Sh'ma outside, away from her crucifix, and when she finally bites him, she complains that his blood is "ice water" and cannot nourish her (212). On the one hand, this reinforces the notion that Jews will always be fundamentally different from Christians; on the other, this difference saves the protagonist. Unable to find nourishment, she dies, and he sorrowfully buries her.

While the protagonist is less violent than many fairytale heroes in his situation, the story clearly warns of the danger of intermarriage, with sensual Christian widows eager to lure Jews to destruction. "Unchanged by the violent episode with the lady, the peddler continues to wander with his wares on his back, the archetypal Wandering Jew—without the characteristics that frightened British readers of nineteenth-century gothic. He is not threatening but pathetic, not cunning but naive, not evil but kind" (Grumberg 52). As such, the tale unravels the Wandering Jew stereotypes. In fact, the man is not predatory, cunning, or invasive—hardly a metaphor for the frightening immigrant. "Agnon's depiction of a lady as a bloodthirsty vampire threatening a foolish but kind peddler not only disrupts the Christian-versus-Jew dynamic of violence and power but also upends the notions of femininity and masculinity that so often inform this dynamic, from gothic tales of helpless heroines imprisoned and dominated by evil men to Nazi images of hook-nosed men leering at Aryan milkmaids" (Grumberg 60). Instead, the woman is predatory, inviting him into her home so she can devour him. In context of pre-Holocaust Europe, this functions as a warning to Jews who assimilate—their welcoming hosts have a cruel agenda.

Another story of folkloric tropes and inverted stereotypes, "Meh.olat ha-mavet" ["The Dance of Death"] from 1919 is the most gothic of Agnon's works. In a Polish town, a father's petition to allow his daughter to wear silk for her wedding is denied. At the ceremony, a nobleman arrives on horseback.

Overcome by lust, he slits the groom's throat and kidnaps the bride. The helpless townsfolk bury the bloody groom before the great synagogue where he fell, believing that burying him here in his bloodstained clothes will help avenge his murder. "Besides enhancing the macabre atmosphere of the story, the juxtaposition of the bloody garments—the count's hunting attire and the groom's pure white kittel—forcefully announces their difference and coalesces the tension between power and powerlessness even as it laces both with ambivalence," explains Karen Grumberg in her *Hebrew Gothic* (2019, 65). The bride, meanwhile, gazes endlessly out of the tower where she has been imprisoned and finally dies of grief. Each night, however, the couple rises from the grave and dance together.

> The groom's kittel, a key image in the story, offers a direct parallel to the danse macabre: the kittel, a simple white linen robe worn by Ashkenazi Jews in weddings and on certain holidays, is also used as a burial shroud for men. Emblematic of purity and simplicity, the pocketless kittel disallows the deceased to bring his earthly possessions to his grave, signifying the equality of all in death—precisely the motivation of the danse macabre. In the story, however, burying the groom in his bloodstained kittel will not only equalize power relations but will also compensate for his powerlessness in life by fueling his vengeful resurrection: folk belief transforms the kittel into a vehicle of revenge. Yet the groom declines this opportunity, instead using his supernatural ability to return from death to consummate his interrupted love. (Grumberg 49)

The concept of the blood libel and lustful foreigners stealing brides are subverted here as the groom is a figure of peace and purity—foregoing vengeance to dance with the bride stolen by the wicked and entitled count. "The Dance of Death" and "The Lady and the Peddler" both use gothic tropes to share Agnon's vision of Jewish history "in the emphasis on fear and anxiety as defining features of the Jewish presence in Europe; in the depiction of time as cyclical and the past as perpetually returning to and rupturing the present; in the thematization of these phenomena through supernatural figures; and, finally, in the portrayal of historic Jewish experiences in terms of certain key motifs that mediate between the gothic and the Judaic" (Grumberg 40).

The gothic, based in folkloric elements as it was, looked to nostalgia even while struggling for equality. Austrian author Gustav Meyrink's novel *The Golem* ([1915] 2017) follows Athanasius Pernath, a jeweler and art restorer in Prague's ghetto as he wrestles with "a horde of fantastic impressions and visions" (83). "Part dream-like expressionist melodrama, part creepy horror, part eerie evocation of the magical city of Prague and its shadow-haunted ghetto, *The Golem* occupies a singular niche in fantastika. And it is hard to re-read without placing the narrative against the clouds of war which were gathering over Europe" (Barnett 2014). The serial concluded in 1914, as unheard-of violence transformed the world. After selling 200,000 copies in Europe, it was translated into English in 1928. In his "Supernatural Horror in Literature" essay, H. P. Lovecraft ([1927] 2009) said the novel is one of the "best examples" of Jewish weird fiction "with its haunting shadowy suggestions of marvels and horrors just beyond reach." All this is written as a memorial to the twisting, dark, mysterious ghetto, torn down at the time of writing thanks to gentrification and assimilation in the area. As such, it explores Jews' imaginings and fears. Interwoven tales of mass murders and casual anti-Semitism blend with the mystical threats to create a shadowy realm of threat. The golem itself lurks through the murder mystery, mirroring the ghetto's history of suffering, now embodied as the ghetto's inhabitants' collective psyche, as well as of the ghetto's own "self." Meanwhile, Pernath finds *The Book of Ibbur*, which guides him on the path of life, as opposed to death, in a mystical kabbalistic journey. This arguably stretches beyond the bounds of credulity when he learns that Tarot and Torah are the same word (121) but the philosophy of looking deeper and following a spiritual path is thus extended across multiple belief systems as the hero seeks truth.

It's gradually revealed that Pernath has amnesia, possibly from a prior mental breakdown. Through this point of view, blended with hallucinations and questionable events, many details are called into question. Life in the ghetto is thus surreal and fantastical, blending memories and tales from different times. Pernath's mental fogginess makes him especially helpless as others assert authority over him: in prison, accused of the crime he's investigating, he "is plunged from one nightmarish scenario to another at the behest of shadowy powers, unknowable bureaucracy and individuals with covert agendas: perhaps his is the story of the Jews of the Prague ghetto and their centuries of subjugation at the hands of others" (Barnett 2014). When he's finally released, it's into a ghetto he no longer finds recognizable. The world is changing, and his mental fog only exacerbates his conflict.

The non-Jewish Hans Heinrich Ewers (1871–1943) was involved in the new German film industry, working with Director Paul Wegener to produce a number of films for the Deutsche Bioscop G. M. B. H., such as *Die Verführte* and *Der Student von Prag* (both 1913). He spent the Great War in America, campaigning for the German cause. As a German national, he was sent to the internment camp at Fort Oglethorpe, Georgia. Thus, his subsequent novel was quite autobiographical.

In *Vampir* ([1921] 1934), Braun is most obviously a heroic image of the author, spying in Mexico during the Great War and becoming a vampire through drinking the blood of his Jewish mistress. His character Frank Braun, an incarnation of Nietzsche's Übermensch, lives his life in violation of the "normal" values of society. En route to Germany, Frank Braun announces to the passengers that they will be put in concentration camps, but they all laugh. Baum ruminates on the question of nationality, even as he feels cut off.

> To be part of it, to be one with the crowd might mean new life for millions of people who were nothing in themselves, who were created only in this hour of need when they became an atom in the huge body of a unified nation and thus breathed, lived, fought with it. But he wanted none of this—for him it would mean the loss of everything he stood for. It would reduce him to a mere speck of dust like millions of others, to a tiny, miserable scrap of flesh on the bleeding body of the nation. (31)

In *Vampir*, identity is consistently expressed through the language of blood and through a blood mythology that links Germans and Jews. Even as the author felt the rising hatred and Fascism from Germany, he maintained that Germans and Jews were bound together, albeit through the rather flimsy characterization of his stand-in's Jewish lover Lotte Levi.

After the war, Ewers returned to Germany and joined the Nazi party, but his rebellious writing, homosexuality, and protection of Jews angered the Nazis. His books were promptly banned and burned, along with his final collection of stories, *Die schönsten Hände der Welt* (1943) (The Most Beautiful Hands in the World), which contained several stories satirizing the Nazi regime. The hardly politically correct "The Dead Jew" is gothic in Poe's realistic style. It features a coach ride with a corpse the drunken passengers all swear to have heard talking to them but leaves room for doubt. This emphasizes the insidious nature of rumor and its ability to make people believe outlandish fantasies. Condemned by his society, Ewers died of tuberculosis in Berlin in 1943.

Arguably, anti-Semitic stereotypes appear in many early German horror films, especially *Nosferatu* (1922), in which a vampire arrives in Bremen, Germany. He's a lascivious, blood-sucking extravagantly hook-nosed Eastern foreigner who arrives with a plague of rats, hitting all the publicized tropes. The vampire Orlock is introduced buying property before he preys on the local women. Even more than the original *Dracula* novel, he evokes the image of a monstrous foreigner from the east, staggering with a distorted gait. Adding to popular conspiracy theories of the time, there's also an invisible enemy pulling the strings. The filmmakers were not known for anti-Semitism, and in fact the writers were of Eastern European Jewish descent, but they repeated the stereotypes, perhaps to capitalize on pop culture moments familiar to the audience.

Some American horror films from Universal were produced as a counter to the German stories. *The Black Cat* (1934), Edgar G. Ulmer's vehicle for Bela Lugosi and Boris Karloff, was released just over a year after Hitler came to power. It was an incredibly loose adaptation of Poe's story, as this version marooned a naive pair of American honeymooners in Europe's heart of darkness, where they became unwitting pawns in the death struggle between a hysterical Hungarian psychiatrist (Lugosi) and a proto-Nazi, Satan-worshipping Austrian architect (Karloff) in a steel-and-glass deco castle overlooking the site of World War I's bloodiest battlefield.

Curt Siodmak, a German Jewish engineer, reported on the film *Metropolis* and got to be an extra. As part of the "German Hollywood," Babelsberg in suburban Berlin, he worked on the film *Menschen am Sonntag*, or *People on Sunday,* in 1929, which later became known as a masterwork of neorealism. Gernsback reprinted Siodmak's "The Eggs from Lake Tanganyika" in 1926. However, Germany was growing more dangerous. With his books confiscated and forbidden to work, Siodmak fled to France, then England. In 1937, he joined 1,500 other filmmakers from Babelsberg in Hollywood.

His big break came with his script for *The Wolf Man* in 1941, bringing the dark European folktale to the American big screens. Starring Lon Chaney Jr. along with Bela Lugosi and Claude Rains, it used music by Jewish composer Hans Salter, an Austrian refugee whose film scores would eventually be nominated for six Oscars. Siodmak created the now-standard werewolf lore about werewolves being marked by a pentagram, being practically immortal apart from being shot by silver, and the beast's monthly emergence during a full moon.

Of course, there's a deep allegory here. The film is about an ordinary man, Lawrence Talbot, suddenly turned into a monster, and thus echoes the German Jewish experience of the thirties. Filled with self-loathing for his new monstrousness, Talbot fears not only what he might do to his friends but also being hunted down and killed. He struggles very clearly with identity, giving his story more nuance than Hollywood's competing monsters. "The original title was 'Destiny' because he believed it was the story of an outsider whose destiny was cursed by forces he could not control," documentary producer Constantine Nasr says. "There was going to be no way out for him" (King 2010). Even the pentagram in Talbot's hand signifying a werewolf is a "very obvious substitute for the Star of David, and if you had that symbol you were going to be cursed," adds says (King 2010). Being marked with a star meant doom. "I am the Wolf Man," Siodmak said in an interview. "I was forced into a fate I didn't want: to be a Jew in Germany. I would not have chosen that as my fate. The swastika represents the moon. When the moon comes up, the man doesn't want to murder, but he knows he cannot escape it, the Wolf Man destiny" (Martin 2000).

BRITISH STEREOTYPING

H. G. Wells is most famous for the science fiction novels that began the genre, like *The Invisible Man* and *The War of the Worlds*. Most of his career, however, was spent writing books like *A Modern Utopia* and *The Shape of Things to Come*, which predicted World War II erupting in Europe. "He was a major celebrity—sort of a cross between Isaac Asimov and Carl Sagan, although vastly more famous than either. His opinions and presence were sought by heads of state from Roosevelt to Stalin," Darrell Schweitzer (2018) notes in "The H. G. Wells Problem."

He did care about the "problem" of the Jews. "I met a Jewish friend of mine the other day," wrote Wells, "and he asked me, 'What is going to happen to the Jews?' I told him I had rather he had asked me a different question, What is going to happen to mankind? 'But my people—' he began. 'That,' said I, 'is exactly what is the matter with them'" (Schweitzer 2018). Wells in this scene dictates that his friend should worry about everyone equally and give up tribalism. However, he is painfully wrong as in a few years the European Jews are nearly destroyed entirely. His criticism of the Jews' difference—both politically and outwardly—appears as a trace through his and his contemporaries' science fiction just as the genre began. In contrast with American science fiction—largely authored by Jews and containing almost no Jewish characters—the pulps across the pond were sprinkled with the anti-Semitic tropes common in Europe, as a standard warning against foreign cultures.

The War of the Worlds ([1898] 2018) offers a disturbing stereotype during the evacuation of London involving a "bearded, eagle-faced man" (suggesting a long nose) carrying a satchel of gold coins. As he flings himself down to collect his spilled coins, a horse runs him over, breaking his back. "Clutching the man's collar with his free hand, my brother lugged him sideways. But he still clutched after his money, and regarded my brother fiercely, hammering at his arm with a handful of gold" (118). Even with his back broken, he continues trying to gather the money. The unsympathetic onlookers heave him out of the way like trash. Likewise, Wells's invisible man has a conflict with his landlord, "an old Polish Jew in a long grey coat and greasy slippers" with "German-silver spectacles," emphasizing his foreignness and unwashed appearance (110). The text then paints him as something of a coward who sneaks away when the narrator arrives. He also has two "thick-lipped, bearded," Yiddish-speaking stepsons. The invisible man feels driven to strike one of the stepson's right smack in his "silly countenance," but instead he sets the house on fire and flees (115).

Similarly, Jules Verne's *Off on a Comet or Hector Servadac* ([1877] 2008) strands a small group on an asteroid, including Isaac Hakkabut, a stereotyped

German Jewish trader. "The heartless, wily usurer, the hardened miser and skinflint. As iron is attracted by the magnet, so was this Shylock attracted by the sight of gold, nor would he have hesitated to draw the life-blood of his creditors, if by such means he could secure his claims." He obsesses over money and payment though it's worthless on the asteroid. Notably, the narrator insists—without evidence—that Hakkabut is an opportunist and cheat, validating this stereotyping when it proves correct later in the novel.

"Now, casual anti-Semitism is pretty common in Victorian fiction, so we learn to brace ourselves for this sort of thing," Schweitzer explains. Indeed, anti-Semitism has a long history in English literature. As Orwell observed in 1945, Chaucer had anti-Semitic traces and "without even getting up from this table to consult a book I can think of passages which if written now would be stigmatized as anti-Semitism, in the work of Shakespeare, Smollett, Thackeray, Bernard Shaw, H. G. Wells, T. S. Eliot, Aldous Huxley, and various others" (1971, 385). In a strike against this sort of depiction, laudable characters at the turn of the century and a little earlier appeared in Sir Walter Scott's *Ivanhoe*, George Eliot's *Daniel Deronda*, Dickens's *Our Mutual Friend*, Charles Reade's *It Is Never Too Late to Mend*, and finally, James Joyce's *Ulysses*. In this trope, these Jewish protagonists were all idealized and feminized, emphasizing their role as harmless minorities.

Some Jewish British writers joined in. Benjamin Disraeli, first Earl of Beaconsfield and prime minister of Great Britain, wrote many works of fiction, including an early epic alternate history in *Alroy: The Prince of the Captivity* (1845) 2006. (The first version was published in 1827.) The hero, David Alroy, begins the story defending his sister from a lout, only for her to warn him, "Fly, David, fly; for the man you have stricken is a prince among the people." This alludes to the story of Moses, casting Alroy as a particularly biblical figure before he journeys into the wilderness. He also invokes the story of Samson as he dreams of killing all the "Philistines" who have attacked them. This second image is that of the Jewish warrior, and indeed, Alroy fulfills this role, breaking stereotypes. Off he goes into the wilderness like so many biblical heroes: "As thou didst feed Elijah, so also hast thou fed me, God of my fathers!" he prays. All this imagery is recognizable to a Jewish audience as well as a Christian one, building him up as the great hero of prophecy.

In exile, he has visions of his great destiny, rendered with elevated language and again evoking the Bible. As he explains:

> A flaming light spread over the sky, the stars melted away, and I beheld, advancing from the bursting radiancy, the foremost body of a mighty host. Oh! not when Saul led forth our fighting men against the Philistine, not when Joab numbered the warriors of my great ancestor, did human vision gaze upon a scene of

so much martial splendour. Chariots and cavalry, and glittering trains of plumed warriors too robust to need a courser's solace; streams of shining spears, and banners like a sunset; reverend priests swinging their perfumed censers, and prophets hymning with their golden harps a most triumphant future. "Joy, joy," they say, "to Israel, for he cometh, he cometh in his splendour and his might, the great Messiah of our ancient hopes."

Aiding him in his quest is his mentor, the kabbalist Jabaster. He has previously failed to establish God's kingdom, but he hopes David can succeed. David insists he can with the words "The Lord, who knoweth all things, hath deemed me worthy of His mission. My fitness for this high and holy office was not admitted without proof. A lineage, which none else could offer, mystic studies shared by few, a mind that dared encounter all things, and a frame that could endure most, these were my claims." His strength is not only through physicality but birth, wisdom, and studies of the mystical. As such, he's a quintessential British hero—educated as well as muscular. He is not a Jewish outsider but a biblical paragon.

He travels to the Middle East and, in this British imperialist fantasy, becomes the majestic and beloved conqueror-king as well as the Messiah. He achieves all this by the halfway point and then appoints his mentor High Priest of the Temple in the old tradition. Pomp and ceremonial splendor are constant, with much gorgeous description. Alroy's allies include his idealistic and loving sister Miriam. There's also the fascinating Esther the Prophetess, who believes in him wholeheartedly. Of course, she warns him his ambition will doom him. "Mené, Mené, Tekel, Upharsin!" is inscribed in the garden, foreshadowing his tragic downfall in another recognizable biblical allusion.

Next, Alroy marries a local princess in a lavish ceremony. However, all his friends warn him that if he accompanies her to her mosque, he is sinning like Solomon, and like him, he will lose the kingdom. The hero eventually falls— captured by his enemies, accused of sorcery (including the magical seduction of his bride) and is executed. It's a tragic death but still a noble and admirable one. It also evokes sympathy, not only for its Jewish hero, a celebrated conqueror brought down by betrayal, but for the dream of Zionism: since it's described as "a glorious prime when Israel stood aloof from other nations, a fair and holy thing that God had hallowed," Here, Christians are invited to participate in the dream and help rebuild the Kingdom of God.

This work is an exception: Even pro-Jewish British writers fell into racist depictions. Samuel Butler's utopian *Erewhon* ([1872] 2002) uses the mythology of the Second Coming, in which the Jews are to return to the Holy Land, to speculate on whether his utopia is made up of the "lost ten tribes of Israel awaiting the final return to Palestine" (75). However, their achievement comes from their power of acquiring wealth. Taking this image to a darker place, George Allan England wrote the socialist story *The Golden Blight*, in which a Jewish financier buys up the world's gold and insists he'll enslave everyone.

Echoing this trope in his *The Golden Bottle* (1892), Ignatius Donnelly imagines a utopian Jewish state in Palestine where a Jewish plutocracy utilizes Zionism for the good of mankind. *Caesar's Colum: A Story of the Twentieth Century* ([1890] 2012), Donnelly's dystopian political satire, frames a world in which "the aristocracy of the world is now almost altogether of Hebrew origin." As a character explains:

> "Well," he replied, "it was the old question of the survival of the fittest. Christianity fell upon the Jews, originally a race of agriculturists and shepherds, and forced them, for many centuries, through the most terrible ordeal of persecution the history of mankind bears any record of. Only the strong of body, the cunning of brain, the long-headed, the persistent, the men with capacity to live where a dog would starve, survived the awful trial. Like breeds like; and now the Christian world is paying, in tears and blood, for the sufferings inflicted by their bigoted and ignorant ancestors upon a noble race. When the time came for liberty and fair play the Jew was master in the contest with the Gentile, who hated and feared him."

Having risen through the world, Jews now inhabit the great palaces where they were driven out. Here, the fear that cruelty will beget equal cruelty (seen in the harsh treatment of many minority groups in America and worldwide) creates the imagery of a Jewish-run future. The words are complimentary, but they explain the threat Jews pose to the Christian world.

George Griffith's *The Angel of the Revolution* and sequel *Olga Romanoff* feature the brave, beautiful half-Jewish Natasha. The pulp adventure begins with airship pirates led by a hideously crippled, brilliant Russian Jew and his alluring daughter. Like a more successful Captain Nemo, the team, called "The Brotherhood of Freedom" establish a "pax aeronautica" over the earth. Natas, the Master of the Terror, is described as "the man whose wrongs, whatever they might have been, had caused him to devote his life to a work of colossal vengeance, and his incomparable powers to the overthrow of a whole civilization" ([1893] 2010). As he insists, clumsily mixing Bible stories and Jewish belief: "I believe myself to be the instrument of vengeance upon this generation, even as Joshua was upon Canaan, and as Khalid the Sword of God was upon Byzantium in the days of her corruption." Russian atrocities against the Jewish people are described in depth, eliciting sympathy. Still, if the heroes are Jews, it seems they must fall into all the stereotypes, from secret controllers of the British hero with strange mesmerism powers to the monstrous revenger with his lovely daughter (of which Shylock is the most famous). It ends with a European slaughter of outside nations, complete with heavily imperialistic language, and the triumph of socialism.

In light of all these stereotypes, Romanian science fiction author Felix Aderca spoke in praise of ethnic "indifference." In the late 1930s, he blamed not only the anti-Semites, but the philosemites too who, he claimed, "are much too well spoken of." As he adds, "He who explicitly declares himself, even in the best of faith, to be fond of our nation above all the others is himself the author of discrimination. . . . My dream is to deal with fellow men who do not care a rap whether I am a Jew or not" (Oisteanu 2009, 23). Admiration for having hypnosis powers or being secretly wealthy is just as dangerous as condemnation.

The British Jews acknowledged the ongoing typecasts and tried to flip them. In fact, Jews of the time wrote propaganda fiction emphasizing their goodness and harmlessness. Benjamin Farjeon, Grace Aguilar, and Celia and Marion Moss embarked on this type of apologist Jewish novel, differentiating good Jews from bad. Jewish "novels of revolt" struck back against these and countered the stereotypes—these were led by Amy Levy's *Reuben Sachs* (1888), followed by authors Julia Frankau, Cecily Sidgwick, Leonard Merrick, and Mark Herbert. Likewise, Israel Zangwill's *Children of the Ghetto* (1892) and *King of the Schnorrers* (1896) did not spend their time advertising Jews' goodness, but told fun, lively tales for his community that were much beloved.

Science fiction was rare from European Jewish authors of the nineteenth century and early twentieth century, who largely wrote realistic tales. However, Victor Rousseau's dystopia *The Messiah of the Cylinder* ([1917] 1974) has the hero frozen to awaken in a new century. The narrator seeks his true love Esther, frozen alongside him, even as he discovers the people have found a new Messiah, Sanson. Indeed, he evokes biblical Samson, also considered a savior only to fail. This relationship has a particularly Jewish sensibility. "Only the very ignorant believed that the Messiah would be a supernatural being . . . the world awaited, rather, the inevitable leader who must come to set free a people grown over-ripe for freedom" (200). Admittedly, Judaism goes unmentioned in the novel, reflecting the author (born Avigdor Rousseau Emanuel) who conceals his own identity beneath a penname. As a stand-in for Judaism, Christianity is the forbidden religion for which "dozens had died under torture rather than disclose the hiding place of their treasured Scriptures" (201). The novel's triumphant ending, with the people rededicating the Temple (admittedly on Easter) "with the unleavened bread of sincerity and truth" feels recognizable too (319).

In this future, only a few fragments of the Bible have survived, though the author gets in some direct commentary when he adds, "The world has gained immeasurably by the removal of the scaffolding of the Temple of Truth . . .

never again will literal interpretation be placed upon Old Testament mythology" (203). More social commentary appears as this is a frightening socialist world, in which the government kills the elderly and dictates marriages and procreation through eugenics, while sorting people into übermenches and untermenches. As such, it suggests early National Socialism. "We know each age has its own cruelties and wrongs: the Inquisition of the sixteenth century; religious massacres in the seventeenth; in the nineteenth, factory slavery and the prisons with their silent cells," the narrator concludes, calling back to massacres of the Jews even as he uses science fiction to plead for tolerance (318).

However, much of British literature ignored these appeals to a common humanity. As Russian pogroms sent 70,000 Jews flooding into England, Jewish literary villains appeared en masse, threatening British women in *The Picture of Dorian Gray* and *The Sorrows of Satan*. Echoing these, George du Maurier's *Trilby* (1894) was overwhelmingly popular with a lasting effect. Chapter 1 introduces Svengali, "of Jewish aspect, but sinister," "very shabby and dirty," with "thick, heavy, lustreless black hair," a long black beard, twirling moustache, and heavy German accent (11). He's suggested to be the Wandering Jew, living in torment as he wields strange potion bottles and kabbalistic powers. Later he's described as an "incubus," with a caricature of a spider as illustration. His obsession with music leads him to hypnotize the heroine Trilby into being his star pupil and mistress until an Englishman slays him and frees the damsel. With this, the dangerous magical foreigner's control ends.

This theme appears more figuratively in *Dracula*. This villain comes from Romania and has studied English customs well enough to blend in, before he begins preying on the upper-class women. All the Christian imagery used to repel him is suggestive, as Jews were the rare non-Christians in Europe. Observing that "vampire stories and the blood accusation against Jews have a family resemblance, if not more," critic David Biale (2007) connects "the same kind of anxieties over race, nationalism, and sexuality that pervade modern vampire stories" to the blood libel: "It may well be a coincidence that Bram Stoker's *Dracula* (1897) was published just as the modern ritual murder accusation was reaching its crescendo, but both traffic in the same idea that those who threaten the stability of the nation do so by sucking its blood" (172). An unfortunate stereotype appears more directly as the heroes hunt Dracula. Dracula has hired "Immanuel Hildesheim" to transport his coffin, and he betrays his master for a bribe. The novel describes him as "a Hebrew of rather the Adelphi Theatre type, with a nose like a sheep, and a fez" (477).

Beloved children's author E. Nesbit has similar problematic moments herself. *The Story of the Amulet* ([1906] 1996) offers a shop owner named Jacob Absalom, who has a "large, dirty, short-fingered hand with a very big diamond ring" (27). He sells them half a magical amulet, and is infuriated when the children ask for the rest. After the children time-travel to 6000 BC Egypt and bring back the Babylonian queen, she scatters largess. However, stockbrokers with "curved noses" and names such as Levinstein, Rosenbaum, Hirsh and Cohen protest (in exaggerated Yiddish-inflected dialogue) that the queen is wasting good food on poor people. "All along Bishopsgate," Levinstein tells the clerk, "I haf seen the gommon people have their hants full of food—goot food! Oh, yes, without doubt a very bad tream!" (153). They threaten the queen and the children, until the queen's guards slaughter them all. In historical context, this scene is even more chilling: "It is in fact a pogrom. Subsequently, this bloody scene is turned into a dream—but nonetheless, it happens" (Wise 2000, 334). Her *The Story of the Treasure Seekers* ([1899] 2006) has the protagonist children try to get rich by taking a loan from the hook-nosed Rosenbaum, who charges 60 percent interest. Granted, her *Harding's Luck* (1909) amends this with a Mr. Rosenberg, who is "dark, handsome, and big nosed" (63). While these stereotypes were typical of the time, it's a bit more chilling to reflect that E. Nesbit's books are still popular children's works, presented without censorship or explanatory footnotes.

Aldous Huxley, author of the dystopia *Brave New World,* added many moments of anti-Semitism to his short stories and other novels. In "Farcical History of Richard Greenow" (1920), a nurse takes over a house from Jews "anxious to live down a deplorable name by a display of patriotism," the story explains (69). Much worse than the suggestion of disloyalty was that of war profiteering. In *Those Barren Leaves* ([1925] 1994), Chelifer is appointed to the Air Board and narrates: "I spent my time haggling with German Jews over the price of chemicals and celluloid, with Greek brokers over the castor oil, with Ulstermen over the linen" (115). Even in the midst of the worst war the world has seen, Jewish merchants, allied with the enemy, are trying to make money. In "Chawdron" ([1930] 1957), the narrator and Tilney discuss Charlotte Salmon, a famous "blackly Semitic" cellist: "And her playing! So clotted, so sagging, so greasy" one character explains, and then the other agrees: "So terribly Jewish, in a word" (17–18). There is deniability as the point-of-view characters are the ones having racist thoughts, not the narrator or author. Granted, this technique makes the Jews representative figures rather than characters. As critics like Claudia Rosenhan posit, "The 'Jew' is hated for what he is taken to represent, e.g. cosmopolitanism, otherness or sexual perversion, and not treated realistically. Huxley presents anti-Semitism in the context of a plausible social and ideological narrative frame and does not voice his personal anxieties" (7). Still, the prevalence of these incidents is certainly problematic.

Later, in the face of Hitler's cruelty, Huxley spoke against Hitler's anti-Semitism, observing, "Performing a magical rite as old as history, Hitler has symbolically loaded all the sins and misfortunes accumulated by the German people during the last nineteen years onto the backs of the Jews. Staggering under the burden, these unfortunate scapegoats have been beaten and booted into the wilderness" (quoted in Rosenhan 2003, 16). His actions likewise revealed kindness as he helped Jewish children escape Germany.

Clearly, he realized how much of the scapegoating was cultural. In *Ape and Essence* ([1948] 1992), Huxley's post-apocalyptic morality play, the Arch-Vicar explains the "Hots" and their position: "Remember your history. If you want social solidarity, you've got to have either an external enemy or an oppressed minority. We have no external enemies, so we have to make the most of our Hots. They're what the Jews were under Hitler. [. . .] If anything goes wrong, it's always the fault of the Hots. I don't know what we'd do without them" (76). Even as characters show off their racism or not, the authoritative depiction of the Jews as scapegoats remains the most pointed.

George Orwell criticized all the unthinking hatred with one of the most groundbreaking dystopia novels ever written, *1984*. (Some think George Orwell learned that the Jewish year *Tashmad* (meaning destruction) numerologically corresponds to the Jewish year 5744, which fell in 1984, and that is why he chose the title.) His character of Emmanuel Goldstein, mythic leader of Big Brother's opposition and thus a scapegoat for the public's constant fury, suggests Stalin's, and indeed, the world's, baseless anti-Semitism. In his essay "Antisemitism in Britain," Orwell (1945) describes the many people he interviewed who insisted that they were not anti-Semitic but nonetheless disliked Jews or did not want to be around them. Over and over, he points out these people's lack of evidence, and yet their insistence on sticking to their prejudices. "It is at bottom quite irrational and will not yield to argument," he concludes. Orwell also observes that, while prejudice had risen during the war, previous generations of British barred Jews from certain jobs, bullied them at school, and otherwise treated them unkindly. As he continues:

In private, antisemitism was on the up-grade, even, to some extent, among sensitive and intelligent people. This was particularly noticeable in 1940 at the time of the internment of the refugees. Naturally, every thinking person felt that it was his duty to protest against the wholesale locking-up of unfortunate foreigners who for the most part were only in England because they were opponents of Hitler. Privately, however, one heard very different sentiments expressed. . . . This feeling that antisemitism is something sinful and disgraceful, something that a civilized person does not suffer from, is unfavourable to a scientific approach, and indeed many people will admit that they are frightened of probing too deeply into the subject. They are frightened, that is to say, of discovering not only that antisemitism is spreading, but that they themselves are infected by it.

Postwar, the revelation of where such prejudice could lead put a stop to much of it, but the traces remain in even the most foundational works of science fiction and fantasy.

TOLKIEN'S DWARVES

Beloved fantasy author Neil Gaiman notes, "Tolkien was the bowling ball in the rubber sheet; Tolkien changed things. Before him, things weren't published, regarded, or reviewed as fantasy. They were reviewed in the *New York Times* by W. H. Auden. We live in a world where the idea of fantasy as being 'something else' is prevalent, where its success means it has to be replicated to keep it commercial" (Wagner, Golden, and Bissette 2008, 503). After his *Hobbit* and *Lord of the Rings*, a host of fantasy novelists followed his tradition and created a massive genre. Tolkien was famously Catholic. However, his characters and languages display distinct, deliberate Jewish influence, sometimes to the point of allegory.

When Tolkien published *The Hobbit* in 1937, the Zionist dream of a Jewish homeland was still unfulfilled. Thus, Tolkien paralleled his invented dwarves and the exiled Jews: both were, as he put it, "at once natives and aliens in their habitations, speaking the languages of the country, but with an accent due to their own private tongue" (Carpenter 1981, 176). Other moments are recognizable to modern readers beyond this: "The dwarves' sorrowful song of longing to return to their homeland might have been lifted from a Middle Earth *Kinnot Tisha B'Av*" (Saks 2013).

"I didn't intend it, but when you've got these people on your hands, you've got to make them different, haven't you?" said Tolkien ([1965] 1979) during a BBC interview. "The dwarves of course are quite obviously, wouldn't you say that in many ways they remind you of the Jews?" The dwarves, like the Jews, are noted craftsmen, workers of stone and metal. They have a strong work ethic and take great joy in life, whether fighting or celebrating. Politically, they are insular, worrying little of matters outside their own nations. Beyond this, the dwarf calendar invented for *The Hobbit* reflects the Jewish calendar in beginning in autumn (Tolkien and Rateliff 2007, 79–80).

Though Tolkien's dwarves remember their traumatic past with mournful songs, most are assimilated and ambivalent about reclaiming Erebor, their lost country. Back at the Lonely Mountain, hidden somewhere beneath the dragon Smaug's treasure mound, there's a self-glowing "Arkenstone" gem, called "the heart of the mountain." The divinely inspired Arkenstone—say some observers—represents the Ark of the Covenant, with the Lonely Mountain standing in for Jerusalem's Temple Mount. (Lebovic 2013)

Of course, one must watch for the negative stereotypes. These characters physically are shorter than other races, with large hooked noses, long beards, and often red curly hair (a common trope to indicate Jewishness). Their obsession with acquiring gold, to the point of bringing about their doom, is problematic. This concept was already embedded in the mythological dwarves from the Norse Eddas and the legend of Siegfried, but Tolkien's combination has particularly unfortunate aspects.

At the beginning of *The Hobbit*, Thorin indicates that the wealth matters as much as his lost homeland: "We have never forgotten our stolen treasure," he tells Bilbo, "and even now, when I will allow we have a good bit laid by and are not so badly off . . . we still mean to get it back" (24). When they find it at last, seeing the treasure "rekindle[s] all the fire of their dwarvish hearts" (231). Here, they fiercely defend their dwarvish interests and they harden themselves against helping those who have helped them. The narrator notes, "When the heart of a dwarf, even the most respectable, is wakened by gold and by jewels, he grows suddenly bold, and he may become fierce" (218). Nonetheless, Thorin ends the story learning the Talmudic lesson: Naming Bilbo "child of the kindly West," he tells him that "if more of us valued food and cheer and song above hoarded gold, it would be a merrier world" (266).

Despite the thirst for gold, the dwarves in *The Hobbit* are positive characters, though often bumbling. Writing the sequel, *Lord of the Rings*, Tolkien became increasingly influenced by medieval texts on the Jewish people and their history (Tolkien and Rateliff 2007, 79–80). Gimli is a more developed hero with a clearer-defined culture. Here, Tolkien's dwarves are revealed as having been created to endure and battle the darkness while living apart from mainstream society. This reflects the Jewish concept of being "Chosen," with additional duties and responsibilities, rather than special favors. Finally, the close friendship that develops between Gimli the dwarf and Legolas the elf can be seen as the final reconciliation of Jews and gentiles, when they learn to each value the other.

"According to some Tolkien scholars, the author's heroic dwarves are a conscious inversion of Wagner's negatively 'Jewish' dwarves, meant to flip the switch on damaging stereotypes. As a lover of Norse mythology, Tolkien despised the Nazis' distortion of ancient tales to incite hatred" (Lebovic 2013). Richard Wagner's operas had several anti-Semitic stereotypes, such as Klingsor from *Parsifal* or the evil underground dwarves, the Nibelungs. Though some hold up Tolkien as a defense of the "Nordic race" and other Nazi propaganda, in the thirties, Tolkien's publisher, Allen & Unwin, planned a German translation of *The Hobbit*. When the publisher, Rutten & Loening, requested a statement of the author's Aryan origins, the South African-born Tolkien haughtily wrote back that he didn't understand how they were using the word "Aryan," as he had no connection with the Indian language group.

He added, "If I am to understand that you are enquiring whether I am of Jewish origin, I can only reply that I regret that I appear to have no ancestors of that gifted people." In addition, he commented: "I have become accustomed, nonetheless, to regard my German name with pride. . . . I cannot, however, forbear to comment that if impertinent and irrelevant inquiries of this sort are to become the rule in matters of literature, then the time is not far distant when a German name will no longer be a source of pride" (Carpenter 1981, 37–38).

While he had no ancestors "of that gifted people," he did speak Hebrew and incorporated it into his world. Adunaic, the language of Numenor, is based on the Semitic triple consonant roots. Most words are not identifiably Semitic, but in Adunaic the word for "she" is *hi*, "ear" is *huzun*, and "to, towards" is *ad, ada*. This is a logical cultural choice, as Tolkien imagined those people, like Jews, as the inventors of monotheism. In 1954, Tolkien composed a letter to Father Robert Murray in which he writes: "The Numenoreans thus began a great new good, and as monotheists; but like the Jews (only more so) with only one physical centre of 'worship': the summit of the mountain Meneltarma" (Carpenter 1981, 204). These were Aragorn's ancestors, the race of kings.

Khuzdul, dwarfish, shares the triple roots. Tolkien ([1965] 1979) adds, "Their words are Semitic, obviously, constructed to be Semitic." In Khuzdul, G-B-L means large. In Hebrew, it's G-D-L. Gimli's battle cry at the siege of the Hornberg is *Baruk Khazad!* (Axes of the Dwarves!). *Baruch* means bless in Hebrew and Gimli's war cry has the sound and construction of the traditional Jewish blessing *baruch HaShem*, bless or thank God, as Zak Cramer notes in his essay "Jewish Influences in Middle-earth" (2006). The language was chosen because it was significantly different from European languages, creating a distance, as with that between the Jews and other European cultures. The dwarves, like the Jews, speak their sacred ancestral tongue and also the languages of the countries they enter. As the Jews believe of Hebrew, dwarfish is the "language of heaven," given to them by their creator. Tolkien's notes, compiled by his son into *The Peoples of Middle-Earth* (1996, 323) explains:

> According to their legends their begetter, Aulë the Vala, had made this [tongue] for them and had taught it to the Seven Fathers before they were laid to sleep until the time for their awakening should come. After their awakening this language (as all languages and all other things in Arda) changed in time, and divergently in the mansions that were far-sundered. But the change was so slow and the divergence so small that even in the Third Age converse between all Dwarves in their own tongue was easy.

This echoes the connection between Jewish dialects worldwide—many of which, like German Yiddish versus Russian Yiddish, had only slight differences. In the early days of Middle-earth, humans of these regions had friendly contact with the dwarves, who "were not unwilling to teach their own tongue to Men with whom they had special friendship, but Men found it difficult and were slow to learn more than isolated words, many of which they adapted and took into their own language." This reflects the adoption of Hebrew roots and words like "Hallelujah" or "Amen" into English, as observed by Tolkien, the linguist.

Elvish too has correspondences: Having left their own mythic homeland, their race is experiencing "the spiritual Yiddish culture of the Diaspora—a culture of memory, mysticism, and light" (Cramer 2006). Notably, the Elvish alphabet, Tengwar, uses only consonants, like Hebrew. Critic Zak Cramer (2011) explains:

> Names like Aman and Gil-Galad might reproduce the Hebrew triliteral root, and names like Amroth or Morgoth or Nan Elmoth reproduce a triliteral root with a Hebrew plural ending *oth*. The name Melkor echoes the Biblical Moloch. Elvish might also be seen to contain numerous examples resembling the Hebrew genitive. The genitive of a female noun ending in *ah* changes its ending to *ath* and precedes the noun it is in a genitive relationship with. Sammath Naur, the chambers of fire in Mount Doom where The One Ring was made and unmade, would seem to imitate just such a construction. This is especially so when one considers that Naur recapitulates the Hebrew word for lamp or fire.

It's also notable that many elves like Galadriel, Tinúviel, and Glorfindel have angel names, ending in "El." In Hebrew, this means God (as in, the Voice of God, the Shield of God, etc.) and is given to angels (Michael, Gabriel, Uriel). In Elvish it's star, or "elf" as the elves are the star people, the heavenly people. Tolkien's own middle name, Reuel, follows this pattern, meaning "Friend of God." This was a family name that he inherited from his father, and that he in turn gave to each of his four children, who gave it to theirs. The prefix "Ben," as in Tolkien's Iarwain Ben-Adar, is also Hebrew, meaning "son of," and used to construct names in this pattern. In fact, this is the Elvish name for Tom Bombadil, Middle Earth's riddling dispenser of wisdom, with "Ben-Adar" translating as without a father. "Rohirim" is a word recognizable for the Hebrew plural at the end.

The Silmarillion, known as the history or "Bible" of Middle-Earth, has even more correspondences. "Chapter 2 tells of the creation of the Dwarves, which tells a founding myth not too removed from the story of *Akeidat Yitzhak* (Abraham's binding of, and near slaughter, of Isaac), and the notion that while born first the race of Dwarves was superseded by the race of Elves," explains R. Jeffrey Saks (2013) in his "Tolkien and the Jews." This last, as he says, functions as "a hint to the status of Jews vis-à-vis God within the

Christian worldview." Cramer (2006) likewise mentions "the Biblical style of *The Silmarillion*, the echoing of Cain's murder of Abel in Feanor's kinslaying and in Smeagol's murder of his friend Deagol, the two trees of Valinor and the two trees of Eden, and salvation on the back of eagle's wings." However, he adds, "All of these and many other Biblical echoes can be ascribed to Tolkien's Christianity, without reference to anything specifically Jewish."

Instead, Cramer focuses on the *tzohar* (an obscure single-use word from the Bible) that Noah is told to place in the ark (Genesis 6:16). Some translate this as "window," but in Talmudic and Midrashic tradition, the *tzohar* is a jewel that contains the primordial light from the first day of creation (Schwartz 2004b, 85–88). After Noah carried it, it became the eternal light hanging in the tabernacle and in Solomon's temple. If as Cramer posits, Tolkien knew this Jewish legend, the Silmarils are the *tzohar*, recurring throughout the history of Middle-Earth until Eärendil the Mariner sails across the sky each day bearing a Silmaril as a beacon of heaven's light, in "an echo of Noah, who carried the *tzohar* across a flooded world" (Cramer 2006).

A few more stories reveal Tolkien's encounters with Judaism and the Jewish fandom that followed. During the World War II, Tolkien was on air raid duty in a bomb shelter with a fellow Oxford scholar, famed Jewish historian Cecil Roth. He writes that "I found him charming, full of gentleness (in every sense); and we sat up till after 12 talking." But what impressed Tolkien the most was that Roth "himself came and called me at 10 to 7: so that I could go to Communion!" He was so touched that his Jewish friend cared so strongly about Tolkien's own faith, "it seemed," he writes, "like a fleeting glimpse of an unfallen world" (Carpenter 1981, 67).

The first translation of *The Hobbit* into Hebrew was undertaken in Egyptian captivity by four Israeli Air Force pilots held as POWs in the early seventies. After they received an English copy from the Red Cross, they began to read. "We were a group of about 20 prisoners," recalled Rami Harpaz, "including many who couldn't read English. So that they could also enjoy the book we decided to translate it to Hebrew." When they were released after three years of captivity, they carried with them seven notebooks with the draft of the translation, which was published with funding from the Israel Air Force (Saks 2013). Following this, it was also translated into a Hebrew version with more grandeur of language and a Yiddish version too. Today, the Israeli Tolkien Society organizes activities, conferences, and research on Tolkien and his works in Israel.

Most dwarves in fantasy and gaming derive straight from Tolkien, though there's little indication that the authors are invoking Jewish tropes. In Terry Pratchett's Discworld series, however, the jolly, gold-loving dwarves grow more fiercely attached to tradition as their children move to the city and adopt its modern ways. By the late books, the dwarfish priests show a bigoted, fundamentalist element that echoes some aspects of extreme Orthodox Judaism (or other types of orthodoxy). The novel *Thud!* (2005) tackles this topic head-on. On the anniversary of the Battle of Koom Valley, troll-dwarf tension is high each year. Ardent, the interpreter of the deep-down dwarves' decrees, insists, "They will not listen to you. They will not even look at you. They have nothing to do with the World Above. They believe it is a kind of bad dream" (76). Their religion insists words are sacred and should never be changed (an analogy for Jewish teachings). However, the young city dwarves and city trolls have set aside the hatred to play a board game called Thud in which they've set aside their grandparents' hatred. Among them is Grag Bashfullsson, something like a reform community leader. The other dwarves call him "A little modern, perhaps. A little young. Not the kind of grag we grew up with, but . . . yes, we'd vouch for him" (257). When the human commander Vimes solves the mystery, he discovers the deep-down dwarves were trying to hide the truth, that at the Battle of Koom Valley, both sides were there to make peace and they died all together, negotiating in good fellowship. Of course, the story works well as analogy for any two races with ancestral hatred who nonetheless have younger, liberal descendants seeking a better world.

Chapter 5

Eastern Europe's Social Science Fiction

THE HASKALAH

The Haskalah, or Jewish Enlightenment, swept through Europe and encouraged a secular approach as Jews moved to cities and integrated with the populations there. In Central Europe, the Haskalah occurred around 1790–1840, spreading to Eastern Europe between 1840 and 1880. Rabbis got university degrees, and Jewish children attended public school. Religion no longer dominated in all spheres of life. The feminist question was trickier; with some rabbis supporting suffrage and women's taking a more active role in the synagogue. Conservative Judaism—known as Masorti Judaism in Europe—emerged in Germany in the latter half of the nineteenth century and accepted limited changes. Through it, the bat mitzvah was held for the first time in 1922. (Lacoue-Labarthe 2016). Sciences too were flourishing:

When the mostly East European readers of *Ha-tsefirah* opened the January 30, 1878 issue, they would likely have been surprised to see an etching of a strange and mysterious creature: a monstrous beast with leathery wings, clawed feet, and ravenous teeth. *Ha-tsefirah*, a Hebrew-language weekly journal based in Warsaw and devoted to the popularization of science among Jews, often published strange and mysterious images. Prior issues contained diagrams for the construction of an electric battery, the mechanism of a telegraph, a cross section of a steam engine, the composition of coral reefs, and a boa constrictor poised to devour its prey. What made this image different from the others was that it was an artistic representation of a long-extinct animal, described by the editor as "a kind of flying scorpion that hardened into stone from the days of the Flood." This was the first image of a dinosaur ever published in a Hebrew newspaper. (Blutinger 2010, 67–68)

The editor and founder, Hayim Selig Slonimski, used his journal to promote science from astronomy to engineering, discoveries in biology, chemistry, and metallurgy, and news of the Haskalah itself.

Jews all over the world, Slonimski wrote in his first issue's introduction, were embracing the Enlightenment and modern science, but it was only "our people, the House of Israel who dwell in the land of Poland, who will still oppose and fear approaching the gates of science," for they believed, like many fundamentalists, that "with the knowledge of any science, Torah will lessen," so they had tried to block the spread of information (Blutinger 2010, 68). As Europe embraced modern technology, the Jews had the opportunity to join in. By choosing to write in Hebrew, however, Slonimski had a difficult time, as the ancient language lacked a scientific vocabulary. Hebrew was the scholarly and religious language (in contrast with everyday Yiddish) and choosing to write in it followed the quest within the Haskalah for a formal literary canon. To solve the vocabulary problem, he invented many words, which later integrated into the Modern Hebrew language.

Aware of his audience, he carefully presented Darwin's theory of evolution and the geologic evidence that the world was older than 6,000 years, while reconciling the facts that he could with the Bible. In this cause, he went on to argue that the biblical Flood had played a key role in the extinction of dinosaurs. Slonimski also focused on rejecting ideas that dinosaurs were never living beings. The idea was that God had begun to create these creatures but then changed His mind. It was "an offensive imaginary fantasy," one "that would never arise in the heart of any man enlightened in the nature of creation and the perfection of the Creator of all," he wrote, to believe that these creatures were merely "a sort of experiment," which had no life and thus "remained like golems who had not completed their tasks." In fact, Slonimski argued, science has shown that these animals "were truly created as living beings and existed in the world," that they became extinct from various causes, and that "it seems they were from the days of the Flood" (quoted in Blutinger 2010, 79). This connection between the Flood and the elimination of the dinosaurs appears several times in *Ha-tsefirah*. The pterodactyl discussed above is described as something that had fossilized "from the days of the Flood," and Slonimski argued that the power and violence of the dinosaurs were causes of the Flood; in turn, the Flood was responsible for their final extinction. With this, he bridged science and the Bible, urging Jews to embrace modern discoveries.

The author Isaac Euchel (1756–1804) was one of the first Hebrew writers of the German Haskalah. Incorporating many European genres, he wrote utopian satiric travelogues including the first Hebrew epistolary story *Igrot Meshulam ben Uriyah Ha'eshtemoi* (Letters of Meshulam ben Uriyah Ha'eshtemo'i), and *Igrot Isaac Euchel*. The eastern protagonist travels with a Spanish Jew to learn about the hidden Jews of Spain and Catholicism. More fantastical travelogues appeared in the seventeenth century through the fantastic stories of Gershon ben Eliezer ha-Levi in his *Gelilot Eretz Yisrael* (Scrolls of the Land of Israel). He explains that in his journey through India in 1630, he found the Sambatyon River (across which the Ten Lost Tribes were apocryphally exiled). This river, he adds, refuses to flow on Shabbat. As he proceeds to describe three-eyed beasts and headless living men, a strong fantasy element appears. Manasseh Ben Israel in his 1650 *Mikveh Yisrael* (Hope of Israel) similarly wrote his belief that Ecuadoreans were the Ten Lost Tribes (with an agenda of getting immigration to England legalized). He too claimed to have found the river and claimed that even when its sand is kept in a glass, it is agitated during six days of the week and rests on the Sabbath.

With the rise of nineteenth-century Zionism and its call to establish a Jewish state in Israel, the Hebrew language (in contrast with everyday Yiddish) rose in popularity. A few Hebrew novels sprang up around the 1850s, though the limited language made writing them a difficult prospect, so they were generally set in biblical times. For the same reason, Hebrew translations of other works proved more difficult and might more appropriately be called adaptations.

Joseph Perl's *Megale temirim* (The Revealer of Secrets, [1819] 1997) has been called the first Hebrew novel. The narrator uses the power of Kabbalah to make himself invisible, thus kicking the narrative off with a truly Jewish science fiction premise. As it goes on, he gathers letters that form the text of the novel. Perl satirizes both the traditional Hasidism and the pro-science Maslikim, the story's villains. Their insistence that there is a natural scientific order in which everything makes sense is misguided and fanatical, the narrator insists. Even as the novel reveals the daily routines of Jewish culture at the time, it considers the movements and outside relationships that define it. Adding metafictional depth, the Hassidic community in the book spends their time chasing a scandalous book that reveals their many immoral acts. (This actually stands in for a critical unpublished pamphlet of Perl's.)

As with traditional science fiction, the structure and genre—in this case, epistolary—provides the culture and social commentary. "The technology of the postal system itself provides both a metaphor and a structuring device for representing how tentative our control of our surroundings is, whether because of the machinations of other people or the unseen hand of fate" (Caplan 1999, 95). Writing in biblical Hebrew adds an extra challenge—its translation of Yiddish idioms gives it the feel of a bilingual novel. In short, it's an Enlightenment satire meant for a Jewish audience in which "Perl mocks the inability of his opponents to even understand him, much less refute what he has to say" (Caplan 1999, 97). He wrote two subsequent satires, *The Test of the Righteous* and *Tale of the Loss of the Prince*, a parody of Reb Nahman of Bratslav's *The Tale of the Loss of the Princess*. In the former, Obadiah ben Petahiah, the fictious editor of both books, acquires a *shraybtafel*—a writing tablet that can do speech recognition and audio surveillance. He goes seeking someone so righteous that the device will work for him and allow him to transfer the data and empty its storage capacity in this satirical work with its delightful futuristic technology.

Other early works explored the inventions entering the culture. Ukrainian author Y. Y. Linyetski's 1876 (2006) Yiddish short story "The Hasidic Steam Engine" stands out as it blends the classic folkloric tradition with imagery of progress. The characters wonder about what appears to be a magically jumping train. One of the characters insists that his rebbe is so magical that he wears seven-league boots and can travel great distances in an instant (this in itself may be a borrowing from German folklore or possibly a reference to the Talmudic power of "jumping the road"). Another local man retorts, "Morons, morons! You can see for yourselves that all those engines run on the energy of pure smoke—on steam! Well, so why are you surprised? Why are you amazed that smoke has the strength to push millions of pounds?" (238). As he adds, humanity clearly learned that smoke could push a weight from their rebbe himself. "Why, his pipe was the first steam engine in the world! And the rebbe uses it every day to transport the sinful souls as well as the prayers and requests to heaven. And to carry the steam engine back down for blessings and successes!" (239). Using this link with heaven and the angels, the rebbe can perform God's will on earth. Moreover, it has resulted in the steam age, in a fascinating blend of religious mysticism creating science fiction. Even as the warring traditions defined daily life, authors tried writing early science fiction to reconcile them.

RUSSIA

The Jews largely immigrated to Russia from former Polish territories in the late 1700s. Between 1791 and 1917, Russian Jews were consigned to the Pale of Settlement (comprising much of present-day Lithuania, Belarus, Poland, Ukraine, and parts of Western Russia). The czars made this decree to find a home for the Jews, but the separation led to their culture remaining apart from the mainstream. This Jewish concentration also made pogroms easier to commit. Conditions were so poor that when they were permitted to emigrate, two million of the roughly five million Jews living there departed, mostly for America.

At the time, Russian literature centered on aristocrats in central Russia, and thus rarely featured the Jews. The Shylock archetype of the cruel usurer and his beautiful daughter began appearing in nineteenth-century stories and plays like *Ispantsy* (The Spaniards, 1830). In the mid-nineteenth century, middle-class writers took over, blaming Jews for plotting against Russia's traditional values and inciting revolution. Alexander II was assassinated in 1881, followed by pogroms, anti-Jewish riots, and laws removing Jewish rights.

Sholem Yakov Abramovich (better known as Mendele Mokher Sefarim or Mendele the Itinerant Bookseller), traveled through the Ukraine writing in Hebrew then Yiddish. His satires of Jewish Russia, *Di kliatche* (The Mare, 1873) and *Masa'ot Binyamin Ha-Shelishi* (The Travels of Benjamin the Third, 1878) are considered classics today: He is considered the grandfather of modern Yiddish literature and the father of modern Hebrew literature: He wrote in Hebrew as part of the Haskalah, then switched to Yiddish, causing something of a literary revolution. In 1886, he returned to Hebrew but modernized it for ease of expression.

The Travels of Benjamin the Third nods to legendary twelfth-century traveler Benjamin of Tudela while subtly criticizing Jews' insular estrangement from the world. Through their history, messianic fantasies staved off despair but gave Jews the excuse of passively accepting slaughter instead of striving for justice. In the story, Benjamin mirrors their fantasies, and finally sets off to find the legendary Red Jews beyond the River Sambaton. A dreamer ungrounded in reality like Don Quixote, he's much more gullible than the epic hero and cowardly as well. His book learning works against him as he mistakes a river for the ocean and believes he's reached the end of the earth.

The Mare has the hero Isrolik attempt to attend university only to find that he must master Russian folklore—abandoning his Jewish beliefs for equally impractical Russian superstitions. Exhausted, he collapses in a field where he sees bullies beating a beautiful horse, a symbol of femininity and the natural world that appears like a sparkling bride. This in turn evokes biblical imagery of the Jewish people with God as bridegroom, awaiting God's protection and love. As the hero bursts out, "One moment, I felt as if my life were about to end out of pity for the poor, broken-down mare. The next moment, I was furious. How could she just lie in the mud, calmly, nonchalantly, as if she didn't grasp her awful situation!" (560). Isrolik seeks benefactors for her from the Society for the Prevention of Cruelty to Animals, representing the St. Petersburg Society for the Promotion of Enlightenment among Jews. They promise to help, but only after the mare improves herself "with all due process" in this Swiftian satire (608). The horse in turn is disgusted that she must dance before receiving food, while other horses are treated far more generously. Isrolik describes her as Job, constantly tormented and adds, in a clear reference to the Wandering Jew, "How long will you be the Eternal Mare, the Wandering Mare?" (600). Until humans become better and wiser, with justice and mercy ruling, is the reply.

When Isrolik, startled at her eloquent argument, insists the devil has gotten into her, the devil indeed emerges and takes Isrolik on a fantastical tour of the world's pogroms and tortures. Continuing the satire, a hen's life is described in the poignant metaphor of pogroms with "her mate and her son seized and tied up before her very eyes" (593). The pair—her son just recently bar-mitzvahed—are subjected to the Jewish ritual of kapparot and slaughtered in front of her. After seeing such cruelty everywhere, the hero falls into madness, which ironically, is finally blamed on devilish possession. The political satire is biting—"Through a succession of duets—Isrolik with his mother, with the mare, and with the despotic devil—the modern Jew is shown trapped between a defensive and decaying orthodoxy and an energetically antagonistic regime, he is stripped of his faith in divine intervention and equally, of trust in positive political reform" (Wisse 2000, 335).

Jewish poetry of the time offered a number of fantastical elements, employed to counter attacks. Ruvim Kulisher ([1849] 2007) in *An Answer to the Slav*, compares Jews to ghosts, demons, witches, and Satan himself, emphasizing the public's irrational fear and hatred. In a very personal approach, he insists that the peasants have no God, faith, or love, so they have tried to extract these from his body. He ends by painting a picture of the more modern Jew, dressed in the new style and embracing theater and city life, even while hoping for a homeland and the brotherly love of their neighbors. Likewise, Simon Frug ([1890] 2007) uses mythology to convey his people's plight. Calling himself an Aeolian harp to echo his people's heartache, he paints images of sorrowful ghosts surrounding him, lending him their mournful songs: "Now phantoms of sadness, now specters of suffering/ Bequeath me their doleful refrains." Dmitri Tsenzor ([1903] 2007) offers a similar metaphor, as near the synagogue, he's surrounded by sobs from "the lonely ghosts of a dark and bloody year."

M. Z. Feierberg (1874–1899) likewise wrote Russian-Hebrew stories highly dependent on the folkloric tradition, even as his themes explored being caught between two worlds. "In the Evening" ([1900] 1975) offers his protagonist Hofni a transcendent experience when a boy tells a story of the synagogue filling with ghosts praying. Outside, Hofni staggers home through the darkness, "through the perilous world, which was teeming with ghosts, demons, phantoms, sorcerers" (73). In this, a single lantern shines, drawing back the darkness like the *Ner Tamid*. At home, his mother tells another folktale, of a Jewish boy stolen away by a greedy landlord. This boy is instructed by his Christian adoptive father that Jews are devils, even as the father trains him in self-rejection. However, after the unkind children tell him the truth, his own ghostly father visits to advise him. At last, he puts aside his fine clothes and goes to study in the Great Yeshiva. On the road, wolves attack, but cannot penetrate the holy circle of his camp because he has followed all the mitzvot. All the magical occurrences are left in retold tales within the frame, giving the story a technical realism and yet welcoming the spirits of the folkloric tradition—even blending them into the ordinary world. As Hofni narrates during the story, "Something hung in the air and I didn't know what—whether it was good or evil, holy or unclean, but I did know that whatever it was, it was dreadful . . . and in this dreadful life, we had to battle every minute with dreadful powers that lay constantly in wait for us" (83). These are the goyim, tempting Jews and burning down the temple, so Hofni knows he must always be vigilant.

As the twentieth century began, Russian Jews began sharing their experiences with a wider audience, though they were left out of the literary canon. Such Jewish authors, writing to protest their oppression and better the Jewish situation, included Osip Rabinovich, Grigori Bogrov, Lev Levanda, Osip Mandelstam, Moyshe Kulbak, Andrey Sobol, and Semyon Yushkevich. Isaac Babel is the most famous for sharing the Jewish experience, while Boris Pasternak, a poet of the time, went on to win the Nobel Prize for *Doctor Zhivago*. Meanwhile, socialism was seen as a solution to the Jews' outcast status, and the Yiddish socialist movement urged a new way to join mainstream society. At the same time, Yiddish newspapers and theater rose, creating a distinct culture.

After the Russian Revolution of 1917, however, Jews mostly de-emphasized their cultural identity to avoid the accusation of "Jewish nationalism," especially in an era of heavy censorship. "Because of its theoretical internationalism, Communism offered modern Jews the unique opportunity of quitting Judaism not through defection (conversion to another religion) and not through assimilation (conversion to another nationality) but through national self-transcendence" (Wisse 2000, 119). Nonetheless, Communism emphasized the distinction between Jews and non-Jews, even as its precepts called for erasure of such categorization. Nonetheless, when Stalin took charge in the twenties, a Commissariat for Jewish Affairs was established. In 1928, the Soviet government actually established an agrarian Jewish Autonomous Region near the Sino-Soviet border. (Potentially it could have become a Yiddish-speaking Jewish homeland to rival Israel, but few Jews emigrated there.) Stalin's Soviet state supported homogenized Yiddish language institutions and Yiddish education, though religion was de-emphasized in the program. Still, many modern Jews preferred to learn Russian and assimilate.

While Russian science fiction's golden age tied in with the later space race, space voyage stories were popular in the early twentieth century. In 1915, Yakov Perelman wrote the first serious book on space exploration, *Mezhplanetnie puteshestviya* (Interplanetary Travel), along with guides to inventor Nicola Tesla's works. Shalom Ben Avram published *Komemiyut*

(Resurgence, 1921), a pointed and surprisingly accurate portrayal of a future mass aliyah.

Other Jewish writers found welcome from the political left. In Saint Petersburg, members of the loose-knit group Obshchestvo Izucheniia Poeticheskogo Iazyka (Society for the Study of Poetic Language) examined literary devices. Many Jews were in the group, including Iurii Tynianov and Osip Brik, though two of the most famous, Viktor Shklovskii and Boris Eikhenbaum, were Jewish only through their fathers.

Osip Brik and his wife Liliia Kagan entered a ménage à trois with the poet Vladimir Mayakovsky, adding their culture to his life. Mayakovsky, a leader of Russian Futurism, became a vehement defender of the Jews. His play *The Bedbug* ([1929] 1970) is surreal, if not quite science fiction. The hero, Ivan Prisypkin, is frozen for fifty years and wakes in a shocking future. Abandoned even by his bedbugs, he panics. He is a caveman to the locals in their shining paradise with no drinking, smoking, swearing, or poverty. They put him in a zoo as a paragon of uncivilized man and howl, "The children! Remove the children! Muzzle it . . . muzzle it!" (302). While he is not identified as Jewish, the public's determination to silence him as well as his symbolic link with an insect (in itself evoking Kafka's cockroach) is suggestive.

This was a time of early speculative fiction, often more surreal and dystopian than emblematic of the genre. Ilya Ehrenburg's *The Adventures of Julio Jurenito and His Disciples* (1921) satirizes the great European national myths with a Candide-style adventure (Ehrenburg himself is the first disciple and the author-narrator as skeptical Jew). The narrator begins the story in a riotous café, hoping for someone to pay the bill, when a man with a pointed tail walks in. This is Julio, visiting from Mexico. At the narrator's exclamation, as the novel puts it, "He looked quietly and clearly into my face and said: 'I know who you think I am. But he does not exist'" (17). This moment of deep insight and philosophy blends with marvelous inventions and abilities. In one scene, Julio is "simultaneously reading the Bible, dictating a letter to the Minister of Fine Arts of the Republic of Chile to a shorthand-typist, listening to yesterday's cattle prices over the telephone from Chicago, chatting with us, smoking a fat cigar, eating a soft-boiled egg and looking at the photograph of a plump actress" (26–27), while his armchair is "equipped with all kinds of lathes, tubes, mechanical holders in the shape of ladies' fingers, and a whole keyboard of incomprehensible buttons" (27). With heavy irony, one chapter begins with engraved invitations for all the nobility to attend a pogrom. "This is unthinkable! The twentieth century and such vile doings!" a student bursts out. He's told the frivolity of the era will lead him to accept such violence as a matter of course, as so many ethical people do (111).

Many have observed the prophetic nature of the book—foreseeing the Holocaust in villages the Germans have brutally emptied, depicting an early

Nazi type called Schmidt, and even predicting the nuclear attacks on Japan. Later, the author and Vasilii Grossman became the best known of the war correspondents. They documented Nazi atrocities against Jews, in *Chernaia kniga* (The Black Book, with a companion account, *Krasnaia kniga*, The Red Book, describing Jewish heroism in the Red Army).

Envy by Yuri Olesha ([1927] 2004) stars Nikolai Kavalerov, who's disillusioned with the increasingly industrialized USSR even as he hearkens back to an age of imagination and romance. However, as the book reveals, the more man discovers about himself, the more he is lost. The character is like Chaplin's tramp, fully aware he will always be the underdog. As such, it has a distinctly Jewish dystopian sensibility. Jews appear sporadically in the text—the narrator passes Shapiro, "a melancholic old Jew with a nose like the number six" who compliments the sausage amid jokes about eating pork. Mentions of Hebrew letters and the tree of life remind readers of a Jewish presence even as the fantastical elements subtly pervade the text.

Other Jews found their own way to petition for respect. Ilya Selvinsky's "Bar Kokhba" ([1920] 2007) adapts the story of a Jewish revolutionary to show what a Jewish epic in European sonnets would resemble. It begins, "And he was huge/his whole frame filled with might/As if Leviathan's own nursling splendid" (228). Indeed, the historic warrior is powerfully built with a divine light bursting from within. He even battles Jewish demons great and small as he stabs Asmodeus into dust" (228). Though his people serve the Romans, Kokhba leads his people in a great war for redemption, presumably echoing the Jews' need in more modern times. He falls, but majestically and memorably, offering a powerful hero for Jews to hold as a paragon.

In the same tradition, Vladimir Jabotinsky's *Samson the Nazarite* ([1926] 1930), a biblical epic that reflects the Russian situation, tells of a Jew surrounded by a hostile gentile population. His Samson is attracted to the surrounding culture and conflicted over how much to assimilate. In fact, Samson sneaks off to the Philistines to drink—breaking the rules of the Nazarites while on furtive sprees within the foreign culture. They accept him for a time, but start taunting him with his inferior origins, highlighting Jabotinsky's point that Jews will never be accepted.

H. Leivick, wrote the poem "The Wolf," in which a rabbi, last survivor of anti-Semitic violence, rises from a mound of ashes and transforms. This rabbi-wolf haunts a new generation of Jews when they move in to rebuild the destroyed town. When they ask the rabbi to resume religious services, he bitterly insists that the ruins be retained as a memorial for his dead generation. They dismiss him. Eventually, in his despair, he attacks them in the synagogue on Yom Kippur, where he is released from his suffering when they beat him to death. At this point, the newcomers need no longer fear this last survivor who spoke for the murdered generation but can resume the reconstruction of a new communal life. "It is interesting to gauge Leivick's reaction to the pogroms of his homeland; the wolf, rather than turning his rage upon those who wronged him, instead terrorizes his kin. Leivick, it seems, is using the wolf to warn that blood for blood is pointless, for it makes the Jewish victim no different from his non-Jewish oppressors. It is not a revenge fantasy, but rather a revenge nightmare," comments Esther Sacks (2017) in "What's So Jewish About Werewolves?" The dark metaphors of alienation and persecution continued, even for the refugees who found safety in the new world.

Rochel Broches, a Yiddish writer who perished in the Minsk ghetto in 1942, called attention to the plight of the poor. "Little Abrahams" ([1940] 2007) in particular tells its story with fantasy imagery. The orphanage, from which loud wails emit, is described with a bed: "in the huge pile of rags, are feet and hands moving, heads with contorted faces, gaping mouths" (92). The child pulled out of there howls until "it" appears a cat or dog (92). "The little creature," chided for eating the babies' food, runs off (92). As the orphanage head explains, using darker dehumanizing imagery, "Who would take care of these children if she didn't? They would be lying around on the street, in a barn, in the alleys because they aren't really children. They're dust, garbage, that's what everyone believes and that's what happens" (95). The protagonist is called Avremelech (Little Abraham) but confusingly, all the children at the orphanage are—identityless, interchangeable; the girls, who are not registered with a bris, go nameless. Everyone in town agrees that the protagonist is a beautiful child, but when he is abandoned, no one wants to take him in.

Post-Holocaust, Jewish authors continued to reflect the state of minorities, using aliens, outrageous situations, and mad inventions to reflect the human condition. Many of the early authors were lost to violence or disease, adding tragedy to their already sorrowful works. They foretold the horrors of nationalism, in a world growing ever-darker.

POLAND AND ROMANIA

Sholem Aleichem ("peace be unto you") is the pen name of Sholem Rabinovitch (1859–1916), whose Yiddish stories inspired *Fiddler on the Roof*. He was born in Poland but traveled through Europe after the 1905 pogrom in Kiev, finally arriving in America. His literary acclaim only grew, and his funeral procession was witnessed by 100,000 mourners. Of course, the shtetl culture he wrote of blends realistic stories with goofy folktales of Chelm and lavish adventures among demons and angels. In his works, Elijah visits on mysterious errands and a tailor brings home a gilgul disguised as a goat. Thus a few of his short stories, though folkloric in their feel, arguably cross over into pure fantasy.

Mendele Mokher Seforim, Sholem Aleichem, and I. L. Peretz (1852–1915) are considered the three great Yiddish authors. All were modern, as the novel and formal short story were late to assimilate into Yiddish culture. Adapting to the modern style, Peretz reimagined folklore in his *Folkstimlikhe geshikhtes* (Folktale-like Stories). In his story "Bontsha the Silent" ([1894] 1955) a meek porter dies, unnoticed. However, the story follows him to heaven, where angels greet him joyously. The man is so humble, he assumes he's in the wrong place: "In his veins ran ice and he knew this must all be a dream or simply a mistake" (225). Only when the Angel for the Prosecution tells his life story does he realize he's where he belongs. After all the sorrows of his life are revealed, moments of constant injustice always met by silence, he's offered whatever he most desires. He chooses only a hot bun daily, with butter. While the character is sympathetic, Peretz suggests that his humble death was a waste—that his meekness led to a meaningless death, smashed by a carriage and neglected at the hospital and still not uttering a word, instead of striving for equality. "The meek porter's life is made a protest against man's abuse of man, an oppressed man's cry for human justice" (Madison 1968, 115). The angels' sympathy for him gives the readers a model for understanding.

Peretz's "The Three Wedding Canopies" ([1901] 1987) begins like a Jewish fairytale indeed. "Far, far away, beyond the Mountains of Darkness, on the other side of the Sambatyon River, there is a country known as Wonderland, where the red-haired Jews dwell, the descendants of the Ten Lost Tribes" (60). The king, Solomon XXVII in his beautiful palace, has a beautiful daughter, Princess Shulamite. When she goes out on Lag B'Omer, the birds sing to her of her future husband. Seeking such a paragon, the king feasts the suitors (with perfectly kosher food) and challenges them to a riddle contest. Robbers, transformations, and talking animals set up the classic fairytale plot. Still, as a sorceress blows the traditional sounds of the shofar and the characters reference the Book of Esther, it's a delightfully Jewish fairytale space. He also published tales of the golem, of the Prophet Elijah visiting the pious with a feast, and other traditional folklore.

A darker story, "The Dead Town" ([1895] 2002) features a Jewish town in which anyone with a soul that wasn't very good or bad keeps it after death instead of going to the afterlife. "It goes right on living in the World of Illusion. It never leaves its body at all. The only difference is that before it dreamt it was living on the earth and now it dreams it's living in the earth." Such souls, still in the bodies, return to the town and eat all the food, leaving the people to starve. All the officials like the rabbi exist in such a dream state, so nothing gets done. Besides a ghost story, this works as a parable of leaders suck in the past or oblivious to present-day hardships, unable to modernize.

In this tradition, Peretz's surreal play *A Night in the Old Marketplace* ([1906] 1992) explores the entire modern Jewish experience, with nearly one hundred characters: a wedding jester, young lovers, musicians, wealthy Jews, impoverished pious Jews, and also the revolutionaries and political prisoners of his modern time. A frame story shows the theater cast struggling to stage the drama, even as it's shown as the dream of a mysterious wanderer. As the play continues, the dead join the living, along with talking gargoyles, zombies, and dancing statues. The local drunk marries a young woman who rises from her grave, and they perform the Dance of Death. Like many Jewish stories, it incorporates grief into what should be scenes of joy, revealing the sensibility of the Jewish experience.

While assimilation was heavy in Germany, Czechoslovakia, and the Austrian part of Poland, native Yiddish speakers most often wrote in Yiddish and kept to their own community. Prior to World War I, Yiddish publishing was centered in Warsaw and Vilna. In 1931, almost 80 percent of Polish Jews identified Yiddish as their primary language (Wisse 2000, 133). About 300,000 Jews (a third of the population) lived in Warsaw prewar, publishing 11 daily Yiddish newspapers. Peretz helped found Yiddish schools, along with the Association of Jewish Writers and Journalists, which not only wrote but translated many secular works by Jules Verne, Jack London, and H. G. Wells, among others. During the Soviet regime, the field expanded and introduced important presses in Moscow and Minsk, with more in Petrograd, Kharkov, Odessa, and especially Kiev.

In the late 1930s, Polish Jewish writers for children clustered around *Okienko na świat,* a weekly edited by Marta Hirszprung. Its contributors included well-known writers Juliusz Feldhorn and Chaim Löw (pseudonym of Leon Przemski, 1901–1976), and poets Maurycy Szymel (1903–1942), Horacy Safrin (1899–1980), Maria Hochberżanka (1913–1996), and Minka Silberman. *Okienko* published Jewish fairy tales and legends, historical and Talmudic stories, Polish translations of Yiddish classics, and biographies of prominent Jewish leaders in Europe and Palestine (e.g., a short story about Yosef Trumpeldor). It sponsored literary competitions and published the winning entries. *Przegląd Społeczny* (Lwów) published literary criticism pertaining to children's literature written by Dvora Vogel (1900–1942) and Hermann Sternbach (1880–1942). ("Children's Literature: Polish Literature" 2010)

Meanwhile, Yiddish theater, cabaret, and cinema boomed. Yiddish theater began in Jassy, Romania in 1876. An 1882 performance in New York cemented this genre's popularity, and troupes toured from Eastern Europe to the United States. Plays mostly consisted of historical and Bible legends adapted along with modern melodramas and comedies (Goldberg 1983, 18). Yiddish films repeated these tropes, adding many interwar stories about patriotism and discrimination. Between 1910 and 1941, roughly 130 feature films and 30 short Yiddish films were created in Russia, Poland, Austria, and America, first silent and then with sound (Goldberg 1983, 17).

The tiny number of Yiddish fantasy films include *Jeden Z 36: Der Lamedvovnik* (One of the 36). Filmed in Poland in 1925, it merges the legend that thirty-six righteous Jews maintain the world with the story of Jewish heroism in the Polish uprising of January 1863, evoking a patriotic image of Polish-Jewish brotherhood. *The Yiddish Queen Lear* (Jacob Gordin's *Mirele Efros*) added trades of the fairytale epic. The best known and most celebrated film is the Polish adaptation of Ansky's *The Dybbuk* (1937). Finally, New York's *A People Eternal* (1939), advertised as the "First Million Dollar Yiddish Spectacle with a Cast of 10,000," adapts the British *The Wandering Jew*, toning down original antisemitic and Christian elements to follow the Jew's survival in different eras (Goldberg 1983, 97).

Itzik Manger, called the "Shelley of Yiddish," traveled throughout the world but was particularly part of the Warsaw literary scene. He weaves a hilarious satire in *The Book of Paradise* ([1938] 1965). In the story, Shmuel-Aba retains his memory of heaven by avoiding having the customary angel touch above his lip to make him forget. Heaven is divided into Jews, Christians, and Muslims, with the Jews relying on Christian difference. "Eden is inhabited mostly by angels and pious Jews. There are few Lithuanians, but a great number of Polish Jews. And the rest are Galician Zaddikim." It's a place of conflict—the "Zaddikim" (holy men) argue among themselves as well as with the angels. The latter even request a quota on humans. Manger thus appeals to readers to set aside prejudice and accept one another's humanity. Peasant angels labor for the three patriarchs, and there are too many souls for anyone to budge—a problem for which the tzaddikim are blamed. Though it's a story of angels, the political satire files it near early science fiction.

> Science fiction stories offering a social commentary on contemporary society usually place the action in the distant future on earth, on an alien planet, or in an alternate universe or world. While authors like Itzik Manger did not write science fiction, their use of Heaven/Paradise as an alternate world, forms a bridge between traditional mystical tales and the contemporary science fiction alternate world format. (Troen 1994, 35)

Yiddish culture's blend of folklore, faith and tradition is memorialized even as the author pokes fun at it all. The book was published in Warsaw in August

1939, but nearly the entire edition was destroyed by the invading German army. Only a handful of review copies mailed to America survived.

Jews who wrote in Polish at this time include Antoni Slonimski, Julian Tuwim, Józef Wittlin, and Bruno Schulz. Polish non-Jewish writers looked on them as intruders, while Yiddish writers tended to maintain a distance. Isaac Bashevis Singer explains, "We Yiddish writers looked at them as people who had left their roots and culture and become a part of Polish culture, which we considered younger and perhaps less important than our own culture. They felt that we Yiddish writers were writing for ignorant people, poor people, people without education" (Roth 1975, 248).

Antoni Slonimski (grandson of the founder of the science newspaper *Ha-tsefirah*) wrote *Torpeda Czasu* (Time Torpedo) in 1924. While the characters time-travel to prevent the nationalism of the nineteenth century, they finally discover that time cannot be altered. Riffing on H. G. Wells's *The Time Machine*, the book argues for pacifism and education, even as Slominski suggests that technological progress will not cause happiness.

Romanian author Felix Aderca (1891–1962) adored art for art sake and the city life, while being influenced by literary trends of many nationalities, like psychoanalysis and modernism. As discrimination increased, Aderca proposed civic nationalism and assimilation, even as he valued his dual heritage. Romanian literary critic Călinescu notes, "In the manner of many Jewish writers, Felix Aderca is obsessed with humanitarianism, pacifism, and all other aspects of internationalism" (Oisteanu 2009, 253). He also celebrated all the different cultures within Judaism. *Aventurile D-lui Ionel Lăcustă-Termidor* (The Adventures of Mr. Ionel Lăcustă-Termidor, 1932) uses fantasy to depict the author's nonconformity through poetic expression. Breaking the conventions of style and form, it ignores linear time as well. The eponymous hero, Ionel, a modern Romanian writer, has a second identity that hails from unmeasured spaces and times. The artwork depicts these past lives: an African dancer, a head of cabbage, a tree, a polar bear. With this, he celebrates the many voices within each individual, something he, as a pacifist Romanian Jew, must have channeled as he pursued art and beauty. All these past lives, across racial and biological lines, are meant to criticize the ridiculousness of nationalism. Another theme is a love of enthusiasm and experience, even tiny ones. Many small stories merge into the larger narrative, like one of a superior life in Atlantis, a city sunken by the Norwegians and Greenlanders.

Aderca's other novel, *Orașele înecate* (Sunken Cities, 1936), set the foundations for Romanian science fiction. In Bucharest of 5000 AD, humanity has built a new civilization of five spherical cities on the ocean floor, where they can channel the heat of the earth's core. Under Hawaii is the beautiful crystal-enclosed capital, while the Mariana Trench houses a massive pyramid. As their power decreases, however, they lessen to simple aquariums where the fish can observe the remnants of humanity. Intelligence has decreased massively, and the fascist President Pi rules cruelly, imposing eugenics and taking people's children to raise communally. He also imposes a socialist economic system and forbids ethnic affiliation. When the president dies, the cold wave advances, and humanity stands on the brink of annihilation. Meanwhile, scientists worry that biological devolution is turning the last remaining humans into mollusks. One engineer and his faction favor building spacecraft and taking to the stars, while the other wishes to dig further into the seafloor. Clearly, isolation is dooming the people, emphasized by their bubble cities and suggestive transformation into shellfish.

Later came the Kafkaesque pamphlet-novel satire *Revolte* ("Revolts"), first published in 1945 but completed in 1938, which celebrated nonconformity to social conventions. Criticizing middle-class docility, the book stood out for its protest of the eroding freedoms. Istrăteanu, a sales representative for Buştean's gristmill, clashes with the accountant Lowenstein, who investigates Istrăteanu's credit system. The book satirizes the unfair and incompetent judicial system as Istrăteanu succeeds and rises to the top.

In early 1938, a new Romanian government was formed and Jews fired from their positions in public administration. Aderca, a veteran, was allowed to keep his, but exiled to the countryside. In the autumn of 1940, after the far-right Iron Guard took over, Aderca was fired. While in the Jewish ghetto, he became artistic director of the Baraşeum Jewish Theater. After the rebellion of 1941, Aderca was caught in the Bucharest Pogrom, though he was beaten and survived. His books banned, he went on to teach at a private college for Jews. He protested the concept that Jews were prevented from actively engaging in any other economic branch but trade, and parodied anti-Semitic accusations: "Since they could not live on land, the fish monopolized the ponds." (Oisteanu 2009, 149–150)

He was to be sent to a concentration camp but escaped because of his past war service. He survived through the coup of 1944, and in 1945 was appointed director of artistic education in the Ministry of Arts. Much later he created the parable play *Muzică de balet*, (Ballet Music, 1971) about the pogrom at Bucharest. It is often classified as Holocaust literature and is one of the few post-war Romanian writings to openly discuss the slaughter.

GERMAN INTERWAR UTOPIA/DYSTOPIA

Generally known as the first science fiction film, *Metropolis*, a 1927 German expressionist science fiction drama, shows a dystopia in which Freder, the rich son of the city master, and Maria, a leader of the workers, fall in love and try to unite their classes. Freder hallucinates that the machine running the city and hurting many workers is Moloch and the workers are being fed to it in heavy biblical allegory, while the workers' triumph at the end is very communist-sympathetic. The workers' eagerness to scapegoat Maria to the point of trying to burn her at the stake also resonates with the rising bigotry of the time. The film was cowritten and directed by Fritz Lang, who was raised Catholic by his Jewish mother in Vienna. He began his directorial career in 1918 at UFA, the principal German film studio during the Weimar Republic. However, in 1933, Joseph Goebbels, the head of the Ministry of Propaganda, banned his *Testament of Dr. Mabuse*, reportedly "because it proves that a group of men who are determined to the last . . . could succeed in overturning a government by force" (Bernardi et al. 2012, 10). Goebbels invited Lang to meet nonetheless, but Lang fled to Hollywood, where he made twenty-three films.

The interwar period in Germany saw Jews writing dystopia even as they increasingly found themselves within one. Karl Kraus, apocalyptic satirist, wrote the play *The Last Days of Mankind* to criticize the prejudice, fearmongering, and stupidity of World War I. The play begins with "the Grumbler" (counter to the other universal character The Optimist) announcing that the play is meant to be performed on Mars since "Earthly audiences could not bear it" (159). The Grumbler predicts a wave of religious war between Asia and Judeo-Christian world destruction (a phrasing that pointedly includes Jews in the blame), while praising Tsarist Russia for stopping Jewish intellectualism. He also compares Hindenburg with Joshua, cynically equating Jewish and German belief in being Chosen People and so beginning world conquest. In the play, the Jews worry over how they're perceived but do little to change their lot, a situation that proved tragically prophetic.

An interesting addition to this list is *Bambi: A Life in the Woods* by Felix Salten, which first appeared serialized in 1923 Vienna. Though the Disney film cuts this, animal culture in the novel is complex, with the animals debating assimilation and a plan for their own land that parallels Zionism.

> One of the deer uses the loaded verb verfolgen to ask whether humans and deer might get along: "Will they ever stop persecuting us?" When another deer answers that "reconciliation" with humans will eventually come about, Old Nettla, a third deer with vastly more experience of the world, will have none of it. Indeed, her response foreshadows a line from Salten's Zionist book *Neue Menschen auf alter Erde* (loosely translated, new people on ancient ground), which expresses impatience with the enduring "dream of full integration." Old Nettla seethes that humans, "have given us no peace and have murdered us for as long as we've existed." (Reitter 2014)

Few of the deer believe they can live harmoniously with the hunters, whatever they promise. Of the deer that do, two are killed by hunters. One of those, Bambi's cousin Gobo, is captured, and when he returns to the forest boasting of how well he was treated, Bambi is appalled by how much his captors have transformed him. Further, Salten's hares use Yiddishisms, stressing their vulnerability in the forest hierarchy. The hares were "perhaps using mimicry as a defense against persecution," as Karl Kraus observes (quoted in Reitter 2014). It's an allegory of survival in the forest of Nazi Germany, though its most famous adaptation is a simplified children's cartoon.

Austrian-Bohemian novelist Franz Werfel's *Star of the Unborn* was published posthumously in 1946. Werfel was forced to leave the Prussian Academy of Arts in 1933, and his books were burned by the Nazis. He fled to France and then America, narrowly escaping. Today, the Franz Werfel Human Rights Award is awarded by Germany to those who oppose genocide through their art. His novel takes place in California 100,000 years in the future. The author himself is protagonist, revived by a spiritualist to be the wedding entertainment. This self-aware travelogue is slow and rambling, with a personal, *Gulliver's Travels* feel of wonder exploring a foreign world.

War, old age, poverty, and violence have been conquered, leaving the people existing underground in a tranquil state of youthful pleasure-seeking. However, little remains of earth flora after a devastating solar event killed and mutated everything above. Nearly the only thing that has lasted is religion—both Jewish and Catholic. Werfel also pictures the Germans recovering from the madness of Nazism as "Between World Wars Two and Three the Germans took the lead in humanitarianism and good will," choosing this as a better path to influencing society (177).

Jews include the Orthodox "King Saul" and his radical son, Io-Joel Sid (short for Sidney), who as his father insists "sold his birthright and for something less than a mess of pottage" (261). The narrator, on seeing his dress style, calls him "a case of extreme assimilation . . . a person who has to be constantly on guard" (261). He's moving the young people forward, in a way that seriously dismays his traditional father. This in itself reflects Europe at the author's time. Both characters conform to typical gentile stereotypes of the Jew as they debate Catholic and Jewish theology. Meanwhile, their nature as relics is emphasized through their activities: King Saul runs a curio shop filled with ancient tablets and candelabra, like remnants of the past: "The Jew of the Era disappeared into the next room and returned a little later with an antique silver salver. It looked ancient enough to have come from the tabernacle of Shiloh" (253). As the narrator adds, he speaks in "that bitter, witty, reproachful, and self-ironizing manner that I and every other knowing person would have expected of him" (253). He is called the Official Jew of the Era because "the meaning of the word itself indicates . . . that there are always ten who simultaneously answer to the name of Minionman. They represent the race that, by the will of God, must not die out" (258). This echoes the traditions to the thirty-six righteous people but also sets the king apart for his religion. A final message appears in that civilization is moving farther from God but also invariably closer as humanity approaches its end. Philosophical, utopian, and speculative, the novel considers how much is fundamental to humanity.

THE BROTHERS ČAPEK

Like the rest of Europe, Czechoslovakia brimmed with anti-Semitism in its everyday life and its literature. The wicked Jew was a traditional stereotype, even as many writers speculated about mixed loyalties and the impossibility of full assimilation. Still, since nineteenth-century Czechs lacked a state of their own, some wrote allusions to the homeless Jew longing for a country.

Few biblical themes appear, and these come mostly from Jewish writers. J. Vrchlický wrote over 100 poems on Jewish themes, including the dramatic epic *Bar Kochba* (1897). Julius Zeyer published a biblical drama, *Sulamit* (1883), a story about Joseph in Egypt called "Asenat" (1895), and many biblical poems. Stanislav Lom's drama about Moses, *Vůdce* (The Leader, 1917) took its place beside many radio plays based on the classics.

Some of the most famous science fiction of the country was written at this time—Kafka, who was Jewish, dreamed up his "Metamorphosis," and Karl and Josef Čapek, who were not, invented the term "robot."

As their country became increasingly threatened by German aggression, the brothers wrote pointedly anti-Fascist science fiction. Further, beyond the many stories of the oppressed seeking justice, the many Čapek works stood out for their sympathetic attitude toward the Jews. In their cowritten play *Adam the Creator* (1929), the authors ridicule racism when the superman Miles insists he hates Adam "Because you belong to another race" (120). Adam himself embodies pathological hatred as he holds up a sign saying "The World Must Be Destroyed." He insists as the play opens that religion is a sham, government is tyranny, compassion a crime, and all must be torn away (10). This appears the authors' view of Communism. After Adam destroys the world, God allows him to remake it in his own image. Oddly, Eve and Lilith switch places, with Eve the superwoman who arrogantly abandons Adam and Lilith the adoring submissive bride. Adam next creates Alter Ego, a darker copy of himself who creates the masses with a "crowd soul" of followers that support Alter Ego in everything (105). Soon enough, they invent war. With this, the largely philosophical play lets the Čapeks use the biblical retelling to criticize the world's shortcomings.

As the Nazis rose in power, Karl wrote the anti-fascist plays *The White Disease* and *Mother*. The latter follows a family that has sacrificed most of their sons to the cause, with pithy comments on the destructiveness of war. In *The White Disease* (1937), also translated as *Power and Glory* (1938), the doctor who can cure the plague is a Greek, named Galen, so those in charge try to dismiss him for being a foreigner. Considering that Galen shares his name with a Greek physician and also the anti-Nazi bishop Count Clemens August von Galen, pointed satire appears here. In fact, Čapek had originally intended to name Galen the Jewish "Herzfeld," but "To have made Galen a Jew would have changed the meaning, even the sub-genre of the play" (Pynsent 2000, 345). Since Galen is not utterly benevolent—he distributes the cure to the poor but uses it for political leverage against the powerful—such an association would have tied into the Jewish world conspiracy stereotype. He's nonetheless an intellectual and the voice of reason as he advocates for an end to war. As the play goes on, Baron Krug offers twenty million for a cure for himself but won't agree to Galen's price—that he stop making munitions. At last, his superior, the marshal, becomes so desperate for the cure that he shifts from insisting God demands they go to war to insisting "God wants me to make peace" in a satire of European warmongering and self-interest (95).

The financial director of *R.U.R.*, the robot company in the play of that name ([1923] 1987), is a stereotypical wealth-loving Jew named Berman. He tries bribing the robots not to kill him and his colleagues (though he plots to destroy them and their factory after). This attempt fails and he is the first of the board of directors to be killed. His colleagues varyingly call him "a genius of finance" and "a great self-sacrificing comrade" (86). While he's an unfortunate stereotype, the larger story deals with the rights of the oppressed—the enslaved robots themselves who seek freedom if not equality. The main story ends with two endearing robots escaping as a new Adam and Eve. The play is famous for inventing the term "robot," with constructed people based in local legends of the golem.

The Absolute at Large ([1927] 2019), a novel, follows the discovery of unmaking matter, and with it, the appearance of a spiritual essence called the Absolute. The people of the world, of all religions, throw themselves into belief and with it, nationalism. Of course, some irrationally blame "the Freemasons, the Jews and other progressives" (219) for perpetuating a hoax. Soon enough, the population are burning Jews at the stake. A holy war ensues that eclipses World War I, written at a time when the world was still recovering from it. The Absolute aids soldiers on both sides and produces so many free manufactured goods that economic collapse ensues but it is only a neutral force enabling the people to enact their desires. They in turn come to worship it—in a ceremony, the Absolute is proclaimed God. "As for the Jews, a secret doctrine spread among them to the effect that the Absolute was

Baal of old; the Liberal Jews announced that they would in that case recognize Baal" (204). Clearly, the schism between modern and traditional Jews is satirized here.

Bondy, a rather clichéd Jewish moneylender, is a central character, though he does have some depth. When asked his views on God, Bondy replies, practically, "Perhaps there's a God but he's on some other planet. Not on ours. Oh, well, that sort of thing doesn't fit in with our times at all" (33). Later he adds, "I haven't anything against God. Only he oughtn't to interfere with business" (45). This could function as a stereotype but also could comment on the smaller war within the Jewish community of secularism versus spirituality. "Although a Czech discovers the world-shattering Absolute, Bondy the Jewish cosmopolitan frequently attacks Czech smallness and small-mindedness. His dismissal of the small-scale nature of everything Czech becomes something of a refrain" (Pynsent 349). Bondy is himself mixed up when, asked to represent his community, he prays for God to "remove this cup" (78) and at story's end comments that he's been baptized. Symbolically, he is so removed from Jewish tradition that he uses Christian allusions, before he gives himself over to the trendy new religion. Since this is under the influence of the Absolute, this twist explores his spiritual evolution—but one away from the ways of his ancestors.

Karel Čapek's *War with the Newts*, written during Hitler's rise, is pointed in its satire. The story opens with J. van Toch, a crusty sea captain who parodies Joseph Conrad sea stories. He calls on Bondy for financial backing. When he reminds Bondy of their time as schoolmates, Bondy recalls how the captain used to shout "Jew, Jew, the devil take you" (31). The oblivious captain recalls these as "great days," ignoring any blame for being an antisemitic bully. Here, the author highlights how prevalent and hurtful such cruelty is. In the present, the captain has been hunting pearls and has worked out a colonial arrangement with the local giant newts. "Those are shells which cling to the rocks as fast as the Jewish faith," he drops into his story in more obliviousness (34). The newt population has been kept down by sharks, but when Captain van Toch teaches them to throw stones and soon provides knives and harpoons, the grateful newts supply him with pearls. Under his training, the newts show a genius for underwater engineering and build breakwaters to keep out sharks.

Uninhibited by sharks, the newts multiply rapidly and van Toch schemes to export newts to other pearl islands and establish farms. However, he soon dies and his old-fashioned colonial attitude is replaced by unscrupulous businessmen. Pearl markets are glutted and newt expansion is unchecked. The newts are soon used for slave labor—likely a reference to the German abuse of minorities in the thirties. As a consequence, the newts revolt, committing dramatic sabotage with their marine engineering skills. Further, their population has grown so much that they dig away at Europe to create new shorelines. The Germans ally with them "so that generations of racially pure original German salamanders could develop in German waters everywhere" (193). Germany also bans vivisecting salamanders—but only Jews are barred from doing so, in a quick parody of Hitler's anti-Jewish laws.

In a scene reminiscent of Hitler's request to annex Czechoslovakia, the newts send the following message: "We regret the loss of human life. We do not want to inflict unnecessary losses on you. We only want you to evacuate the seashores in the places we will notify you of from time to time. If you conform, you will avoid regrettable accidents" (215). This immediately escalates in a scene that parodies Hitler's demands as well as the Nazi hymn and Spengler's *The Decline of the West*: "Hello you people! No need for alarm. We have no hostile intentions towards you. We only need more water, more coastline, more shallows to live in. There are too many of us. There's no longer room for us on your coasts. That's why we have to dismantle your continents. . . . You wanted us. You spread us all over the globe. Now you've got us" (216).

The nations of the world meet in the Alps, one of the last safe places. "It was legally and practically impossible to declare war on the salamanders or to bring any international pressure to bear on them; each state was entitled only to take action against its own newts; it was in fact a purely domestic matter. For that reason there could be no question of any collective diplomatic or military campaign against the newts" (222). They invite the newts to the next meeting, and the newts send human delegates, signaling the arrival of collaborators as well as the newts' increased power and political savvy. The Chief Salamander agrees to end hostilities in return for Britain ceasing their embargo. The extortion escalates as the newts' lawyers suggest it would be better for mankind to accept Chief Salamander's generous offer of buying the world from the human beings instead of taking it by force. The delegates offer loans and then propose surrendering central China, ignoring the Chinese delegate, whom no one can understand anyway. During the discussion, the newts promptly invade Venice. Those familiar with Hitler's grab for territories will see the parallel.

As the book concludes, the European countries are being overrun one by one and all the world is lending them money to do so. Bondy's doorman Povondra finds himself regretting admitting the sea captain who began all this and wonders how he will ever make amends to future generations. Meanwhile, he insists to his son that their neutral country can't be invaded and everyone else must fend for themselves, seconds before a newt's head pops up. The final chapter, "The Author Talks to Himself" suggests pitting the newts against each other is their only remaining option. The narrator finally gives up, throwing himself into promoting newt nationalism as there's

no defeating the creatures. This fatalism in the face of Nazi invasion is under-
standable, even as the author directly appeals to his readers.

Karel Čapek died on Christmas Day, 1938, just after the Munich
Agreement. In September 1939, Josef was arrested by the Gestapo for his
protest cartoons and writings. He died at Bergen-Belsen in 1945.

BRUNO SCHULZ: REAL AND REIMAGINED

Lost books are particularly mesmerizing in the world of Jewish fantasy, like,
on occasion, their authors. The murder of famed Polish author Bruno Schulz
in the Holocaust encapsulates much of literary scholars' grief at an entire
culture of art and expression so suddenly destroyed. Famously, he was shot
in the street by a Nazi to get back at the SS Commander who was having
Schulz (an art teacher as well as writer) paint murals on his child's bedroom
wall (these murals themselves have since been liberated by Israel's Holocaust
museum, Yad v'Shem). "Schulz's importance to Polish literature is now
recognized to roughly the same degree as Chekhov is to Russian, and Israel
esteemed him a predominant enough part of the Jewish cultural heritage to
have warranted a commando-style fresco-cutting operation (the so-called
'Schulz-gate')" (Zalmayev 2016). Since 2004, Drohobych (a Polish city in
Schulz's day, now part of the Ukraine) has hosted the biennial International
Bruno Schulz Festival.

Schulz's writing shares snapshots of his family in Drohobych through
the lens of fantasy. "Mannequins" has the character of the narrator's father
describing how unused rooms can wilt and, lost to memory, become lost to
existence as well. His father enters this sort of lost passage and reports, "From
every crack in the floor, from every molding and frame, thin sprouts shot out
and filled the grey air with a glimmering filigree of lacy foliage, with a con-
servatory's openwork thicket, full of whispers, shimmers, swinging, a kind of
spurious and beautiful spring" ([1934] 2018b, 32). The sudden, elusive flow-
ering of the forgotten space becomes a metaphor for lost memories, suddenly
returning and blossoming into gorgeous fulfillment. The fantasy is subtle but
strong. Singer comments, "He reimagines his hometown of Drohobycz into a
more terrifying and wonderful place than it actually was" (Roth 1975, 247).
"Pan" likewise brings a garden to fantastical life, calling its unkempt corners
"a paroxysm of madness, an explosion of fury, a cynical shamelessness and
debauchery" ([1934] 2018c, 40). The title, here, celebrates the pagan wild-
ness of unconquered nature as it revels in its own liveliness.

At the same time, Schulz reveals the opposite can happen—that neglected
people can wither into inanimate objects, giving readers rather heavy food for
thought. A cranky old aunt, shocked at the loss of her possessions in a fire,

shrinks, dwindling and spitting curses until she shrivels into dust. An uncle likewise sinks into a pulsing stupor; his inner juices cycling round and round. In another story, the father has actually turned into a cockroach, even as the mother takes refuge in denial. His decline into madness is shown through his physical dwindling through the stories, but also by his symbolic transformations into dust, paper, birds, and the artifacts that surround him. Translator John Curran Davis (2012) observes: "Reality adopts certain forms only for the sake of appearance, as a joke, for a game. One person is a person, another a cockroach; but such forms do not reach the essence, they are merely roles, assumed momentarily, like an outer skin that is cast off a moment later."

As the story continues, the narrator's father's bizarre imagination takes over the narrative, even as the boy uses fantasy to free himself from his claustrophobic world. Davis (2012) notes: "Once one is initiated into Schulz, the world itself becomes more amazing. In winter, it becomes a labyrinth; come the spring, a great revolution. In summer, the world is like a great book; and all those books accumulate in the library of the season we call autumn (or fall). One simply begins to look at the world with slightly wider eyes." The narrator's whimsy provides the lens through which people transform, leaving it ambiguous whether he has imagined it all.

In "Cinnamon Shops," the young speaker is sent home from the family's trip to the theater to fetch his father's wallet. The streets open around him, confusing in their make-believe patterns. From here, a magical horse arrives and carries him into a fantasy world, leaving the boy skipping off happily after, delighted with the wonder in the world. The horse, meanwhile, shrinks as small as a wooden toy. As the story charmingly concludes, "Like a silver astrolabe, the sky opened its inner mechanism on this magic night and revealed in endless evolutions the golden mathematics of its wheels and cogs" ([1934] 2018a, 32). Another tale has the narrator rouse a set of wax figures to life, to fight as soldiers in a great battle, and then he grants them their freedom. All these moments of personification and antipersonification blur the lines between humanity and surrounding objects, calling into question what it is to be real. Schulz doesn't send his characters to fantastic worlds—he emphasizes that this world is fantastical when viewed correctly.

The title story of his other collection, *Sanatorium under the Sign of the Hourglass*, has the narrator going to visit his father at the sanatorium, where the patients always sleep but night never comes. Further, his father is in a nebulous existence. As the doctor puts it, "You know as well as I that from the point of view of your home, from the perspective of your fatherland, your father died. That cannot be entirely undone. This death casts a certain shadow on his existence here" ([1937] 2018b, 188). The sanatorium cures by setting back time. As the doctor adds, "We have turned back time. We are late by an interval whose length is impossible to define. This boils down to a simple relativism. Here, your father's death, the death that has already reached him in your fatherland, has simply not taken effect" (188). They reactivate past time and through it enact a recovery. Thanks to this, his father can lie sleeping in the sanatorium and also manage a popular shop in the town—where, in fact, the residents drop to sleep themselves at any moment in the strange timelessness. The doctor is both performing surgery and hasn't been there for years. The halls are a labyrinth, the mirror fogs when he looks in it. There are no other patients, no nurses—in fact, the bell has been ripped out by the wires. Food must be smuggled in from outside. He sleeps in his clothes. This is a commentary on the sameness of life in the ghetto, crowded in, jobless, with only an eternal drifting existence.

The story takes place in a sudden war that is quite recognizable: "A war not preceded by diplomatic moves? War in the middle of blissful peace, not distrupted by any conflict? War with whom and over what?" (200). In the village, the narrator sees a tied-up man: "Judging from his black suit and the cultivated form of his beard, one might take him for an intellectual, an educated man" (202). However, he transforms into a brutish lout and then a dog—alluding to the perception and legal treatment of Jews at the time. At last, the narrator drifts away to become a beggar on the local train: his father dead, himself rootless in this new twilight world. Singer believes Schulz wrote in parody "because he was not really at home, neither at home among the Poles nor at home among the Jews" (Roth 1975, 250). Whether or not it's true, the stories are deeply psychological, with trauma brought into physicality and loss followed by death and then possibly rebirth.

Schulz's second collection offers more fantasy scenarios—a neglected child is blown away on a gust of wind, and his irate teacher strikes his name off the roll list. Another tale celebrates the beauty of spring, with mysterious passages from the underworld found in gnarled tree trunks. The first story, "The Book," lovingly celebrates a beloved book filled with beauty, and the narrator's horror on hearing it's being used to wrap his father's lunch. The story has the young hero gazing on this forbidden talisman on his father's desk with worshipful awe. Even the Bible doesn't satisfy him, as he longs for the magical book he once beheld. At last, he discovers it, and as he says, "Bent over the Book, my face aflame like a rainbow, I burned in silence from ecstasy to ecstasy" ([1937] 2018a, 90). He describes ordinary books like meteors that blaze for a moment and go out, unlike this one, which soars like a phoenix. In fact, this book is filled with "pure poetry"—the characters and exotic instruments of far-off times (87). Not only does he discover that books are eternal, but as author, Schulz is the ultimate creator here. Once again, the magic of the otherworld blends with the everyday, exploring how much one intrudes into the other.

More intriguing than Schulz's two surviving collections is his lost final manuscript, *The Messiah*. Reportedly, he entrusted all his papers to gentile friends as the war began, but they have never surfaced. "Because Schulz was killed by the Nazis, he comes to stand in these texts for a whole generation of Jews slaughtered in the Holocaust," notes Emily Miller Budick in *The Subject of Holocaust Fiction* (2015, 128). Unsurprisingly, people of the book long for this vanished manuscript with its secrets—to the point where its loss has inspired its own fantasy fiction. Isaac Bashevis Singer, John Updike, Salman Rushdie, Nicole Kraus, and Danilo Kiš all wrote about Schulz. Adding to the mystique of course is the name of the piece as well as the lack of details: "That Schulz's masterpiece, *The Messiah*, might well be apocryphal adds still further support to the idea that such Jewish messiahs as exist are firmly transient creatures of the human imagination" (Budick 145).

Jonathan Safran Foer loved the book so much that he published a fascinatingly sliced-up tribute. *Tree of Codes* (2010) is actually chosen snippets of *The Street of Crocodiles*, with gaping squares cut out through the book to resemble the peepholes to the next page sometimes seen in picture books. It's a delicate, fragile work, like the Jewish communities so completely destroyed. As *Guardian* reviewer Michel Faber (2010) comments, "The idea of *The Street of Crocodiles* surviving in disguise, chopped to within an inch of its life but still clinging to its soul, strikes me as a bittersweet irony, an oddly fitting homage. It has also given rise to the most potent work of art that Jonathan Safran Foer has yet produced."

> Snip seven letters from the title *Street of Crocodiles* and you get *Tree of Codes*—and so on, for 134 intricately scissored pages. A boutique publisher called Visual Editions, working in tandem with die-cut specialists in the Netherlands and a "hand-finisher" in Belgium, has produced a £25 artifact that, if you share Foer's aesthetics, has "a sculptural quality" that's "just beautiful," or which, if you're an average reader, might make you think a wad of defenseless print has been fed through an office shredding machine. (Faber)

Further, it makes the reader participate: "Insofar as we the readers must insert either our hands or blank sheets into the text, we are made into coauthors of the text, replicating an aspect of Foer's relationship to Schulz's text. Thereby we are forced to conspire in the conjuring of ghosts, the ghostwriting of the text" (Budick 153). It's a reviving of a ghostly text, made more ghostly from the words that peep out from behind others. "This material object literally reincarnates another material object, another text, even if in the process Foer produces a text of his own" (Budick 153).

Certainly, the book-as-cut-out-art is a gimmick. Still, it functions as loving homage and comment on intertextuality—the words that are absent echo Schulz's lost words, while those present represent how new authors can carry on the legacy of those gone. "Jonathan Safran Foer's is the most inventive of these Schulz-derived novels, even if it is not a Holocaust text, although Foer's status as a writer of another important Holocaust novel, *Everything Is Illuminated* (2002), helps put one in mind of the Holocaust while reading *Tree of Codes*" (Budick 2015, 132).

Like *Street of Crocodiles*, *Everything Is Illuminated* is a series of vignettes describing the narrator's ghostly, fanciful world. Foer writes, "I saw on the far side of living, the constellations were lit by the city. I shall never forget that luminous journey" (83–84). It's like found poetry, keeping the glimmering essence of words poking startlingly from half-chopped-up pages. Cutouts from two paragraphs form the next sentence, "The air shimmered, trembling" (84). Foer can also be remarkably self-referential as he writes, "We find ourselves part of the tree of codes. Reality is as thin as paper. Only the small section immediately before us is able to endure" (92–93). "We are attracted by the pretense of a city," (93) the text explains, a remark offered of course, in the pretense of a complete book. In this book, all traces of the shtetl are destroyed, condemning it to the dark places of history. However, Lista, the last survivor of Trachimbrod, can still testify and has brought forth an archive of gathered possessions. This distinction between preserved and lost history creates a border between the history and the imagined that one of the characters confronts directly. "How can you do this to your grandfather, writing about his life in such a manner? Could you write in this manner if he was alive? And, if not, what does that signify?" (179). The present-day protagonist (Foer himself) investigates this lost world while discovering nebulous, fantastical stories of his ancestors. With this, he blends fancy and history to emphasize how much of the past cannot be reconstructed once lost.

Other authors chimed in on adapting Schulz's story or elements of it. Like Foer's work, Appelfeld's *Age of Wonders* offers a character named Bruno whose father, an Eastern European writer, was condemned by the Nazis. Bruno returns to his childhood home seeking his father's writings but discovers much more about him and the lost community. Chabon's *The Final Solution* follows a mute frightened Jewish refugee child, whose father was kept alive to aid a German much as Schulz was. Singer's "The Manuscript" has a woman risk her life seeking a precious lost manuscript in Nazi Poland, only to burn it in front of her lover when she returns to find him bedding an actress. Danilo Kiš's *Peščanik* (Hourglass) and Aleksandar Hemon's *The Question of Bruno* join the list. Nicole Krauss's *The History of Love* follows a character named Bruno, an Eastern European writer. However, he is only a memory, as Bruno perished back in the old country—it's his near-miraculous escape to America that is the fantasy. "Evading these texts, one has the eerie sensation that perhaps there is only a single Jewish author and a single Jewish text, which, in some breaking of the vessel, has shattered into fragments, each retaining its reflection in and of the others" (Budick 2015, 136). Maxim

Biller's novella, "Inside the Head of Bruno Schulz," has Schulz compose an excited letter in which he reveals his survival. This, too, feels more fantasy than reality.

The more mainstream author Philip Roth, who also speculated about Anne Frank's and Kafka's survivals, writes a short farce called "The Prague Orgy," in which his hero Zuckerman tries getting the locals to part with the manuscript. All have objections, from spite to nationalism to greed, to block his claiming the papers. "Amid the descriptions of frenetic and blackly humorous 'orgies' among Prague's dissident artists and intellectuals, and insights into the bureaucratic repression that pervades Kafka's bleakly beautiful city, the true or false story of the improbable Yiddish manuscript evokes the pain and the sense of irretrievable loss that is characteristic of Holocaust literature" (Fried 1988, 430). As the police finally throw him out of the country, sans manuscript which he couldn't read anyway, the story seems more than a little autobiographical. "The recovery of another writer's Jewish manuscript would, for Zuckerman, serve an ethical purpose. However, it might also put an end to or at least overshadow his own creative career" (Budick 2015, 130). All consider the tantalizing search, which most often fails.

In a similar reinterpretation of his legacy, David Grossman's *See Under: Love* (1986) tells of Schulz's tragic death. Grossman continues the story, however, as Schulz escapes into the water and is reborn as a fish, safe and free, though bereft of his beloved stories. With art imitating life imitating art, Grossman's novel increased Schulz's fame, and new editions of his work were subsequently published worldwide. In this way, all these adaptations brought new life to the author's reputation.

Schulz has, indeed, become a literary "Messiah" for scores of famous writers, incarnating in the pages of their novels. . . . The nooks and crannies of Schulz's "Street of Crocodiles" became the nooks and crannies of the Andalusian town in Salman Rushdie's "The Moor's Last Sigh." A worm-hole leading into Drohobych's parallel dimension was found when Jonathan Safran Foer die-cut into Schulz's "Street of Crocodiles," to discover his own appropriated work "Tree of Codes." "The letters that were before beetles had turned into eyes, into the eyes of Bruno Schulz, and they were opening and closing again and again, some eyes clear like the sky, shining like the sea's spine, which was opening and blinking, again and again, in the middle of total darkness," comments the protagonist of Roberto Bolaño's novel "Distant Star," while reading Schulz's story. (Zalmayev 2016)

Cynthia Ozick's *The Messiah of Stockholm* (1987) tackles this subject as well, from the point of view of the survivors. Schulz's son, an infant refugee, grows up obsessed by his father's legacy, especially the lost manuscript.

Hallucinations of his father's eye follow him, a gaze from the past seeking to reconnect. Here Schulz "is recalled in such a way as to figure not so much as an object of mourning as an idol or fetish, or a golem or a messiah" (Budick 2015, 134). A woman arrives, claiming to be his daughter and to have inherited the manuscript. Creating the lost manuscript is in itself a fantasy, and it gives Lars the abandoned son a nearly transcendent experience as he pictures "That despoiling, withdrawing light, a lightning-explosion. As though—for an inch of time—he had penetrated into the entrails, the inmost anatomy, of that eye" (115). As Lars's companions insist the public must come to believe in it, *The Messiah* represents the lost author, and, in fact, the potential coming of the Messiah himself. The story ends ambiguously—probably a forgery, a false hope like so many rumored saviors of Jewish history. "Whether genuine or not, however, the manuscript recovered in Ozick's novel winds up in ashes, like the many Jewish artists who perished in the Holocaust" (Budick 129). However, the story emphasizes belief's power to transform. All these homages use Schulz to emphasize how much has been lost with all the promising authors and artists suddenly silenced.

Chapter 6

Kafka's Great Legacy

KAFKA'S JEWISH STRUGGLE

Kafka was a Jew in an anti-Semitic age, and he suffered for it. Anti-Semitism colored his relations with his profession, his father, his family, Prague, and his contemporaries" (Stolzl 1989, 53). Emancipated from the ghettos, Jews of the early turn of the century began joining the middle class. Assimilation, it seemed, offered the best path to escape prejudice. There were about 30,000 Jews in 1920 Prague, with a broad intellectual social network (Stolzl 62). "Not yet aware of the gigantic threat that lay ahead, the generation of Kafka's parents had learned to make do with half-measures and compromise. Jews celebrated the birthday of an emperor who would not deign to receive them at his court. They made up for the fact that so many careers would forever be closed to them by redoubling their exertions in the ones that were within reach" (Sokel 1999, 842). In Kafka's father's desperation to fit in, he had his children educated in German, though young Franz learned Czech as well. His friend and editor Max Brod later described Franz's childhood as "unspeakably lonely" (Blunden 1980, 12).

Guilt inhabited both his language and his art, the two being inextricable. A Prague Jew assimilated to German language and culture, momentarily drawn to rising Czech nationalism but in essence an outsider, even a traitor to it, stood on condemned ground. Compelling alternatives loomed: significant literary work was being done in Yiddish, the renascence of Hebrew as a modern tongue immemorially rooted in Jewish experience, was palpably imminent. Kafka looked with wary pathos in both these directions. Yet he chose German for his truths. (Steiner 1992, viii)

As the city Jews assimilated, they reproached other Jews with anti-Semitic stereotypes as they struggled to fit in. As Kafka explains, "We see each other better than other people, because we are together on a journey" (Stolzl 55). Assimilated as Kafka's generation was, he and his peers were particularly hurt by the anti-Semitism in the literature they read. Kafka describes "Jewish self-hatred," noting, "I have vigorously absorbed the negative element of the age in which I live, an age that is, of course, very close to me, which I have no right ever to fight against, but, as it were, a right to represent" (Stolzl 57). He felt danger and threats everywhere, especially in a simple question about his background.

> On one side stood the possibility of marriage, of children, of human connection and contentment—everything he understood by life in the world (what he called Canaan)—but also defection from his own spirituality; writing and the freezing solitude of his own subjectivity and spirituality stood on the other (what he called the wilderness). He had to die as a human being to live as a writer, to lose in order to win. It was an old (by now it is a conventional) attitude of the modern age, but with him it was not an attitude, it was his life, the antithesis that he lived and died from. (Greenberg 1986, 76)

His father, meanwhile, was massive and powerful in a way young Franz was not but had discarded the heritage Franz sought. "To him, his father's residual Jewishness was a parody of religion and a mockery of the kind of community Kafka longed for. Hermann Kafka, as Franz saw him, was the epitome of a Yom Kippur Jew, that is, the incarnation of half-heartedness, hypocrisy and self-deceiving compromise" (Sokel 1999, 842). He threw himself into his business and to fitting into the urban culture, leaving young Kafka feeling neglected and rootless. "To the young Kafka, Jewishness manifested itself as a double negative. Jews were Jews because they were not like others, because they were different from everyone else. And it also manifested itself as a guilt feeling in reaction to his father's constant accusations of Franz's indifference" (Sokel 843).

He warred with the previous generation, writing, "All parents want to do is drag one down to them, back to the old days from which one longs to free oneself and escape" (Stolzl 1989, 63). Kafka wrote to his sister Elli describing the family as "merely an animal connection" or "a single bloodstream" (Baioni 1989, 107). Further, the Jews of Eastern Europe, still devoted to the insular shtetl life suggested a similarly embarrassing animal family. In an often-quoted letter from 1921, Kafka wrote, "Most young Jews who wanted to write German wanted to leave Jewishness behind them, and their fathers approved of this. . . . But with their posterior legs they were still glued to their father's Jewishness and with their waving anterior legs, they found no new ground" (Friedlander 2013, 42).

In December 1897, the imperial government headed by Count Casimir Badenia issued a decree giving equal standing to Czech and German in the Bohemian crown lands, precipitating furious riots and then counter-riots when the decree was withdrawn. Czech-speakers rioted, looting shops with German names. Hermann Kafka's haberdashery was protected by its owner's Czech-sounding name, but fourteen-year-old Franz remembered the "the terror of being confronted by a rioter screaming Jste zid? (Are you a Jew?)" (Burton 2013, 61). In college, he was drawn to atheism, though faith still tied into his thought process in a fatalistic, very Jewish way. "The Messiah will come," he said, "only when there is no longer any need for him, he will come only the day after he comes, he won't come on the last day, but on the last day of all" (Greenberg 1986, 75). Whether for good or ill, the Messiah will not be humanity's savior, so people must do the job.

In 1911, when he was twenty-eight, Kafka was drawn to the Yiddish theater troupe visiting Prague. He watched most of their performances, fell in love with an actress there, and began a close friendship with one of the young actors. His enthusiasm came from "the unfettered Jewishness of these Yiddish actors, as they played their Jewish roles and lived their unquestioned Jewish lives" (Friedlander 2013, 43). They were proud of their heritage instead of disguising it.

Kafka's "Josephine the Singer, or The Mouse Folk" ([1924] 1993) is likely a salute to this love interest. It follows a member of a community's attempt to explain the art of their only singer, Josephine, and the powerful effect that her singing has on the community that ordinarily has no use for song or diversion. While her people have forgotten how to sing themselves, "a certain tradition of music is preserved, yet without making the slightest demand upon us" (243). Of course, this sounds like the assimilated Jews only celebrating a few holidays in their urban surroundings. The mice, like the Jews, are scattered, yet come together to share certain traditions. "The power which Josephine possesses of unifying her people, especially in times of peril, recalls the role which the songs, psalms, and epics of ancient people played; and there is indeed a perennial sense in which language not only unites but makes a people" (Thorlby 1980, 142). Meanwhile, her singing, like prayer and community, strengthen them all: "Josephine likes best to sing just when things are most upset" (239) and her singing "resembles people's precarious existence amidst the chaos of a hostile world" (241). If, as Brod and others have suggested, the mice are the people of Moses, then Joseph(ine) may reflect a different path, a new leadership under a different patriarch, all the more revolutionary for being female. This final story of Kafka's considers the relationship between art and artist, while Josephine, a gender-flip on his auto-biographical characters like Joseph K., must be seen as another self-portrait. Josephine loves her art and longs for her people to value it. Without knowing why they keep listening, while criticizing, disdaining, and infantilizing her, they allow her to continue beautifying their empty lives.

Immediately, upon encountering the theater, Kafka began studying Jewish history, Talmud, and Kabbalah. He published two of his stories in Martin Buber's Zionist journal *Der Jude* and took a great interest in Zionism, an alternative to assimilation. He also helped set up an evening of Yiddish songs and recitations at the Jewish Town Hall in Prague, introducing his friend with a speech about how Jews might try to escape their Yiddish-speaking heritage out of fear of difference, and even fears of their own alienness, but how the language and culture remained a part of them (Blunden 1980, 17).

This theme, arguably, haunts *The Metamorphosis/Die Verwandlung* ([1915] 1993). In this, "The submerged Jewish self, though buried and over-laid by German, is still strong enough to unmask the German surface consciousness as a distorting, falsifying agency" (Sokel 1999, 848). While the protagonist suppresses this instinct, seeking assimilation and normality, it cannot be denied and finally bursts forth. Promptly, Gregor Samsa, a salesman, turns into "einem ungeheueren Ungeziefer," meaning not just "giant" but "horrendous" and not just an insect but vermin (Miron 2019, 27). His Id prefers garbage to fresh food, makes him scuttle up the wall, drives him to crawl on his belly, and in short, drives him to rebel and do all the primitive things civilization forbids. A life that has always been concerned with the minutiae of "train connections" and "casual acquaintances" has become disrupted forever as his grotesque, alien self emerges for all to see (76). His normal human parents (possibly symbolizing the Christian neighbors) are humiliated and try to hide him. He in turn conceals his disgustingness from the family, especially when his sister feeds him. He slowly gains control over his insect body, but the family is still repelled and finally tries to get rid of him. "If this were Gregor, he would have realized long ago that human beings can't live with such a creature," the sister says bitterly. He finally dies, freeing the family of his loathsome presence. "Gregor's verminous condition functions as the alienated and disgusted perspective with which Gregor's dutiful bourgeois consciousness views his rebellious desire for liberation from his salesman's existence of routinized drudgery" (Sokel 849).

This is an outward manifestation of the loathing and prejudice Kafka himself felt. At the time, the governments made Jews speak and write in German and follow Christian practice. While Gregor's loss of language reflects Kafka's own loss of his native Yiddish, Gregor also finds himself losing his humanity and confined to chirping and hissing.

Letters, sketches, and journal entries supply many details to show, for instance, how much Kafka himself felt like the untranslatably metaphorphosized creature in his story, preferring the solitude of his room to a wedding, often fantasizing about not having to hold a job which stood in the way of his writing, watching his family through a crack in the door, loving his youngest sister, and being inwardly destroyed by his father, before whom his art was a compulsive but futile gesture of self-justification. (Thorlby 1980, 137)

There are more suggestively autobiographical elements to the story. "Kafka was ashamed of his body as a typical Jewish body, characterized in the anti-Semitic imagination of the time by various defects and disgraceful characteristics; the Jewish male body in particular was seen as effeminate and weak" (Friedlander 2013, 45). Anti-Semitic tropes depicted Jews as weak, echoing the recurrent subject of militarization in the story. Keeping to this image, Kafka writes many times of mice, beetles, a fly, a mole, a sparrow—imagery of overlooked insignificant creatures. They are forced to hide away, yet by doing so survive. This story is unforgettable particularly because of the absurd image that speaks to human nature. He crafted a story so universal and transmissible that the absurd "Kafkaesque" image has lasted through time.

"The element of the fantastic, which has come to be known as Kafkaesque, derives from that strange discrepancy between the explicit perspective of the narrative, which is the protagonist's consciousness, and a reality that erupts from within him and overwhelms and destroys him" (Sokel 1999, 849). This is also seen in "The Judgement" ([1912] 1993) and *The Trial* ([1925] 1992). The former follows Georg Bendemann as he lovingly cares for his father, who torments him. As his father rejects him entirely, Georg is stricken. The father wraps up with a final judgment: "So now you know what else there is in the world besides yourself, till now you've known only about yourself! An innocent child, yes, that you were, truly, but still more truly you have been a devilish human being! And therefore take note: I sentence you now to death by drowning" (38). Georg dutifully carries out his father's sentence. As he clutches the railings, "Georg has now replaced his father as the one who is in need of sustenance. This need, here as in other stories by Kafka, can result only in death, withdrawal, and silence" (Thiher 1990, 40). Pronouncing such a curse makes it come true—the son feels forced to the river where he slips over the bridge while "an unending stream of traffic was just going over the bridge" (39). These scenes certainly could represent the power of the angry parent over the child or the artist over the community. They also could allegorize the relationship between the loving, faithful Jews, and the country that turns them into traitors and murder victims with an irrational pronouncement.

Kafka felt a link with the ancient past in the ghettos and wrote to a friend, "We walk through the broad streets of the newly built town. But our steps and our glances are uncertain. Inside we tremble just as before in the ancient streets of our misery" (Stolzl 1989, 61). The ghost of the old architecture remained. "As Kafka writes, while we walk the bright broad modern boulevards, the dank, gloomy alleyways of the old ghetto still live on deep within us" (Sokel 1999, 849). Beneath a modern exterior, of city or person, this dark internal past still rules. "At the time, when Kafka wrote *The Trial*, he noted a similar relationship between surface consciousness and submerged Jewish past, this time expressed in terms of cityscape rather than of language" (Sokel 848).

In this famous novel, K., arrested for a crime he can't identify, calls himself "completely innocent" (163). However, this does not matter to the thugs in their endless chain of bureaucracy as they lock him up and abuse him. As K. realizes, "My innocence doesn't make the matter any simpler." He adds, "I have to fight against countless subtleties in which the Court indulges. And in the end, out of nothing at all, an enormous fabric of guilt will be conjured up" (163). In 1899, Jews were targeted when, in the small Czech-speaking town of Polna, a Jew named Leopold Hilsner was accused of murdering the nineteen-year-old Christian Anezka Hrüzová to use her blood in matzah. "The sixteen-year-old Franz Kafka can hardly have been unimpressed by the plight of a fellow Jew arbitrarily and unjustly accused of an almost unutterable crime" (Burton 2013, 62). Alternatively, *The Trial* may have its roots in Kafka's attempted engagement to Felice Bauer. "A disastrous meeting with her family did actually strike him in the juridical light suggested by that title. The proceedings between them, conducted for the most part through the medium of writing, by correspondence, do often seem to be as endless, one-sidedly obscure, and self-destructive as the legal procedure in the novel" (Thorlby 1980, 137).

At the climax, K. seeks out a priest and confesses his doubts. The priest then tells a parable about a man seeking the Law, only to be blocked by a self-important doorkeeper. The man at the door is foolish to accept the doorkeeper's authority at all. An official lacks freedom from his duties, whereas a man like K. is free to make decisions if he refuses to buy into the chain of authority. After the fall from Eden, as the priest explains, man has had the knowledge of good and evil and must choose between them. At the same time, the Law has replaced God, as the thing man strives for, a mystery that cannot ever be attained or revealed. Though K. does not truly hear the priest's advice, the priest tells him he must not rely on outside help. Whether K. is questing to break free of scapegoating (a metaphor for Jewishness) or for deeper spirituality, he must look within instead of without.

In the debate and elsewhere, the levels of narrative and internal discourse feel Talmudic, while the symbolism owes a debt to Judaism as well. "The arcane wit, the delicacy of probing, the *finesse* of Talmudic, of Midrashic and Mishnaic commentaries, the fine-spun inventiveness of the acts of reading by orthodox and kabalistic masters of textuality are truly accessible only to those schooled in the labyrinth and echo chamber of the rabbinic legacy," explains George Steiner in his introduction to *The Trial* (1992, vi). As he sees it, Kafka's exploration of the fine points of the law here, along with Kafka's parables and fables are just such Talmudic works.

The ugliness of the giant insect also appears here. "Kafka does not idealize the Yiddish world; if he turns it into a myth, he does so by fetishizing its daily life, exalting the aspects which most disgusted him. The unspeakable filth in which the Yeshiva students lived—they don't undress for bed, never wash, and are full of fleas—is already the fundamental characteristic of the court in *The Trial*" (Baioni 1989, 107). At the same time, he values their community of closeness and their natural affection for each other and their upbringing.

After his encounter with Yiddish theater, "He began to be intensely occupied with Jewish history, Jewish tradition, Jewish lore and Jewish culture—an interest which was not only sustained but constantly grew until his death in 1924 at the age of forty" (Sokel 1999, 837). In 1912, he adored Meir Isser Pines's *L'Histoire de la literature Judeo-allemande* with songs, folktales and Yiddish writers like Sholem Aleichem and I. L. Peretz (Friedlander 2013, 50). He enjoyed Eastern European Jewish folklore especially. "The aphorisms are, of course, heavily influenced by biblical texts and by various Rabbinic or esoteric Jewish writings (including Jewish mysticism)" (Friedlander 2013, 62).

"All the Jewish figures that were to recall Kafka to Judaism were rebels with the courage to defy their fathers, to break away from stifling surroundings, and to follow their urge to independence" (Sokel 1999, 851). All his literary friends in Prague and beyond were Jews: Oskar Pollak, Hugo Bermann, Max Brod, Felix Weltsch, Willy Haas, Ernst Weiss, Oskar Baum, Franz Werfel, Georg Langer, and Robert Klopstock (Friedlander 2013, 49). With this, Kafka detected a hidden hypocritical disguise in himself: "I write differently from what I speak, I speak differently from what I think, and so all proceeds into the deepest darkness" (Stolzl 1989, 64). In "The Jew as Pariah, a Hidden Tradition," Hannah Arendt quotes *The Castle* in which the landlady tells K., "You are not of the castle, you are not of the village, you are nothing at all" (62).

His unfinished novel *Amerika* ([1927] 1946) is an immigrant story though also a fantastical one. He learned of the country from travelogues and envisioned a place of senators who dressed like royalty, with fawning workers from the servant class. In his book, policemen demand papers from people on the street, subways exist in small country towns, the bathrooms are packed with showerheads. A millionaire's country house resembles a labyrinthine European castle. All in all, this hybrid country, as the hero's uncle explains, is filled with "the signs and wonders that still happen in America if nowhere else" (27).

Karl Rossman is an obvious stand in for Kafka, as is K. As in *The Trial*, the young hero tries to get ahead but fails as he runs into unknown rules and

unfair treatment. He fights for himself and for the lowly stoker on the ship
that brings him to America, but each time, powerful people in charge decide
everyone's fate, ignoring truth and justice. He's fired from a job and appre-
hended by the police for not knowing the rules, even as a devilish pair of
tramps attach themselves to him. He ends the story more hopeful than in his
other books, playing a trumpet alongside a bunch of women dressed as angels
outside a racetrack, slowly climbing toward some sort of salvation, however
long it takes. "*Amerika* has no closure, for, unlike the incomplete *The Trial*
that nevertheless brings Joseph K. to a final grisly judgement, this novel could
only end in a final judgement that would exonerate the forever innocent Karl
Rossman—and there are no exonerations in Kafka" (Thiher 1990, 30).

His persecution as an immigrant is not explicitly tied to Jewishness, but the
metaphor seems present nonetheless. "Kafka's works are the most complex
internalization in Jewish fiction in foreign languages of the *feeling* of persecution experienced by characters whose identity is determined by their *being
persecuted*" (Fried 1988, 399). Their vulnerability means they are at home
nowhere and always vulnerable to the abuse of authority. "Since the universal
Jew has no identity, is persecuted, and lacks a place in space and time, his
predicament typifies the human condition . . . the Jewish plot takes on the
dimensions of a universal human *metaplot*" (Fried 399).

In Kafka's earliest extant narrative, "Description of a Struggle" ([1912]
1981) the narrator (The Fat Man) cannot look away from a wild exhibitionist
in a church. The narrator calls him "The Praying Man" because he is ostensibly praying, while indulging in grotesque antics. The Fat Man accuses the
Praying Man of having a disease he too has carried—"a seasickness on land"
(33). His true affliction, however, is linguistic, as he cannot remember things'
true names and thus must invent them. Unable to think of the word for poplar,
the man names the tree "the Tower of Babel" then "Noah in his Cups" (33).
This works as a metaphor for being cut off from language, trapped between
cultures until a man stands out as grotesque in a house of worship. The
repeated religious terms and symbols suggest Kafka is obliquely addressing
religion.

Community for Kafka is lodged in the family. As the family disintegrates, community is lost. This is what the sequence of the narrator's associations alludes to.
The metaphor following "Tower of Babel," "Noah in his Cups," alludes to the
rebellion of son against father, reported in *Genesis*. When Noah lies in drunken
stupor, his son Ham mocks him for his exposed genitals. Man's first inebriation
leads to the self-exposure of the second father of mankind—Noah—and his
consequent fall from authority. The first rebellion of son against father. Ham's
against Noah, is in turn followed by mankind's self-assertion against God in the
building of that tower that was to reach into Heaven and ended in the breakup

of the human family into isolated, mutually uncomprehending groups of individuals—the atomized, strife-ridden societies of history. What is hinted at in "Description of a Struggle," in thickly veiled form and abstractness, becomes personalized and concretized eight years later in "The Judgment," Kafka's first mature work. Georg Bendemann's sanctimoniously concealed disrespect for his apparently senile father marks that self-assertion of the uprooted ego, which, as in "Description of a Struggle," ends in obliteration by drowning. (Sokel 1986, 172)

The result is the speaker's total isolation. The Praying Man foreshadows Gregor Samsa, who can no longer make himself understood. Uncertain of every aspect of his own existence, he needs others' opinions to push him into a concrete identity, even as he attempts prayer to find such self-meaning. Like Kafka himself, he speaks in fantasy words that cannot be understood, and like Kafka, he seeks out the place of worship for spirituality and connection. "One fears a number of things—that one's body could vanish, that human beings may really be what they appear to be at twilight, that one might not be allowed to walk without a stick, that it might be a good idea to go to church and pray at the top of one's voice in order to be looked at and acquire a body," he protests (44). Meanwhile, stories feed into stories as in *Arabian Nights*, trapping readers in multiple layers of meaning. "The narrator recognizes that he has entered a realm that, as he says, may be that of the imagination" (Thiher 1990, 5). The Fat Man finally sinks into the water, still begging passersby to identify him and measure his height. He too is like Samsa, transforming and within his change, begging for certainty.

In "The Married Couple" ([1922] 1993) Kafka describes the distasteful social aspects of Jewish society (without specifying it as Jewish). The barrenness of Jewish life with its single-minded business drive is the subject. The narrator distracts his agent from spending time with his son, and when the man suddenly dies, conceals it from his wife to avoid a scene. "Oh, how many business calls come to nothing, and yet one must keep going," he decides (465).

Continuing this theme, "A Report to an Academy" ([1917] 1993a) satirizes assimilation. In this, a man tells of his previous existence as an ape. "I could never have achieved what I have done had I been stubbornly set on clinging to my origins, to the remembrances of my youth" (295). He had been captured on the Gold Coast and shut in a cage to suffer terribly, as he describes in poignant detail. Still, he describes the goodness of his captors and the calmness that kept him from struggling to escape. He acquired skills he hated, like drinking schnapps and speaking. When presented with a future in the zoo or on the variety stage, he struggled to get into the latter. Because of his need to achieve this, he became his own taskmaster. "One

stands over oneself with a whip; one flays oneself at the slightest opposition" (203). He has achieved humanness, though his mate "has the insane
look of the bewildered half-broken animal in her eye" (204). Critic Roy
Pascal (1980) explains that the word "evasion" in this story can also mean
"a way out." As he adds, though the ape improves, "He has no grandiose
hopes of these accomplishments; they are only 'ways out' that keep the
future open" (115).

The unfinished sketch "Blumfeld, an Elderly Bachelor" ([1915] 1971)
certainly may comment on Prague's Jewish search for spirituality. Blumfeld
is a crotchety, irascible and lonely bachelor, living in a state of suspicion of
and aggressive hostility toward neighbors and colleagues. "His barren routine
is ruptured, like Joseph K.'s by a mysterious visitation, but in his case, it is
an explicit wish fulfillment" (Pascal 1980, 116). He has been wishing for a
pet that would not disturb him or require care. A magical pair of bouncing
balls supply just this, dancing around him during the day "like children" who
resist all efforts to stifle them (191). However, in a fit of irritation, he locks
them away. If the Jews of Prague seek more religion, and then reject it when
it appears, they are mirroring his behavior. Here, as in other stories, there
is a demonic or angelic visitor suggesting a primitive part of the self that is
banished from consciousness but still, like Kafka's hidden Judaism, intruding
on the personality (Miron 2019, 84).

"Jackals and Arabs" ([1917] 1993b) could be a parable for Palestine but
also fits well with Diaspora Judaism as a jackal tells the narrator that he values northerners over Arabs. It suggests they ally and attack the local Arabs.
More jackals hold him down with their teeth as the first insists, "Sir, we want
you to end this quarrel that divides the world" by doing the killing himself
(177). The jackals endlessly ask this of Europeans, hoping that they will stop
the eternal conflict while keeping the jackals' hands clean.

"In Our Synagogue," written around 1920 (1961) was Kafka's only
explicitly Jewish work. A mysterious animal, a blue-green martin, mottled
and ugly, lives in the synagogue of a small community in Slovakia. It, like
Kafka's other images, suggests the outsider. "Aren't we faced with the inde-
terminate aspect and the uncertain 'color' of Jewishness as Kafka perceived
it?" (Friedlander 2013, 60).

Above all, it keeps away from human beings, it is more shy than a denizen of
the forest, and seems to be attached only to the building. And it is doubtless
its personal misfortune that this building is a synagogue, that is, a place that
is at times full of people. If only one could communicate with the animal, one
could, of course, comfort it by telling it that the congregation in this little town
of ours in the mountains is becoming smaller every year and that it is already
having trouble in raising the money for the upkeep of the synagogue. It is not

impossible that before long the synagogue will have become a granary or something of the sort and the animal will then have the peace it now so sorely lacks.

The animal and people are frightened of one another, but the people gradually become accustomed to its presence. With this, tension is heightened between it and them, between the men and women (who are ridiculed and have no voice here though the animal adores their balcony), between the secular community and the ancient "secret power" of the Ark, which captivates the creature while the humans take it for granted (Miron 2019, 47). The animal is unclean, atavistic, embarrassing; much like the old shtetl traditions or the stereotypes perpetuated by anti-Semites, but the narrator insists it's harmless. The religiosity of the past, however primitive and embarrassing, cannot and should not be exorcised. "The paradox in the synagogue is, in fact, occasioned by the lack of attention drawn to the animal . . . like the leopards in another of Kafka's temples, the intruder has broken into the sanctuary so often, and emptied the sacrificial pitchers so completely, that the violation may be calculated in advance until it becomes part of the ceremony" (Baum 1986, 151).

Still, "It is in terror that it comes running out, it is in terror that it performs its capers, and it does not dare to withdraw until divine service is at an end." The narrator wonders whether its terror comes from past memories or future premonitions. Once they had tried to drive the animal off in ancient memory (so its terror has some basis) but now they have all given up on the concept. Still, the center of the temple holds the numinous ark, like the key to Kafka's parables. The animal's attraction to it emphasizes its desire for the central tenants of Judaism, even as the synagogue goers take them for granted. "Similar codices may be discovered at the center of almost any of the labyrinths in which Kafka's heroes find themselves" (Baum 1986, 152).

The Castle ([1930] 1992), a quest through just such a labyrinth, describes a study in futility. "In German the word for castle *(Schloss)* also means lock—the castle of the novel is locked against all K.'s efforts to fight his way into it, a fortress of impersonal mediate authority which expresses the tyranny of automatic social, biological, and psychological processes, barring the way to the ultimate self-authority of the individual person freely choosing himself and choosing to be free" (Greenberg 1986, 68).

K. (a nod to the author once again) is a Land Surveyor, already summoned to the castle, but, when his status is denied by the townsfolk, he sets out on an epic quest to have the authorities there validate him. He quests to speak with Klamm, the one identifiable Castle official, only to be blocked over and over. "K is possessed by only one thought: that he must come to grips with Klamm; yet at the same time, he knows that his very obsession with this thought precludes him from reaching what he mistakenly believes only Klamm can give"

(Heller 1986, 147). He takes up with Klamm's mistress Frieda. He attempts bribery, blackmail, back-door channels, and anything he can think of, but the path to the Castle remains mysteriously closed. His vision of the hidden power in charge in *The Castle* and *The Trial* reflects Kabbalah and also his position at the bottom of the Austrian bureaucracy.

No clear antagonist blocks K.'s quest, suggesting that his mazelike world is the real enemy. The Land Surveyor's job, as critic Erich Heller notes, is "consisting precisely in what K. desperately desires and never achieves: to produce a workable order within clearly defined boundaries and limits of earthly life, and to find an acceptable compromise between conflicting claims of possession" (139). The word *vermesser*, surveyor, also alludes to *vermessenheit*, "hubris" as well as mistakes in measuring (139). Klamm, meanwhile, suggests "a sound producing a sense of anxiety amounting almost to claustrophobia" (139).

Final authority's taking a realistic shape—that of a Castle—is complicated. There is a glimmer of enlightenment waiting there, but one K. cannot reach. "It is the paradox of spiritual absolutism that the slightest touch of concreteness will poison the purest substance of the spirit, and one ray of darkness blot out a world of light" (Heller 1986, 147). The Castle has been said to represent self-sufficiency, God, spiritual fulfillment, deadly bureaucracy, and anything else one can imagine. From a Jewish perspective, the character can be seen questing for acceptance—the locals wrote for a Land Surveyor, he is one, and yet, everywhere he goes he encounters a slippery disapproval, hotels where he does not qualify to stay, employers who deny any interest in employing him. As with *The Trial*, the author-substitute does not fully understand the shifting rules, only that he is unknowingly transgressing them over and over. "In Kafka's fiction, the Truth remains inaccessible and is possibly nonexistent. The messengers themselves (or the commentators) have but hazy notions regarding the messages they carry; this very uncertainty and the never-ending query that ensues are the main contributions of Kafka's Jewishness to the world he created" (Friedlander 2013, 65).

One character who stands out is Amalia, chosen to be the mistress of a Castle official in a moment described as "such an abuse of power" (193). She firmly refuses and the family is ostracized—not by the Castle but by the villagers. So ingrained is service in their minds that refusal is deadly. One critic compares this to Abraham's binding of Isaac—God truly did not want his child's life but was testing his obedience. While an angel is unlikely to intervene and save Amelia if she submits, Amalia epitomizes moral convictions in contrast to K.'s shady maneuverings. If the Castle is where cold, cruel deities live, she and K. follow contrasting solutions and Amelia may represent the path K. should have taken in the face of this cruelty—refusal rather than trying to meet their incomprehensible demands.

Klaus Wagenbach notes that the village's description suggests Osek (Wossek), where Kafkas had lived since the eighteenth century as part of "the Bohemian Jewish provincial proletariat" (79). Kafka's own father was born there, and he visited family on occasion, including at the time of writing. The lower village was peopled almost entirely by Jews, with a synagogue, cemetery, and so on. However, by 1890, the village had dwindled to a few Jewish families, who finally left for the big cities, "following the general pattern of the retreat of the Jews" (81). The massive castle above had a large administrative staff with corrupt officials. It "can hardly be seen; it is hard to reach, and the gates are shut; children are not let in, least of all Jewish children. The owners are not in residence, for it is a summer castle. Only the bailiffs, keepers, secretaries, and servants are there" (84). The owner, a knight, always "had a lot of women around" (82). Since the castle owned all the land about, there was certainly pressure from above and yet, appeals to the absent owners were impossible. Meanwhile, there was a significant separation between the Jewish and Catholic villages.

Some of the language used to reprimand K. criticizes him for being an undesirable outsider—a Jewish metaphor. His landlady protests, "You are not from the Castle, you are not from the village, you aren't anything. Or rather, unfortunately, you are something, a stranger, a man who isn't wanted and is in everybody's way" (50). She hates that her dear adopted daughter Frieda has lowered herself to sleep with him and describes his "obscure" intentions, an allusion to Jews' constantly being described as foreigners lacking allegiance to their country. Later the landlady insists "she woke up to your tricks" and that "you couldn't deceive her even if you did your best to hide your intentions" (156). He is crafty, deceptive, slippery, even in his heartfelt protests that he only wants to reach the Castle to do his job.

The Castle, like the rest of Kafka's fiction is "concerned with questions such as exile, assimilation, endangered community, revelation, commentary, law, tradition, and commandment" (Howe 1992, viii). His friend and editor Max Brod was convinced Kafka was questing for an unreachable God, as *The Trial* and *The Castle* feature unreachable authorities. Brod reports that *The Castle* was supposed to end with word coming that K.'s legal claim to live in the village was invalid but that he would still be permitted to live and work there. He would not receive literal validation, but he was to be given a sort of solace, though only as an eternal outsider and only on his deathbed (Howe 1992, xx). This, it seemed, was the constant fate of Prague's Jews and Kafka himself, who fell in love with Jewish socialist Dora Diamant and found a new acceptance, but only during his prolonged illness and death of tuberculosis at forty. He died in 1924 and thus was spared the Holocaust, though his younger sisters perished in the camps.

ALT-KAFKA

Robert Crumb and David Zane Mairowitz wrote the comic *Kafka* (2007), in which they tell his biography of growing up in Prague, interspersed with his stories. It begins with terrifying images of him imagining his own death, then transitions into his early life in the Prague Ghetto, raised among synagogues and legends of the golem, whose story is depicted here. As it explains, "Kafka would have had no way of avoiding [the Ghetto legend's] fantastical imprint on the social memory of a Jewish boy in his time and place" (15). Moments of anti-Semitism follow, melded with fantasy and legend. What excited Kafka "was the mystical, anti-rational side of Hasidism, where earthly reality was continuous with unearthly reality, where mystical value was to be found in the details of everyday life, and where God was everywhere and easily contactable (Crumb and Mairowitz 19). All of this, as the slipstream comic makes clear, contributed to his art. Another children's adaptation, *My First Kafka: Runaways, Rodents & Giant Bugs*, by Matthue Roth, with illustrations by Rohan Daniel Eason, introduces children to the dark gothic with spooky illustrations.

Kafka made such a literary impact that modern stories not only adapt his fiction but reimagine him as a fantasy character. "Franz Kafka, Superhero" by David Gerrold (1994) dresses him all in black as Bug-Man the human insect and master of metamorphosis. "In his ordinary life, he pretended to be just another faceless dark slug—sweaty, confused, trapped by circumstance" with a public persona of a writer of the grotesque (115). His nemesis PsycheMan is actually Freud—hero and villain are both trapped in their neuroses. In their superhero guises, however, they can release many daily struggles and instead revel in the simplicity of their alternate selves. At last, Kafka triumphs over Freud by reinforcing that life is meaningless.

Similarly, "The Jackdaw's Last Case" (2013) by Paul Di Filippo has Kafka becoming a superhero in 1925. He calls himself the Jackdaw (the translation of his last name) and soars around New York fighting crime. A cool intellectual, he answers letters to the editor with puzzles and wordplay. It's a love letter to the great writer, musing on an alternate life he could have led in America. Ironically, the story pits him against the Black Beetle, a Zionist demanding that America help create the State of Israel. The Black Beetle finally unmasks to reveal himself as Max Brod, in this reality a young admirer from Prague whom Kafka never noticed. Now he has become a radical Zionist. He takes his revenge and locks Kafka into a contraption that will tattoo him with "a portion of the Talmud dealing with traitors to the Jewish race" (275). In these stories, the superhero is often following a Jewish metaphor, but it's much rarer to find a Jewish super villain. Brod's anger is externalized by symbolically forcing Kafka to take his cause, incorporating the text of Judaism into his very body, while the American Kafka has abandoned such concerns in the land of luxury.

Philip Roth also offered an alternate version of Kafka, exploring the tragedies and strength of the writer living in a time of affliction: "'I Always Wanted You to Admire My Fasting'; or, Looking at Kafka" ([1973] 2017). Roth creates an alternate 1942, in which the fifty-nine-year-old emigrates to America. He becomes a professor, dubbed Dr. Kishka, by his students, and resolves to save the Jews of Europe. Kafka dates Philip's aunt, but the family deems him crazy. He finally fades into obscurity—with America's safety, his great works go unwritten. "The chill here comes with the confusion of power between life and art, between fact and fiction" (Pierpont 90).

Kafka's Leopards ([2000 2011) is another alt-history adventure by Brazilian author Moacyr Scliar in which the hero is sent on a spy mission. In the story, a Russian Jew named Mousy journeys to Prague in 1916 to receive coded instructions from a Trotskyite revolutionary. As he's instructed, he must approach a local writer to get it. However, he loses the instructions and ends up mistaking Kafka for his informant. Kafka gives him the mysterious story "Leopards in the Temple," which the hero indeed mistakes for a code. The story is inspired by a Kafka aphorism: "Leopards break into the temple and drink up the offering in the chalices; this happens again and again; finally, one can predict their action in advance and it becomes part of the ceremony." There's a theme of contrast between those who can decode the inner meaning of a story and those cannot, as Kafka tells Mousey, "The text is obscure. You are not obliged to get a message out of it," even as Mousey frantically seeks its coded meaning (70). The story is self-referential even as the mistakes of each generation repeat. Later in life living far from all the world wars in Brazil, Mousey discovers the monetary value of the story. Nonetheless, he cherishes it, until finally he offers to sell it for his beloved grand-nephew's education. When his grand-nephew is arrested for political protests, in a never-ending generational cycle that echoes the original quote, Mousey manages to arrange his release. However, in a Kafkaesque bureaucracy of absurdity, the police suspect the story is a code and are only mollified by ripping it up and throwing it away. The hero rescues a tiny scrap, and when he dies, visions of leopards come to escort him away. Thus, literature is weighed against family, with another tantalizing lost manuscript featuring in this story. As the story's introduction notes, "Scliar has created a story that addresses themes of Brazilian and European history, Jewish writing, the travels of literature, and fundamental questions of reading, such as how the rightness or wrongness of a literary interpretation is to be judged" (xii).

Jerzy Peterkiewicz's "A Triptych for the Jackdaw" (1980) and D. J. Enright's "K. on the Moon" (1980) are homage poems. The former has the Jackdaw building nests in the Castle over and over to have them knocked down (likely a nod to Kafka's writing career). When he succeeds, there's a grand ball, but the Jackdaw is left watching from the corner. It ends with his prayer as he endeavors futilely (like Kafka's many characters) to reach paradise: a prayer that those who cannot see can still move forwards and persevere. "K. on the Moon," meanwhile, emphasizes his isolation as he heads for the moon. Thin, tormented, and dying, he still tries to wed and find happiness. Still, his wedding is framed as the proverbial "giant leap" to the unreachable heavens.

J. P. Stern's "The Matljary Diary" (1980) envisions Kafka as a World War II soldier, bantering with his friends as he describes himself as Josephine the Folk Mouse and considers the value of art. While the narrator tries getting him a better job in the army, Kafka, echoing his mouse's dilemma, feels he must refuse it and do his duty. The narrator is skeptical about fighting beside "Prague coffee-house Jews" (238). At the same time, he discovers that "Dr. K." is useful, as he knows the region. As they debate philosophy, the narrator blurts into his diary, "Truly, I've never had such weird conversations in all my life" (242). Still, he's touched by Kafka's "specialness" with his unique view of the world.

Jay Cantor's *Forgiving the Angel: Four Stories for Franz Kafka* (2014) explores Kafka's loved ones, in a collection somewhere between historical fiction and alt-history, with more than a touch of magical realism. The first story has Kafka wrangling with his impressions of the Angel of Death as he slowly succumbs to his final illness. After, Max Brod and an interviewer wrangle over Max and Dora's responsibility to burn Kafka's manuscripts as he had requested. "Dora said Kafka told her to destroy the manuscripts to keep the ghosts from attacking him. Don't you think that you may have left Kafka defenseless, open to the attack of tormenting demons?" the interviewer questions (28). They debate over the treasure of stories, even as they consider the author's superstitions in a story that blends post-modernism and fantasy. Another story follows Kafka's lover Dora Diamant, and her later marriage and child as she fled with her daughter to England and worked with the Friends of Yiddish to preserve her culture. Much of the story comes from her husband, sick with jealousy at his attempts to compete with Dora's memory of Kafka. Marianne, the daughter, describes Kafka as "a broken sort of angel, maybe, crippled when he fell" (137). She has grown up with "the Kafka gospel that all things were linked, so a bird or an old Yiddish writer might speak your secrets" (141). There's much description of the "in-between place" separating living and dying, and its metaphysical effect on the characters. Another story follows his translator and lover Milena, and her friendships in the death camps. The last presents a lost Kafka story, in which Abraham and Moses consider whether God intended mankind to be vegetarian and alter the laws to suit their own interests.

Kafka Americana (2011) is a collection of short stories by Jonathan Lethem and Carter Scholz parodying and offering alternate lives of Franz Kafka and his works. In the funniest, "Receding Horizons," Kafka comes to America, changes his name to Jack Dawson and writes screenplays. After his death, Director Frank Capra wants to make Dawson's "The Judgment" into a film. However, Capra retorts, "This material is hopeless for a movie. No fee is large enough for me to jump through these particular hoops. Find another writer" (34). He and his team discuss making it a Christmas film like Dickens *A Christmas Carol*. They can call the Prague story "Miracle at Progress Falls" with the hero, Aussenhof, translated for an American audience into its meaning of Bailey, so the character is called "George Bailey," with a plot recognizable as *It's a Wonderful Life*. As he dreams of reaching Israel, this plot entwines with the film one, emphasizing what might have been. In his dreams, Kafka moves to Israel and writes propaganda that helps avert the Holocaust. Continuing this ultimate fantasy, Dr. Lowy cures him (a golem reference). However, he wakens to write, "Dr Lowy is dead. The mark, the Shem, placed by his hand upon the golem's head awaits erasure" (48). As he writes, despairing, "Were I able, I would write the story of a patient obliged to a course of treatment that is in reality a penance for failing God. Bit by bit the body is taken away. Then the intellect, the personality, the soul, are broken off and discarded" (48). "I am being erased. As if I had never written," he adds in metafictional fashion (48). As he fades away, however, he decides, "It's a wonderful life" (49). Dawson dies and the film exceeds its budget, becoming an embarrassment for Capra in an anticlimactic ending that nonetheless considers the balance between art and popularity.

A very different story's wish fulfillment considers how Kafka would have adapted his actual works to address the Holocaust. Iris Bruce (2016) imagines Kafka emigrating to Palestine. In 1924, Bruce adds, Felix Salten, the author of *Bambi*, joined him there. "In Zionist circles, Bambi was hailed as a new type of Zionist children's literature. The old King of the Forest was easily recognizable as Theodor Herzl (1860–1904) and the dangers of assimilation were obvious in poor Gobo's fate, who was shot by a hunter" (197). The pair of authors tour the Jewish homeland, meeting other authors who have emigrated there. Kafka becomes inspired to return to fiction and finishes his novels, adapting them for the immigrants to the Middle East. *Driftwood*, adapted from *Amerika*, "took a less optimistic turn and lost much of the light-hearted playfulness" (206). The central character Karl Rossman defends Jewish settlements in Palestine and becomes a spy, aiding the Jews in creating their own state. After his beloved sisters perish in the Holocaust, Kafka returns to writing *The Trial*, "shocked at how many scenes seemed for foreshadow the horrors of war and genocide" (210). He reimagines its protagonist as a Jew, slowly turning to stone as the Nazis invade. This becomes a seminal work of the Holocaust, like his 1963 novel *Hordus' Castle*, of a young Zionist who is named for Herod, builder of Masada. Motivated by Hitler's 1939 speech from Hradcany Castle in Prague, Hordus emigrates to Palestine to build his own castle on Masada in a highly symbolic novel. He wins the Nobel Prize for Literature and ends his days as an Israeli hero.

Many of these stories are outlandish, impossible. Still, they all reflect modern authors' love for the author and their speculative questions of what might have happened had he reached America, reached Israel, or most of all, lived.

Chapter 7

The Old-New Land

From Zionism to Israeli Literature

HERZL'S UTOPIA

Israel was founded on the dream of a Utopia—specifically Theodor Herzel's *Altneuland* (Old-New Land) of 1902 and before this, the lesser known. *A Journey to the Land of Israel in the Year 5700*. Elhanan Leib Levinsky (1857–1910) arrived in Eretz-Israel in 1881. After a two-month trip, he returned to Europe, convinced of the need to establish a Jewish center in Eretz-Israel. *A Journey to the Land of Israel in the 800th Year of the Sixth Millennium* (5700 or 2040), first published in 1892 in the *Pardes* journal in Odessa, and later several times in book form, was called by some the first novel written in Modern Hebrew. In this work of utopian socialist literature, Levinsky imagines what could be: peace, technology, industry, and cultural harmony. Many places in Israel, including the Levinsky Market, Levinsky Street, and Levinsky College of Education are named for him.

Theodor Herzl, the original Zionist, wrote his visionary *Altneuland* (1902) about a paradise of cooperation. In a vision of benevolent colonialism heavily influenced by European views of the time, Herzl envisioned Palestine (at the time, part of the Turkish Empire with a thin Arab population) as welcoming the settlers. His Muslim character explains, "Would you call a man a robber who takes nothing from you, but brings something? The Jews have enriched us, why should we be against them?"

Herzl's colony speak Yiddish and have rebuilt the Temple. There are overhead electric trains and airships. Men and women have equal rights. The new land's spokesman explains, "They have active and passive suffrage as a matter of course. They worked faithfully beside us during the reconstruction period. Their enthusiasm lent wings to the men's courage. It would have been the blackest ingratitude if we had relegated them to the servants' hall or to a harem." Anti-Semitism has even faded from Europe. As the tour guide of the story tells it:

> The vast works of colonization had required a large staff of trained engineers, jurists and administrators. Large opportunities were suddenly opened to educated young men who in the anti-Semitic times had had no sphere for the exercise of their skill. Jewish university graduates, men trained in the technological institutes and commercial colleges, used to flounder helplessly; but now there was ample room for them in the public and private undertakings so numerous in Palestine. The result was that Christian professional men no longer looked askance at their Jewish colleagues, for they were no longer annoying competitors. In such circumstances, commercial envy and hatred had gradually disappeared. Furthermore, the less Jewish abilities were offered in the marketplace, the more their value was appreciated. The value of services always increased with their scarcity. Everyone knew that. Why should not this rule have applied to Jews in commercial life?

One of the central plotlines follows a demagogue politician's rise, as he calls for the expulsion of non-Jews from the New Society. "The villain, Rabbi Geyer, may be read as a composite of Herzl's enemies, especially traditionalist rabbinic leaders in Europe" (Rovner 2016, 220). Nonetheless, the rabbi is defeated at the polls, letting the New Society continue as a haven for all, not just Jews. Elections, newspapers, medical care—all are conducted in a civilized fashion to make sure everyone is protected. There are large bazaars with mass distribution, aided by the transportation system and paid for in shekels. Theater has found a new golden age.

In some ways, Altneuland suggests the Israel that followed, at least in its early decades. The New Society itself is "a syndicate of co-operative societies, a syndicate that comprises industry and commerce [and] keeps the welfare of the workers in mind." This echoes early Israel's Histadrut. No pure kibbutzim are visible, but farming is mainly done by co-ops. They use the biblical forty-nine-year lease later employed by the Jewish National Fund. There was indeed a new art and theater movement, though opera never resurged. Still, it was more fantasy than reality. "The term 'utopian,' even a half century before *Altneuland*, carried pejorative associations of impracticality, naiveté, and wish fulfillment. The Zionist movement—as well as the new Hebrew republic—would move mountains to avoid being stigmatized for what it was—a modern, unabashedly utopian, thoroughly realistic political movement driven, not by imaginative musings or imperialistic hubris but by desperate circumstances and diminishing options" ("Science Fiction and Fantasy" 2018).

Altneuland was translated into Hebrew as *Tel Aviv*, later the namesake for one of Israel's greatest cities. However, it failed to catch on beyond its popularity as fiction. At the time, non-Zionist Jews saw it as just another flight of fantasy, while Eastern Europeans saw it as startlingly western, more a European utopia than a Jewish one. Few readers were convinced to emigrate. Still, Herzl's message kept building through Europe, before, during, and after the Holocaust as the European Jews sought a new home. "The Zionists' most radical act of conception was to re-territorialize their homelands as alien, and a foreign landscape—Palestine—as home. This could not have been accomplished without a modern literature that reimagined the ancient biblical promises. Zionist realpolitik was born of fiction" (Rovner 2016, 45).

> "If you will it," Herzl declared in an utterance that resounds with a science fiction sensibility, "it is no dream." Fearful lest his own dream be dismissed as a frivolous Romantic fancy, however, Herzl initially sought to dissociate Zionism from the utopian discourse that had returned to vogue during the 19th century with the publication, in 1888, of Edward Bellamy's *Looking Backward, 2000–1887*. At least one other such work, Theodor Hertzka's *Freiland: Ein Sociales Zukunftbild* ("Freeland: An Image of Future Society," 1890) is believed to have directly influenced Herzl's decision to craft Altneuland as a conventional utopian novel, quite possibly because of the many editions it had inspired as well as some of the real-world utopian passions it had tapped. ("Science Fiction and Fantasy" 2018)

Other important Zionist fiction works include Abraham Mapu's *Ahavat Ẓiyyon* ("Love of Zion," 1853), a historical novel set in an idealized Kingdom of Judah during the reigns of Ahaz and Hezekiah, and Yosef Luidor's *Yoash* (1912), featuring the Akedah (Binding of Isaac) as a Maccabean myth set against the struggle against the Arabs during the Second Aliyah. More books are Max Austerberg-Verakoff's *Das Reich Judaea im Jahre 6000 (2241)*, published in 1893 and depicting a mass exodus of Jews from Europe and their founding a Jewish state in Israel. *Looking Ahead* (1899), by Henry Pereira Mendes, made an American response to Herzl's *Der Judenstaat* with a similar theme. Isaac Fernh described his own future state of Israel in *Shenei Dimyonot* ("Two Imaginings"). Hebrew-Yiddish writer Hillel Zeitlin published another such tract, *In der Medinas Yisroel in Yor 2000* ("In the State of Israel in the Year 2000"), in 1919, following Great Britain's Balfour Declaration. In 1921, Russian author Shalom Ben Avram published *Komemiyut* ("Resurgence"), weighing the effects of future mass immigration. Already living in Palestine of 1924, Boris Schatz wrote *Yerushalayim ha-Benuyah* ("Rebuilt Jerusalem").

In 1948, the Jews finally achieved a long-imagined utopia, creating a homeland in Israel after two millennia of exile, and reviving their lost language as well. They created an entire country with laws, a national culture, and even new art.

It has been argued that the contemporary State of Israel not only grew out of science fiction, but also has quite literally lived it every day of its unlikely existence. In their most desperately fanciful imaginings, neither Herzl nor his fellow Zionist utopians would have entertained the possibility that a mere century after the first Zionist Congress in 1898, the world would include a Jewish democracy six-million strong with the most powerful economy in the region, a first-rate military able to project devastating force thousands of miles away, seven major research universities, its own satellites and astronaut in orbit, and pride of place as a world-class scientific and technological innovator. ("Science Fiction and Fantasy" 2018)

ALT-ISRAELS

Historically, Herzl considered Argentina, Cyprus, Mesopotamia, Mozambique, and the Sinai Peninsula for the Jewish homeland (Rovner 2016, 45). At the time, the Europeans pictured Africa from the sensational H. Rider Haggard's *King Solomon's Mines,* which described the horde of treasure Solomon used to build the Temple. "For Herzl and the early Zionists, the Uganda Plan twinned the adventures of Stanley with the adventurism of the Age of Empire" (Rovner 47). Noted folklorist Sholem Aleichem believed in the proposal and wrote two plays about it: In one, Herzl and his friends, recast as doctors, attend a deathly ill patient named Israel, and debate whether "Uganda Africana" or a dose of spirit and culture will revive it. In his second, he has a matchmaker trying to set up Zionism with "Miss Uganda." A delegation toured the area in 1905, but it all came to nothing.

Herzl's hope was not the first serious plan for a Jewish homeland: From 1818 to 1848, Grand Island by Niagara Falls beckoned Jews. This was the plan of Sephardic playwright and journalist Mordechai Manuel Noah (a particularly apt name as many noted). After a vicious pogrom in Germany, several German Jews formed the society for the culture and science of the Jews in 1819. As Germany refused to recognize Jewish equal rights, they considered emigration. Noah petitioned America for a Jewish homeland, emphasizing the shame of governments who "were unable or unwilling" to grant Jews "that unalienable protection which is due to a citizen" (Rovner 25).

These rights were granted, and he built the home, beginning with a lavish dedication ceremony. He laid the foundation stone in a church in Buffalo, the nearest town of any size. Many locals came to see, but almost no Jews. There was a parade of soldiers, clergy, and musicians in Turkish dress, while Noah wore "robes of crimson silk, trimmed with ermine" borrowed from a theater production of *Richard III* (Rovner 29). There he laid the 300-pound sandstone block engraved with the Sh'ma for what he called Ararat, the "City of Refuge for the Jews." Today the stone lies at the Buffalo and Erie County Historical Society, as it never founded a building. Despite this homeland awaiting them, the official Jewish response was negative. The Rabbi of Cologna charged Noah with "treason against the divine majesty" for trying to make a Jewish homeland before the Messiah arrived, an argument that appeared repeatedly around the State of Israel in 1948 (Rovner 35). As far as Noah's legacy, many consider him the first to seriously try to arrange a Jewish homeland.

Though his project failed, it inspired several works of fiction. British author and early Zionist leader Israel Zangwill published "Noah's Ark" ([1899] 2011) while collaborating with Herzl. A German Jew, Peloni (a name derived from the Hebrew word for an anonymous "someone") lives in the German ghetto, his people murdered and persecuted. However, Mordechai Manuel Noah proclaims the people have been given a refuge on Grand Island. However, the locals refuse to leave, reflecting the resistance Herzl himself must have encountered. The people insist that persecution will pass and that they have no desire to leave their comfortable homes. The rabbi protests, echoing history, "God alone knows the epoch of the Israelitish restoration; He alone will make it known to the whole universe, by signs entirely unequivocal; and every attempt on our part to reassemble with any political, national design, is forbidden as an act of high treason against the Divine Majesty." Peloni sails for the New World but does so alone. When he arrives, he's disturbed to find that Noah has teamed up with gentile capitalists on his project. Peloni groans. "And Jews will not believe? We must go to the Gentiles. Jews will only put their money into Gentile schemes; will build always for others, never for themselves. It is the same everywhere. Alas for Israel!" With this, he emphasizes European Jewry's lack of direction and commitment to a State of Israel then and in his own time. With each word, the utopia is revealed as more of a pipe dream.

Adding to the fantasy, Noah insists that they can share with the Native Americans as "the Red Indians are the Lost Ten Tribes of Israel . . . in worship, dialect, language, sacrifices, marriages, divorces, burials, fastings, purifications, punishments, cities of refuge, divisions of tribes, High-Priests, wars, triumphs—'tis our very tradition." Of course, this only displays Noah's ignorance. Indeed, historically, his writings reveal "Noah's paternalism toward Indians as well as his esteem of their cultures, as esteem rooted in his belief that they shared a common ancestry with the Jews," making the painful satire more true than not (Rovner 36).

Still, when Peloni goes ahead to plant a flag, he sees the Niagara Falls in the distance and is overcome: "The *Shechinah!*" he whispered. "The divine presence that rested on the Tabernacle, and on Solomon's Temple, and that has returned at last—to Ararat." Noah writes that the dedication ceremony has gone well, with many gentiles in attendance, and now he and Peloni must only await the influx of Jewish pilgrims. Peloni lives there peacefully, but no Jews ever bother coming. Here, Zangwill tells a sad vision of the community failing to rouse to the clarion call in the past, as well as in his present. "Israel had been too bent and broken by the long dispersion and the long persecution: the spring was snapped; he could not recover. He had been too long the pliant protégé of kings and popes: he had prayed too many centuries in too many countries for the simultaneous welfare of too many governments, to be capable of realizing that government of his own for which he likewise prayed."

Yiddish author and publisher Kalmen Zingman (1889–1929) was born in Slobodka, near Kovno. In 1919, Kalmen Zingman published the pioneer newspaper, *Der yidisher komunist*. His utopian novel *In der tsukunft-shtot Edenye* (In the Future City of Edenye) appeared in 1918 under the pseudonym Ben-Ya'akov. After spending twenty-five years in Palestine, the protagonist with the self-referential name Zalman Kindishman visits a multinational city in Ukraine (presumably the grubby industrial city Kharkov, now renamed after Eden). He finds a happy Yiddish-speaking community whose life is built on principles of cultural autonomy. It has many science fiction advancements like flying trains and an artificial climate but also cultural ones, creating ethnic harmony and kindness as children celebrate Jewish holidays in lavish gardens, unafraid of anti-Semitism. Kenneth B. Moss adds in *Jewish Renaissance in the Russian Revolution* (2009):

> In Edeniya, Jews, Ukrainians, Russians, and Poles live harmonious but separate national-communal lives under autonomous administrations. . . . Yet Edeniya is not easily placed among the competing Jewish political ideologies of the day. Politics in the narrow sense is actually absent from the imagined life of Edeniya, although memories of political struggle are central to the city's multiethnic harmony ("together they fought, together they died"). Rather, it is Kultur that stands at the core of the collective and individual lives of Edeniya's imagined Jews. (61)

Edeniya is dotted with memorials exalting Jewish artists and writers as it emphasizes ties to Old Europe. A statue of the Ukrainian national bard Taras Shevchenko stands in the square, and Jewish cultural symbols fill the place. There are art museums, Jewish music, Jewish ballet companies, and Yiddish opera. In the square is a secularized, Yiddishized celebration of the holiday Lag Ba-Omer, "a favorite of Jewish nationalists for its pronounced national and nature motifs" (Moss 61). Two sects govern the country. The Heavenly Ones "renounce all earthly pleasures, all the enjoyments that life can bring.

They maintain that there is an even higher world, a more beautiful one." The second sects are the "Earthly Ones, who say: enrich and improve life, so that heaven can be on earth."

For American-Ukrainian curator Larissa Babij, Zingman "maintains a separation between the realms of everyday activity, where technological advancements have increased the comfort and ease of residents' lives, and the sphere of culture." As she adds, "It's interesting to contrast this vision with that of the early Soviet avant-garde, which envisioned art and its formal possibilities as a means to transform outdated ways of living, to shape and prepare society for new forms of organization, often through a violent break with and obliteration of past cultural traditions" (Goff 2017).

At the climax, Kindishman attends a public lecture about Peretz and his Hasidic stories, "stories that, for Yiddishists, epitomized how East European Jewish religious tradition could be recast as aesthetically compelling Jewish literature" (Moss 61). Everyone greets the lecture eagerly, emphasizing their great literacy. This fantasy shows a majority Jewish culture, updated to modern times.

However, the book was unpopular. Many judged it badly written. Its celebration of Yiddish culture mostly sidelined the Hebrew speakers and dismissed the Zionists. His world was mostly secular, repelling those who sought a homeland based in religion. Further, it overwhelmingly celebrated art rather than history, science, or other areas. Repelling the Russians, it was quite bourgeois in its imagery of music and art lessons for the rich children. Casting the inhabitants of this utopia as cultural elites neglecting their world responsibilities was also an unpopular position.

> Zingman's utopia was of its time and place in many respects: communist in the literal sense (there is no money in Edeniya), cheerfully accepting of the need to use violence to bring about the revolution (it projects this violence safely into Edeniya's past but, of course, Edeniya's past was still the future as of 1917), and unabashed about the role that it assigns to the state in cultural life. Its conception of culture itself, however, is entirely at odds with the ideas we tend to associate with Europe's postwar political and cultural avant-gardes. Edeniya is not an avant-garde paradise in which life itself is remade as art and the distinctions of bourgeois society regarding culture, politics, and society collapse. (Moss 62)

Lithuanian-American Bertha Wiernik's "The Menorah Spangled Ship" (1919) is set in the near future. War refugees have piled into a new ghetto in East London, where the story's protagonists begin building a giant version of the Lusitania, which will be immune to assault and can transport Jews to the Land of the Chosen People. This is planned as "Palestine's first steamship," the worldship/colonyship which in itself will be the future home of the Jews: "The Cunard Company has lately created a new sea-wonder–the Lusitania–which is a miniature vessel of this model. You hear? A miniature! The Lusitania carries about three thousand passengers. Palestine's first ship, according to the model, will carry ten thousand passengers! It will be built and launched on the Jordan." The story ends joyously with a new utopia created: "Justice and permanent peace are the two great laws of the new human race. Light, joy, happiness, prevail on earth and on sea." The Land of the Chosen People is filled with thousands of vessels, led by the Menorah Spangled Ship.

A much more problematic, even painfully anti-Semitic, work of Zionism is M. P. Shiel's *The Lord of the Sea* (1901). The novel begins with England being flooded with ten million refugees. One particular evil Jew named Frankl, with a seductively beautiful daughter, buys the estate where the hero, Richard Hogarth, lives with his sister. Frankl turns them out of their house, frames Hogarth for murder, and commits the sister to an asylum, where she slowly goes mad. Frankl's own sister, meanwhile, has fallen for Hogarth. As in George Eliot's celebrated *Daniel Deronda*, the truth is that Richard Hogarth is, unknown to himself until the novel's beginning, a Jew, Spinoza by name, and heir to a great fortune. Now mimicking *The Count of Monte Cristo*, the hero escapes prison, finds a fortune, establishes himself in society, and plots revenge. With his massive wealth (another painful Jewish stereotype), he constructs eight giant islands, armor-clad and controlling the world's trade routes, and makes himself "Lord of the Sea," surrounded by endless luxuries. Here, the science fiction elements come to play at last.

He collects taxes for using the sea, pushing the author's agenda of a dislike of landownership and its laws and abuses. "All unauthorized ships passing on my domain will in due course be destroyed," he insists. The German Atlantic liner, Kaiser Wilhelm der Groesse, defies Hogarth and flees when "suddenly space seemed to open its mouth in a chasm and bay gruff and hollow, like old hell-gate dogs; and almost at the same moment, quite close by the Kaiser, a column of water belched with one dull humph of venom two hundred feet on high. . . . A six inch shell . . . had half shattered her engines, killing two stokers; and a torpedo-mine had knocked a hole, five feet across, in her port beam." He then saves England from a French-Russian invasion.

At last, Hogarth brings the Jews back to Jerusalem and takes his place as the Messiah. Their new country is a great utopia of progress and learning in which "The University of Jerusalem had become the chief nerve center of the world's research and upward effort." Israel, quite literally, redeems the world and leads it into a new messianic age. The story suggests that, free of Europe, the Jews could do astoundingly well, create a true Utopia. However, in Europe, confined to moneylending and ostracized, they will never integrate.

There were also Jewish efforts to create a refugee colony in Madagascar in the late 1930s, a plan perverted by Anti-Semites. At the time, the plan was seen as a solution by Jews but also hostile gentiles.

Polish nationalists marched and cried out, "Jews to Madagascar!" A novel appeared fantasizing that all but a hundred thousand Polish Jews would be exiled to the island. Jewish journalists reported that anxious members of the community "purchased maps and sought out the location" of Madagascar. A Warsaw theater performed a comic political play, "We're Off to Madagascar . . . or, a gay voyage to the Promised Land." The satirical magazine *Szpilki* (Pins) featured cartoons of "everyday life in Madagascar" superimposed on a map of the island drawn to resemble a bearded big-nosed Jew. And cabaret performers sang a popular Polish satiric number, "Madagascar;" whose lyrics include the lines: "Oy, Madagascar! / beloved country, / long live the dark continent!" In France, a Jewish newspaper published a cartoon depicting an evacuee—a caftan-clad hook-nosed Jew from Kishinev—surrounded by half-naked natives wielding spears. An article decorated with swastikas that appeared in a pro-Nazi Arab nationalist magazine advocated Madagascar as a national home for Jews, Jehovah's Witnesses, nudists, Marxists, and jazz musicians. (Rovner 2009, 136)

An expedition considering the question was dismayed by the climate and mosquito-filled swamps, as well as the cost of resettlement. Hitler, meanwhile, took up the plan, proposing a Jewish "reservation" there, with the British fleet forced to transport refugees from Europe. Adolf Eichmann submitted his "Madagaskar Projekt" in 1940 (Rovner 143). Once the Jews were interned on the island, out of the world's sight, death camps would have been possible. However, the plan came to nothing before the British took over Madagascar in 1942.

Published in 1946, Jacob Weinshall's *HaYehudi HaAchron: Sipur* [The Last Jew: A Story] set the tone for much that was to follow in Hebrew-language alternate histories. The novel depicts the last remaining Jew, stranded in Madagascar. He's the lone survivor in a world run by Nazis whose plan to pull the moon closer so that they may colonize it ultimately fails. Some Hebrew readers consider "The Last Jew" to be the first literary work to imagine a Nazi victory, now a staple plot in the alternate history genre.

LITERATURE IN PALESTINE

The *yishuv* (Jewish settlement), influenced by rising Zionism and violence against Jews, began under Ottoman rule (1905–1917) and then continued through the British mandate after World War I (1917–1948). Those immigrants who had imagined the paradise of milk and honey were shocked to find malaria-riddled swamps and hot, barren landscapes. Even as early writers sometimes described the land realistically, they hoped that a new, tougher kind of Jew would grow up in the land. "Early Zionism conjured a vision of the emancipated Jew striding over his regained homeland, a reinvigorated— male—Jewish body dominating a newly liberated Jewish land" (Levinson 2013, 69).

Soon the Jews came fleeing Eastern Europe, communists who wrote social realism. With masses of immigrants, there was a hesitation to welcome strange visitors. The locals didn't want Jewish literature, while the immigrants were so focused on survival that speculative fiction, especially utopian, didn't fit.

Actual settlement of the land of Israel replaced the yearning for it, dislodging the primacy of the written word as the predominant grounding of a universal Jewish home. This altered condition, the movement from exile to corporeal home, is the background for the imagination of these writers. They inhabit a modern nation-state, though one still viewed by many as the alleged special manifestation of holiness longed for in the ancient texts. Their novels suggest the need for modified narratives, challenging long-held assumptions of what "coming home" means. (Levinson 95)

Nonetheless, fantasy found a niche, generally as social allegory. A series of very popular Tarzan comics were published in Israel from the thirties to the seventies, with a hundred original adventures. Tarzan was shown helping the Jewish illegal immigration to Palestine at the time of the British mandate, for which his fellow British threw him into prison. On another occasion he singlehandedly broke the Egyptian blockade at Suez, and at others, he stopped Nazi-aided Egyptian schemes to conquer Africa and the world. Since the new Israelis, once rather insular Europeans, were trying to forge relationships with their neighbors, they were especially intrigued by stories of Africa. Tarzan stories were their way of building fictional bridges.

Levin Kipnis (1894–1990) emigrated from Ukraine and wrote over 800 Hebrew stories and 600 poems for children. He also edited and wrote a 100 books, collections, and textbooks. The picture books include animal stories, Jewish culture, and lots of holiday learning. He taught at the Levinsky Teachers' College in Tel Aviv, wrote plays and helped found a children's theater, which he managed for twenty-five years. His story "Children of the Field" ([1961] 2020) pictures a new type of liberated child settling Israel. As it begins, "Who has ever seen or heard of such a thing: children sprouting out of the earth like grass in a field?" (40). In this magical scene, birds, butterflies, and angels fly about, blessing them. The Passover story is retold in a paradise of apple trees, which adopt and hide the Jewish babies from Pharaoh. When spring comes, the children blossom from the ground, so that Moses can lead them to a new land. As the sun shines brightly on them, "They began to grow bigger and taller . . . tall and handsome as date palms, strong and brave—a large army of heroes standing at the ready" (44). These are "free children" who have never known slavery, ready to found a new country. As such, it's the dream of the author, raised in exile, that the next generation will gather joyously in Israel. Kipnis wrote this story post-Holocaust, returning to his native Yiddish for this fantasy of freedom. Still, it invokes older themes, that of the children in diaspora seeking a homeland.

While thirties America was beginning science fiction's golden age, the literature of what would be Israel was more influenced by the older gothic works they were receiving. Ya'akov Shteinberg, who emigrated from Warsaw in 1914, wrote in Ashkenazi Hebrew and produced striking stories including "Ha-iveret" (The Blind Woman, 1923). The heroine's mother marries Hana to a mystery man, as her blindness makes her undesirable. Trapped in a marriage with all the trappings of the female gothic, "Hana feels her mysterious husband's beard while he sleeps, slithers across the floor to investigate his boots, listens to his gait as he walks—all to pick up subtle clues about who he really is and what he really does." The sounds are so strange that she wonders if it's not a Jewish house. When her baby daughter dies of diphtheria, the distraught mother reaches into the crib to touch her, only to find it empty. As the story ends, she runs outside for the first time, only discover endless gravestones and realize that she's married the gravedigger.

Dvora Baron's "Shifra" (1927) has a young widow reluctantly leave her baby to be a wet nurse for a rich family. It's a fine house, but the constant observation reminds her of a hospital. Further, the situation deteriorates, and she manages to nurse the baby only once before breaking out in sobs, as the baby reminds her of a vampire or doppelganger of her own beloved child. "A tiny creature was brought to her chest, who fell upon her with a drooling mouth, a strange heat, and a new thirst she had never experienced—the thirst of a bloodsucking leech" (72). She's quickly fired and left to find her own way home. As she walks, she stops and falls asleep by a bridge, where she dreams of her beloved, deceased husband. When she is found frozen, the brilliance her blue eyes had lost in life is now restored in death. They are as bright as eyes that never held a tear—all her suffering has vanished.

Both these stories explore the female gothic—particularly the women's powerlessness in a system where their only value lies in being beautiful wives or nurturing mothers. This lack of choice drives them to despair and loss as the world oppresses them.

Other strikingly gothic stories include "Yatom ve-almana" (An Orphan and a Widow, 1931); "Ha-yalda ha-meta" (The Dead Girl, 1932, 1935); "Kol ha-em" (The Mother's Voice, 1941); "Ha-lev ve-ha-einayim" (Heart and Eyes, 1943); "Hupat dodim" (The Bridal Canopy, 1931), originally published in 1913 as "Ha-hupa ha-shehora" (The Black Bridal Canopy). In these, the Jewish world of the past is filled with gothic tropes specifically blended with Jewish theology: a Jewish girl rises from the grave to fulfill Jewish laws, an orphan's corpse prays with other departed souls in the great synagogue, a Polish king's Jewish wife wanders restlessly after death. "Far from posing a challenge to the 'portrayal of a traditional Jewish milieu,' the gothic mode in these stories intensifies their Jewish mores, offering concrete manifestations of otherwise abstract Judaic notions such as *ha-olam ha-ba* (the world to come), *tohara* (purity), and *galut* (exile)" (Grumberg 43).

Shmuel Yosef Czaczkes, better known as S. Y. Agnon, was born in 1888 in Buczacz in eastern Galicia (now Buchach, Ukraine). He was tutored in German as a child, though Yiddish was his birth tongue and he was skilled in Hebrew and Aramaic. While his father was Hassidic, his mother was descended from *mitnagdim*, rationalist doubters of the ecstatic tradition of religious Judaism, a split that came to define his life. Further, his stories of being born on the Ninth of Av, a traditional day of mourning, link him with sadness. He moved to Palestine in 1907 and lived in the Jerusalem neighborhood of Talpiot from 1924 until his death in 1970; Agnon shared the Nobel Prize in Literature with Nelly Sachs in 1966. His pen name derives from *agunah*, "anchored," referring legally to a "forsaken wife," but symbolically resonating with his ties to his country.

Like Singer and Aleichem, Agnon wrote several stories that cross over into parable and even fantasy. In "Three Stories: Fable of the Goat" (1966), an old man's goat disappears and returns with milk "whose taste was as the taste of Eden." His son ties a cord to her tail and follows her to a beautiful land. "When they emerged from the cave, the youth saw lofty mountains, and hills full of the choicest fruit, and a fountain of living waters that flowed down from the mountains; and the wind wafted all manner of perfumes." This is Israel, reached in a sweet portal fantasy. He writes a note to his father, enjoining him to come. The father sees the goat return without his son, and, in grief and rage, butchers the animal. Only later does he find the message. At this point, the pathway—and perhaps the bond between the father and son—is lost forever. The father cries, "*Vay! Vay!* Woe to the man who robs himself of his own good fortune, and woe to the man who requites good with evil!" He mourns and refuses to be comforted, saying, "Woe to me, for I could have gone up to the Land of Israel in one bound, and now I must suffer out my days in this exile!"

Of course, Jews have long identified with the small sacrificial goat, so vulnerable and prone to literal scapegoating. In a scene rich with symbolism, the son urges the father to follow the cord in a moment of faith—if he does, the miraculous passage will guide him to a paradise-filled land much as Israel of the Bible is depicted. However, the father is spiritually weak and fails the test. In fact, his lack of faith makes him slay his only hope of redemption and he is condemned to exile forever. Since the Torah is also described in terms of milk and honey, this parable could be read as the need to have faith in the Torah, not only in family, miracles, and making Aliyah.

Agnon's *A Guest for the Night* ([1939] 1968), echoes some of these themes in a darker time—the protagonist returns to his Galician town from the Land of Israel hoping to find some of the culture he has left behind. However, he realizes that the townsfolk there lack such a magical passage to safety. At the same time, those in Israel lacked a path back to their birthplace in the Diaspora, especially as the Holocaust destroyed those communities forever. The narrator rescues the key to the Beit Midrash, but nothing more. It should be added that the titular phrase has multiple symbolic meanings, as Jeremiah used it to describe the return to Zion, while it also references Jews' rootlessness and desperation for a homeland. Meanwhile, Agnon, like his protagonist, sees himself as "the traditional modernist, transient native, artistic bourgeois, and sovereign subject of the Jewish God" (Wisse 2000, 181).

Agnon's *In the Heart of the Seas* (1947) is an epic pilgrimage, with events edging on the fantastical. Several rabbis set out for Israel. On the way, they meet a discerning gabbi, who calls them each to read Torah without needing to ask their names. After, he tells them news of their family and friends. On another adventure, they meet a man who had said "There is as much chance for the Messiah to come as there is for hair to grow on the palm of my hand" and then it did! (48). As the rabbis travel, they continue praying to the Lord for protection, which is granted many times along their journey. On one occasion, beautiful music comes out of the sea to show God's blessing on them. They finally reach Jerusalem, where the entire community welcomes them. This is a place of peace and beauty where even the blessed dead return every Shabbat to study and teach. With this, Agnon reveals the beauty of reaching the Promised Land.

In 1951, Agnon wrote a tragically lyrical post-Holocaust story tied into expressionist dreams, called "At the Outset of the Day" ([1951] 1975). Carrying his little daughter from their burned home, the narrator reaches the city and its Great Synagogue on Yom Kippur. He comforts her with the alphabet. "Even as I stood there speaking of the power of the letters, a breeze swept through the courtyard and pushed the memorial candle against my daughter" (220). He tears off the burning garment, leaving her naked. He goes to his old friend Reb Alter's house and finds a small service there. One of the old people tells him, "You are looking at our torn clothing. It is enough that creatures like us still have flesh on our bones" (222). Even as his mind wanders, thinking of the soul as caught between a young girl and an old woman (suggesting the child symbolizes his innocence, occasionally marred with grief), he begs the servicegoers for clothing for his daughter and finds none. "How great was the sadness that enveloped me at that moment, the outset of the holy festival whose joy has no parallel all the year. But now there was no joy and no sign of joy, only pain and anguish" (222). Nonetheless, as they stand together in the courtyard, the Lord guides them to a transcendent service, emphasizing the still-living comfort of God and prayer. His soul wraps itself up within him, finding garments at last.

Chapter 8

Fighting Hitler Onscreen

Marxes, Stooges, and More

THE FILM INDUSTRY

Asimov explains matter-of-factly of the thirties, "I also knew that vast areas of American society were closed to me because I was Jewish, but that was true in every Christian society in the world for two thousand years" (1994, 19). With many professions shut in this era of discrimination, Jews fled to new mediums—comics and television. Within three decades after the mass migration of the 1880s, Jews had transitioned mostly out of the working class. Jews entered the garment industry in droves as well as the revitalized one of motion pictures—now with sound. Just before the thirties, studios were springing up in Southern California, so much that Los Angeles emerged as the nation's fourth largest city and a major Jewish center.

Jews in film go back to Edison one-reelers, as 1903's *Arabian Jewish Dance* and *A Jewish Dance at Jerusalem* recorded Hassidic Jews dancing (Erens 1984, 29). Early classics adaptations including *The Merchant of Venice*, *Oliver Twist*, and *Trilby* were mostly released by the non-Jewish-headed studios and for the most part they left the stereotypes suggestive rather than spelled out. The silent melodramas offered two futuristic stories with Jewish characters—*Levitsky Sees the Parade* (1909, Imp) dreams of a future in which all the ethnic groups "look like regular George Sidney Hebrews" (quoted in Erens 1984, 32). *The Airship or One Hundred Years Hence* (1908, Vitagraph) is more problematic. An identifiably Jewish pawnbroker is pelted by the airship passengers above with vegetables as they laugh. He glares at them and then goes to open his business. A man arrives and pawns a pair of wings. Trying them on, the pawnbroker flies toward the airship. However, the air-cycle cop pursues and clubs him. He tumbles into the ocean where he's swallowed by a fish and finally rescued by fishermen.

It's not just a story of stereotypes but one that models beating and persecuting Jews with no consequences for the perpetrators, while the pawnbroker suffers over and over.

A few more positive Jewish works soon appeared. D. W. Griffith, credited with having made the first Hollywood motion picture in 1910, is more famous for his popular epic *Intolerance* (1916), which confronted anti-Semitism (and then for the notorious *Birth of a Nation*). After this, Warner Brothers directly explored assimilation in the first "talkie," *The Jazz Singer* (1927). Other films of the time had significant Jewish presences: In *The Ten Commandments* (1923) and *The King of Kings* (1927), director Cecil B. DeMille used Orthodox Jews as extras, believing that their "deep feeling of the significance of the Exodus" and their "appearance" would lend authenticity (Wright). At the same time, a repeat message of Hollywood moguls getting their comeuppance, exaggerated for humor, allowed even the producers to get in on the fun. Another famous avant-garde film, crowded with experimental techniques of light and fades, is the silent film *Lot in Sodom* (1933), directed by James Sibley Watson and Melville Webber. It begins with underdressed men cavorting in balletic movements that soon turn orgiastic. Lot, meanwhile, is sequestered at home praying by candlelight with long beard and skullcap. An angel, highlighted with more special effects, appears and guides him out, even as the film ends spectacularly with Sodom's destruction. These Bible stories brought Jews to the fantasy screen, though in rather conventional roles.

By the thirties, six of the eight major studios were managed by Jews: Harry Cohn (of Columbia), William Fox (born Vilmos Fried, of Fox Pictures, later merged into Twentieth Century Fox), Samuel Goldwyn (born Schmuel Gelbfisz, of Goldwyn Pictures, later merged into Metro-Goldwyn-Mayer), Carl Laemmle (of Universal), Louis B. Mayer (of Metro), Jack and Harry Warner (born Wonskolaser, two of the Warner brothers), and Adolph Zukor (of Paramount). Many more Jews were actors but also producers, managers, assistants, agents, and lawyers. Though Jews were about 3 percent of the American population, Hollywood Jews "cut their lives to the contours of their environment and discarded the rest, because only here were they in complete command. The studios were repositories of dreams and hopes, security and power. If one could not control the world of real power and influence, the august world of big business, finance, and politics, through the studio one could create a whole fictive universe that one could control" (Galber 2006, 189).

At the time, stock characters, often racist, worked as shorthand for much of storytelling. With laughable immigrants onscreen, set against rising fascism in the real world, it's no wonder Jews chose to de-emphasize their movie presence. Only as the stories grew more sophisticated did the melodrama decrease:

Many factors, then, influence the changing fortunes of Judaism vis-à-vis the cinema. The ideas and intentions of filmmakers form one element of a complex whole, alongside regulatory, industrial, and artistic concerns. For example, the decline in openly antisemitic treatments of Judaism in the early 1930s is partly a function of changing technologies, and the shifts in narrative and visual idiom that accompanied them. Lacking both verbal soundtrack and developed conventions of continuity editing as means to anchor images and render them intelligible for viewers, very early films relied on strong visual formulae (cues in the form of costume, gesture, physiology) to suggest links between activity, character, and attitude (Ray 2001:24). Caricatures of Judaism existed alongside similarly stock images of other religions. The advent of sound on film and other techniques saw these conventions weaken, but not disappear. (Wright 2010)

The tiny Jewish American population hesitated to make waves or emphasize difference. During the Great Depression, Jews in the film industry were attacked by the political right for "adolescent entertainment" and "immoral practices." This reached the point at which, in two 1937 films, *The Life of Emile Zola*, about the Dreyfus affair, and *They Won't Forget*, based on the Leo Frank lynching, the word "Jew" is left unsaid. After this, the studios, looking for broad appeal, used The Production Code Administration's forbiddance of offensive film depictions to avoid putting clichéd Jewish characters onscreen.

Trying to divorce itself from the racist stereotypes, early American cinema mostly hid Jewish identity, avoiding onscreen representations. Besides Silent Era "ghetto films" depicting Jewish families assimilating, such as "Humoresque" (1920), "His People" (1925), and "The Cohens and the Kellys" (1926), Hollywood avoided clearly identifiable Jewish characters, themes and issues. Soon enough, Jewish humor made its way onscreen but left the explicitly Jewish references far far off.

From the earliest years of vaudeville—Weber and Fields, Dutch jokes [a euphemism for deutch, in turn itself a euphemism for Yiddish], slapstick; to silent movies, Ben Blue, Charlie Chaplin; to early radio, Ed Wynn the Fire Chief, Eddie Cantor, Jack Benny; to talkies, the Brothers Marx and Ritz; to burlesque, Phil Silvers, Red Buttons; to Broadway revues, Bert Lahr, Willie Howard, Phil Silvers, Zero Mostel; to night clubs, Joe E. Lewis, Henny Youngman, Buddy Hackett; to the great days of television, Milton Berle, Sid Caesar; to the cabaret theater, Nichols and May; to the sick comics, Lenny Bruce, Mort Sahl, Shelly Berman, Woody Allen—they've all been Jews. Yet until the 1950s there was never any Jewish humor in the American media. So many Jewish comics and never a Jewish joke! Far from exploiting their identity as Jews, most comics did everything in their power to disguise the fact that they were Jewish. They changed their names from David Kaminski to Danny Kaye, from Joey Gottlieb to Joey Bishop, from Jerome Levitch to Jerry Lewis, from Murray Janofsky to Jan Murray. (Goldman 1987, 80)

There are many theories about why Jews and comedy are so closely linked. Milton Berle commented that one needn't look any further than the Jews for proof that humor can insulate almost an entire people against everything life can dump on them (Samberg 31). Erens (1984) sees Jewish humor as the only alternative to pessimism and a defense which helped the Jews maintain dignity (8).

Jewish comedy arrived separate from films, most memorably in the resorts and hotels of the Catskill Mountains. Around the turn of the century, the Jewish dairy farms there took in boarders to escape the city's summer heat, and business boomed. The resorts were English-speaking but heavy with Yiddish, a place where everyone was culturally Jewish with religious holidays celebrated and kosher meals served. While entertainment began as impromptu sing-alongs and skits, by the twenties, the more formal hotels boasted a large social staff headed by the *tummler*, a comedic master of ceremonies, who also clowned around the resort pulling pranks. In the 1930s, *Variety* nicknamed this the "Borsht Belt," as comedians performed in the all-Jewish space. They took traditions from the *badchens* or wedding jesters of Eastern Europe while adding an American stand-up style. Performers who began there include Jerry Lewis, Danny Kaye, Sid Caesar, Red Buttons, Micky Katz, Phil Silvers, and Jackie Mason—who later took their acts to the big screen. Jewish underdog humor became famous, and some of the most beloved creators, like the Marx Brothers and Three Stooges, satirized society with dystopias and other dips into the speculative. Both comedians and creators of speculative fiction did well with an outsider's perspective, taking control of their marginalization by using it to make pointed entertainment.

THE MARX BROTHERS

The Marx Brothers—Groucho, Harpo, Chico, and Zeppo—were a staple of Jewish comedy, straight from the New York musical and vaudeville tradition. Zeppo most often played the "straight man." By contrast, "Harpo's angelic silence and Chico's Italianate malaprop puns balanced Groucho's sophistic weeds" (Mast 1987, 127). They threw in subtle Jewish jokes, riffing on stars like Sophie Tucker, Irving Berlin, and Eddie Cantor in their first film, *The Cocoanuts* (1929). In *Animal Crackers,* Groucho introduces a program as coming from "the House of David," though he might have used any ethnicity there, and indeed, he and his brothers played unassimilated immigrants of no particular ethnicity (save Chico's Italian stereotype). These second-generation American actors offer fantasies of the new immigrant predicament in the United States—finding acceptance while striking it rich. As Mark Winokur (1985, 161) adds in his essay on immigrant humor, "This anarchy is the voiced solution to the immigrant dilemma of having to choose between the patent culture and the adoptive culture." While the characters don't label themselves Jewish, their Lower East Side street smarts and spirit of debate seem quite recognizable. Highbrow locations like the opera and university, where they clearly don't fit in, stress their outsider status, as do moments where they're literal stowaways in *A Night at the Opera* and *Monkey Business*.

Fantasy and science fiction don't show up much in their beloved comedy films. *A Night at the Opera*, *A Day at the Races*, *Room Service*, *At the Circus*, *Go West*, *The Big Store*, *Horse Feathers*, and *The Cocoanuts* all have the brothers each playing his own ridiculous stock character as they try to get rich in an America filled with opportunity. *Animal Crackers* is a tad more fantastical with an African explorer and a stolen painting mystery, while *Love Happy* features diamond smugglers and a hypnotist, but both are still set close to the everyday.

Still, there's a whimsical trace of fantasy through it all—not only that the underdogs triumph in fairytale style, but that Harpo occasionally disobeys the laws of physics for a laugh. He runs up a backdrop in *A Night at the Opera*, flies on roller skates in *The Big Store*, and occasionally pulls brimming cups of coffee or lit candles out of his coat. While they all have trickster powers, Harpo's cross over into delightful magic. Mute Harpo functions as a real underdog within the stories, often cruelly scapegoated and desperate for rescue. "In class terms, Harpo is similar to Chico. They often operate as partners. Yet his familiarity is different from Chico's. He is the neighborhood crazy man or looney, so off-center that outrageous behavior becomes the norm rather than exception," Leonard M. Helfgott writes in "Groucho, Harpo, Chico, and Karl: Immigrant Humor and the Depression" (2011, 112). This outrageousness, of course, is a source of freedom. Because he is a madman, he can do anything he wishes, including cutting people's neckties and hair. On the bottom of the social ladder as he is, he can tear down those of higher status, to the audience's applause.

Of course, *Duck Soup* (McCarey 1933), the famous anti-dictator, anti-Fascist film, might be described as a dystopia or alt-history. World War II was as yet unimagined, with the world still recovering from World War I. Freedonia's new president, Rufus T. Firefly, declares war on neighboring Sylvania after insulting himself and blaming it on the other country's ambassador. In this, the characters hide their nature as the dispossessed ethnics by claiming great authority. As such, they subtly reveal dictators' own precariousness.

Snarking at the cruelty and hypocrisy of dictators, the *Freedonia Gazette* is subtitled "an independent newspaper published in the interests of the people." Articles are headlined, "Foreign Radio Artists Arrive," "Mayor and Aide in Train Wreck," and "Woman Driver Gets Jail Term." In one moment, Chico adds a greasepaint moustache to resemble Firefly; however, his applying it at Firefly's desk suggests the man wears a similarly fake moustache—he is as fake as his ideals. "Who you gonna believe, me or your own eyes?" Chicolini quips, setting the stage for many political satires that followed.

Meanwhile, Firefly's running joke is that he's rarely more principled than the villains. He shoots his own men, offers to bribe his secretary (Zeppo) to keep this secret, and then takes back the money. His one redeeming feature is his total straightforwardness. Firefly and his people adore war for its own sake, without any pesky moral hang-ups. It's nationalism unbounded by logic. Even as Groucho switches from World War I uniforms to Confederate ones to Davy Crocket and Boy Scout suits, the system is beyond chaos—war for war's sake with no end in sight. While he's unusually powerful as a dictator, he's playing roughly the same character as usual—only more successful.

> Groucho's character served as the hinge on which the Marx Brothers films relied. He connects the world of the ghetto to the outside world of wealth and privilege. He is literate and knows the secrets of both the realm of poverty and the realm of wealth. More or less educated, he is a spieler, a con man, a charmer, a healer, a bit of a gonnif [thief], and, in his own words, a schnorrer [freeloader]. Upwardly mobile, he holds the life of the rich in contempt. He is incredibly clever with words and familiar both with the wordplay of the ghetto and the banter of elites. He often disdains his brothers' characters but invariably sides with them and others of their class against those more privileged. The dislocated intellectual portrayed by Groucho has a long history in ghetto life and has even assumed a centrality in the modern definition of the Jew as wandering or rootless. (Helfgott 2011, 112)

The 1933 movie opened ten months after Hitler's appointment as chancellor of Germany. It was controversial for its time. Benito Mussolini banned it from Italian screens, which delighted the brothers. Hitler likewise banned all the Marx Brothers' films. After this, the team continued fighting the system through satire. The Marx Brothers were particularly subversive as they delighted in demonstrating the fragility and preposterousness of the social order. Mad juxtapositions like the reverent and philosophical jar against popular culture and everyday needs and desires. Shechner (1987, 151) describes "The mayhem of madcap juxtapositions, one frame of reference (popular, modern, awe-struck) bombarding the other (classical, philosophical, reverent) with matzoballs." They somehow always beat the upper-class snobs, striking a blow for the little guy.

A Night in Casablanca (Mayo 1946) has the brothers encountering a Nazi war criminal. As Stubel murders all the hotel managers to try to retrieve the stolen art he's hidden, Groucho takes the manager job. ("Well, gentlemen, I'm a different man behind a desk—as any stenographer can tell you. But, uh, what I want to know, is why they're burying the last manager. And don't tell me it's because he's dead.") Groucho's name this time, Ronald Kornblow, is suggestively Jewish, and at last he battles a Nazi onscreen. Chico plays his bodyguard and Harpo, Stubel's valet. After driving Stubel mad with their shenanigans, they crash his plane into a police station, expose him, and have him arrested. They then chase the Nazi femme fatale off the stage. In itself, this is the ultimate fantasy—revenge for the Jews.

In 1964, Groucho went to East Berlin and visited his mother's birth village of Dornum. When he discovered that all the Jewish graves there had been obliterated by the Nazis, Groucho hired a car, and told the driver to take him, his producer, and their daughters to the bunker where Hitler had committed suicide or as near as possible. There, Groucho actually launched himself, unsmiling, into a frenetic Charleston and danced on Hitler's grave.

The Marx Brothers' final film appearance, meanwhile, did cross over into speculative fiction. In *The Story of Mankind* (Allen 1957), scientists have developed the Super H-bomb, capable of wiping out humanity. A tribunal in The Great Court of Outer Space considers whether to let mankind destroy itself. The devil plays prosecutor, while the Spirit of Man defends humanity. Their evidence comes from a tour of history (with plenty of stock footage from previously made Hollywood films). In this journey, Groucho plays Peter Minuit and swindles the Native Americans out of Manhattan. Harpo gets bonked with an apple as Sir Isaac Newton and then uses his harp as an apple slicer. Chico plays Columbus's companion. With this whirlwind tour, they emphasize their true place in history.

THE THREE STOOGES

The other great comedy team of the era, the Three Stooges, drops plenty of Yiddish phrases into their dialogue, and break out into Klezmer-style dancing when one injures his foot. While the characters' actual ethnicity is never mentioned, their jobs, different in each episode, are clearly those of working-class new immigrants. Jewish humor in mid-twentieth-century America "was the plaint of a people who were highly successful in countless ways, yet who still felt inferior, tainted, outcast; a people who needed some magic device of self-assertion and self-aggrandizement" (Goldman 1987, 83). Certainly, the

Stooges always play the people at the bottom of the culture, financially and otherwise, while the humor derives from their Jewish vaudeville training in the Catskills, where the other two met violin player Larry Fine.

In the thirties, American film was dependent on an overseas market, and the German film industry had forbidden depictions of Hitler. With Hollywood Jews worried about accusations of propelling America into World War II with their propaganda, "Hollywood discreetly avoided making overtly anti-Nazi films, as they were reticent to fan the flames of domestic anti-Semitism or exacerbate problems for Jews in Germany," explains critic Lynn Rapaport (2006, 6). Charlie Chaplin's *The Great Dictator* was an exception, though it met with heavy resistance from studios. Meanwhile, Jewish producers, accused of dragging America into a conflict to save themselves and their loved ones in Europe, treaded lightly in lambasting Hitler. Production Code in Hollywood suppressed all references to Nazism.

Still, the Stooges' popularity let them bend the rules. For twenty-four years, beginning in 1934, the Stooges made eight "shorts" each year, resulting in 190 short pieces. They made five specifically anti-Nazi shorts, with two released before America entered the war—beating Chaplin's *The Great Dictator* by nine months. "You Nazty Spy!" (Jan 1940) punned on nasty with a country motto of Moronika for Morons. The Stooges mock the goosestep, the gestapo, and the swastika (made of crisscrossed snakes in their version). The story kicks off with dictator Moe Hailstone wearing a stunted moustache he calls his "personality" beside Curly and Larry as Goebbels and Göring. Moe takes the dictator job, assured that it's simple: "make speeches to the people, promising them plenty. He gives them nothing and then he takes everything." At last, his cruelties end when he and his pals are eaten by lions. The sequel, "I'll Never Heil Again" (1941), takes a similar angle (with the addition of Mussolini) as the dictators play football with a globe and end up with their three heads mounted on a wall. Both were directed by Jules White, another Jew all too aware of what was at stake. The Stooges were largely apolitical, save for lambasting the upper class, but Hitler was another matter.

These two films are more momentous culturally because of the early dates than the three in 1943: "Back from the Front," "They Stooge to Conga," and "Higher than a Kite," which have them defeating a Nazi sub, discovering spies, and otherwise triumphing in war through general ineptness. In a particularly silly moment, "Higher than a Kite" has the Nazis freezing and saluting each time they see the Hitler photo affixed to Curly's rear end (Lord 1943). In "Back from the Front," Moe does his Hitler impression and orders Nazi officers to blow out their own brains. "But, mein fuhrer, we are Nazis, we have no brains," the captain protests (White 1943).

After these parodies in which the Stooges claimed their Jewish solidarity much more pointedly than the Marx Brothers did, the trio went on to make specifically science fiction and fantasy films, especially *Have Rocket, Will Travel* (1959), *Snow White and the Three Stooges* (1961), *The Three Stooges Meet Hercules* (1962), and *The Three Stooges in Orbit* (1963).

The Stooges' first full-length film, *Have Rocket, Will Travel* (Rich 1959) sends them into space—complete with a sing-along. As janitors, they break into the space agency at night to concoct their own special brand of fuel. They wreck the lab, of course, hide in the rocket, and accidentally launch themselves. More silliness follows, now with a lack of gravity. "Think of it, fellas, the first space travelers. Us three," Moe notes. When they reach Venus, they discover breathable air. "Looks like Death Valley." In quick succession, they also encounter a giant flame-breathing spider, a distressed unicorn, and a talking speeder car that carries them around. They reach a futuristic lab with a many-armed talking robot with great powers. "I shall prove that you are 'little men'," it says, responding to their protest, and shrinks them to tiny size. Of course, that's the point of the story—that the space heroes are actually inept janitors, the working-class heroes who only take the astronauts' place by accident. In context, the film reflects the excitement of the space race and the celebrity status of astronauts (as they end with a characteristically clumsy party and ticker tape parade).

Snow White and the Three Stooges (Tashlin and Lang 1961) is played a little too straight, with more emphasis on the romantic fairytale and less on the Stooges' shenanigans. Olympic skater Carol Heiss stars (complete with skating scenes to showcase her talent). Meanwhile, the Stooges, travelling medicine show hawkers, have adopted an amnesiac boy, who becomes their far more talented fourth player Quatro. As he and Snow White fall in love, he's finally revealed to be the real prince charming. When he regains his memory, he organizes a revolution against the evil queen. With this, democracy, goodness, true love, and the Stooges save the kingdom. This time, the Stooges do slapstick in the background, as supportive rather than lead characters, emphasizing that the romantic and strongman leads are mainstream while Jews remain the ethnic sidekicks.

The Three Stooges Meet Hercules (Bernds 1962) blends sci-fi time travel and magical monsters of ancient Greece in a much goofier story. The Stooges begin in Ithaca, New York, working at Dimsel's Drug Store for a bullying womanizer. He's trying to date Diane, who in turn loves nerdy scientist Schuyler Davis, who is attempting to build a time machine. As usual, the Stooges support the central young couple and try to help their romance along. Amid the usual slapstick, the Stooges get the time machine working, and it whisks them and the couple back to ancient Greece during the reign of the lecherous King Oedious, Dimsel's ancestor. The King lusts after Diane and banishes Schuyler and the Stooges to the galleys. While they quest to restore the rightful King Ulysses to the throne, Schuyler gains self-confidence and manliness, as his rowing builds up his muscles and makes him stronger than Hercules. This is the metaphor of comics' Superman or Captain America, nerdy everyday men who have a superhero just waiting to emerge. Therefore, while Schuyler's character is not identified as Jewish, the story echoes popular metaphors of the time.

The Three Stooges in Orbit (Bernds 1963) is announced with a *Twilight-Zone*-style narration sequence that reaches out to existing science fiction fans, while space imagery fills the screen. As the pompous, rather Rod Serling-like narrator explains:

> No object in the endless sea of space has aroused man's curiosity . . . more than the planet Mars. In particular, the shape and form of Martian life. For centuries, astronomers have searched in vain . . . to solve this mystery. It has challenged the creativity of the world's greatest writers . . . and the imagination of its most gifted artists. Some envisioned Martians as huge, birdlike beasts. Others described fantastic serpents of incredible size . . . grotesque, tentacled creatures. Shapes, sizes and forms beyond man's wildest imagination. Animal, vegetable, mineral . . . even mechanical creatures of enormous destructive power. But all this is conjecture. At last, you will learn the simple truth about life on Mars. As Normandy Productions lights the fuse . . . that puts The Three Stooges in Orbit.

Kicked out of their hotel, the Stooges apply to stay with a nutty professor who shows off his outlandish inventions and then gives a speech that would tip off anyone but the Stooges: "It will be so nice to have earthlings in the house for a change. . . . I'm often bothered by a spy from outer space who's trying to steal my plans. A terrible-looking thing. Claws instead of hands, a hideous green face, sharp yellow fangs. Oh, the regular monster type." It appears and kidnaps Larry and then takes his place in the bed, and off they go.

The aliens are seeking to conquer earth, but, repelled by its popular culture, they decide to destroy it instead. With all the expected hijinks, the Stooges set off in the professor's flying submarine, engaging in aerial battles and saving the planet. This time, at last, they become the central heroes, though pointedly ridiculous ones. "If you can't lick 'em, join 'em," the alien leader concludes.

CHAPLIN'S GREAT DICTATOR

Charlie Chaplin was not Jewish, though his dark-featured, short immigrant tramp fit in so well with his Jewish competition that many believed he was. They saw this small outcast being persecuted unjustly by the authorities and cleverly preserving himself, an underdog anywhere he went. With this, he fit all the Jewish tropes of the shlemiel (a little man with no luck), and the luftmensch (the "man of air" who lives on dreams). His dancing and pantomime, his chaotic mockery of the establishment also felt tied to Jewish theater. "Above all, Chaplin achieved a subtle gender inversion through the graceful, almost balletic eluding of his macho tormentors. Jewish audiences recognized this physical portrayal from the Yiddish stage and read it as a visual metaphor for the disempowered Jew in a hostile world" (Pearse 2018). There are additional Jewish references in Chaplin's bag of tricks like skullcaps and Yiddish newspapers as props, and a scene in *The Vagabond* (1916) in which the Tramp sees a Jewish man eating pork at a buffet and helpfully changes the ham sign to beef.

At the same time, in his famous *The Great Dictator,* in which he lambasted Hitler, he played "Adenoid Hynkel, ruler of Tomainia," babbling speeches alongside Garbitsch (Goebbels), Herring (Göring), and Benzino Napaloni (Benito Mussolini). Playing Hynkel, he falls down the stairs and makes a ridiculous figure of himself. As talkies rose to prominence, this contribution came at a crucial time:

> Hitler, for his part, was known for his speeches, but looked ridiculous in silent newsreels, where his exaggerated mannerisms played more to laughs. When Germans could finally see *and* hear him at the same time, Hitler's onscreen presence had a powerful—and to some, chilling—effect. *The Great Dictator,* which would be the first time audiences heard the Little Tramp speak, toys with this idea: Hynkel's voice, heard over loudspeakers in ghetto streets, is terrifying, though it speaks nonsense. When you actually see him, with Chaplin going to town with his wild gestures, the effect is more comical. The film both ridicules the Hitler figure and explores just what it is that makes him so compelling and frightening. The film reclaims that power at the end, however, as Hynkel's speeches give way to an infamously earnest monologue from the writer-director-star, looking straight into the camera and effectively speaking as himself, proclaiming that "the misery that is now upon us is but the passing of greed—the bitterness of men who fear the way of human progress." It's a speech that's less a rallying cry for war than an appeal for universal brotherhood. Nevertheless, at the time the film came out, the speech was heralded by many as a plea for U.S. intervention in Europe. (Ebiri 2014)

"Chaplin had already run afoul of the Nazis, who thought (erroneously) that he was Jewish, banned his films, and even called him 'a disgusting Jewish acrobat' in one of their publications. When he visited Berlin in 1931 to promote *City Lights*—well before Hitler's rise to the chancellorship in 1933—pro-Nazi media had effectively run him out of town" (Ebiri 2014). Chaplin planned and shot the film in 1939–1940, as France fell to invasion. Chaplin was so determined, that he funded the film himself, amid massive threats of censorship from Germany, from England which was still practicing appeasement, and from anti-war movements in the United States. Chaplin himself tells it in his autobiography:

> Half-way through making *The Great Dictator* I began receiving alarming messages from United Artists. They had been advised by the Hays Office that I would run into censorship trouble. Also the English office was very concerned about an anti-Hitler picture and doubted whether it could be shown in Britain. But I was determined to go ahead, for Hitler must be laughed at. . . . More worrying letters came from the New York office imploring me not to make the film, declaring it would never be shown in England or America. But I was determined to make it, even if I had to hire halls myself to show it. . . . Before I had finished *The Dictator* England declared war on the Nazis. . . . Then suddenly the holocaust began: the break-through in Belgium, the collapse of the Maginot Line, the stark and ghastly fact of Dunkirk—and France was occupied. The news was growing gloomier. England was fighting with her back to the wall. Now our New York office was wiring frantically; "Hurry up with your film, everyone is waiting for it." (quoted in Ebiri 2014)

While American politicians and filmmakers worried about the film's provocative, even possibly pro-communist message and the American Jewish establishment feared that an anti-Hitler film might worsen matters for Jews in Europe, Chaplin stepped forward. "Chaplin's own response—'How can they get worse?'—indicates his own fearlessness. For the Jew in America, it was as if, as Stanley Kauffmann put it, 'a David had arisen—a comic David—to fight Goliath!'" (Pearse 2018).

Chaplin's other character in the film (an offshoot of the lovable tramp) is a German Jewish World War I veteran, now a barber confined to the ghetto. As he comically eludes the cops, Hynkel's voice is heard overhead, railing against the Jews. Ghetto conditions show the Nazis stealing food, breaking windows, and pelting a defiant young woman with tomatoes—cruel but rather sanitized. It's mentioned that the men have mostly been sent to concentration camps, with women and the elderly left in the ghetto. The people are being thrown in prison camps at a rate of thousands a day, as they protest "working hours, wage cuts, the synthetic food, the quality of the sawdust in the bread."

"What more do they want? It's from the finest lumber!" Hynkel demands.

Since his amnesia won't let him realize how much things have changed since he was so recently a respected German citizen, the barber demands Nazis stop painting his shop with graffiti and fights back with a paintbrush when one attacks him. He's shocked to find the police won't take his side. His applying civilized expectations of justice emphasize how immoral Nazi Germany has become. As anyone would be, the soft-spoken barber is utterly perplexed as the Nazis demand he shout slogans and use made-up terms like "Aryan."

Performing the story with American accents and hairstyles and descriptions of how the dictator will take over America and kill all the brunettes there emphasizes this as a conflict where America has a stake. When the romantic heroine, Hannah, sees the persecution let up slightly, she's overcome with joy. "How wonderful if they stopped hating us, if they let us go about our business like we used to. . . . Wouldn't it be wonderful if they'd let us live and be happy again?" she exclaims. However, the Jews' protector, Schultz, is sent to concentration camp himself (after an impassioned speech about how idiotic and destructive Hynkel's policies are). As the Nazis attack in an enormous, brutal mob, the Jews are depicted as ordinary, sympathetic men and women overcome by terror. By the end, Jews are being shot in the ghetto, while Hannah, who has escaped to the beautiful haven of Austria, screams with horror as the Nazis invade there—and brutally slap her in the face, into the bargain.

Chaplin said, "I made this film to show my unity with all the Jews of the world" (Pearse). While Chaplin understood the cruelty of the Third Reich, at the time of filming, he was ignorant of Hitler's intended mass murder. After World War II, Chaplin expressed some regret about treating the subject so lightly, telling interviewers that he might not have made it if he'd known the whole story.

At the climax, the barber, pretending to be Hitler, stands before the public and gives a poignant speech about caring for others. Lines like "I should like to help everyone: Jew, gentile, black man, white" specifically reach out to an American audience, preaching a world without prejudice. He pleads with soldiers in particular—"Don't hate. Only the unloved and the unnatural hate. Soldiers, don't fight for slavery, fight for liberty!" With this, he calls on the entire world to repudiate Hitler and his message. He insists, "Brutes have risen. But they lie! They do not fulfill that promise. They never will!" Some critics were highly uncomfortable with the tone shift from goofy humor to an appeal for peace and brotherhood, but the film certainly made its point.

DISNEY VERSUS FLEISHER

In the forties, two studios were at the forefront of competition for movie theater cartoons—one was owned by Jewish brothers Max and Dave Fleischer. Fleisher Studios developed rotoscoping and added backgrounds, refining the process. "The contrast between its style and that of its major competitor, the Disney studio, was clearly East Coast Jewish versus West Coast WASP" (Brod 2012, 72). The Fleisher cartoons were big-city raucous rather than sweet and juvenile. Their heroes were Betty Boop and Popeye, their animals scruffy and street-smart. (Mae Questel, who got her start in Jewish vaudeville and voiced both Betty Boop and Olive Oyl, loomed over Woody Allen as a giant Jewish mother in the film *New York Stories*.)

Boop began as a Jewish cartoon and a "Red Hot Mama" too. Aligned with [Fanny] Brice's girlish antics more than [Sophie] Tucker's adult humor, Betty Boop gave synthetic body to the voguish baby voice of Jewish actress Mae Questel, and her first cartoons were drawn against a neighborhood of Yiddish shops and immigrant personages. The embodiment of the Jewish "Ghetto Girl" stereotypes, Betty's naive discoveries were sexed up in gartered stockings and innuendo. In her 1934 animation "Red Hot Mama," drawn by Dave Fleisher, Betty inks out the bad little good girl. Her ventures in hell and its freezing over appear sympathetic as Betty's innocence wins out against all odds. As opposed to the vulgar frankness of Tucker's milieu and Brice's defunct femininity, Betty's charms feminize her as an idiot-savant who unknowingly happens upon her sexiness while relying on it to get her out of trouble. (Schwadron 2017, 60)

Jewish characters were rare but memorable. *Betty Boop's Ups and Downs* (1923) shows Betty losing her home to foreclosure even as all of the earth has been foreclosed on and gone up for sale. Saturn, a derby-wearing Hassidic Jew, wins and inherits the earth, so to speak. He takes the gravity with him, and the whole world is briefly sent topsy-turvy. In Betty Boop's "Stopping the Show" (1932), a poster of Fanny Brice's portrait comes to life as Brice asks Betty in her signature Yiddish accent to "maybe giv[e] out a little 'personation' of meeee, nooo?" In other cartoons, Betty experiments with the world of jazz and hula dancing on the South Sea. "This trend of trying on otherness as a fantasy act to put on and take off was hardly her invention. Still, it is important to recognize the ways Betty Boop could cartoon a cultural phenomenon in vogue by other Jewish female acts at the time, such that the very play with identities was a Jewish female comic tradition already taking shape" (Schwadron 2017, 61). Many Jewish comedians brought in impersonation, showing their flexibility in a shifting culture.

Another early Fleischer creation was Ko-Ko the Clown, who crawled out of the artist's inkwell to have adventures. It was quite metafictional, and thus reflective of its creators: As he knew he was a creation, Ko-Ko was always trying to escape or thwart the endless obstacles his creator made for him. This is quite suggestive of the Jewish struggle. "His relation to his creator was the classic Jewish comic response addressed to their Creator on being the 'chosen' people, given the history of persecution that seemed to accompany the honor: 'Thank you, really, but maybe you could choose somebody else once in a while?'" (Brod 2012, 73).

Other cartoons also shared the subtle Jewish sensibility. Bugs Bunny was created in the late 1930s by Leon Schlesinger Productions (later bought by Warner Brothers). Voiced by Mel Blanc and "modeled on the urban, ethnic, Brooklyn type" with some Bronx mixed in, Bugs has Jewish mannerisms, mimicry, voice, accent, and so on, as he outwits human bullies who are western and southern stereotypes. Because such types populated Barbra Streisand's youth, Bugs's street-lingo catchphrase, "What's up, Doc?" became the title of her screwball comedy film in 1972 (Abrams 2018, 205).

Back in the awkward early days of Disney with the painfully stereotyped crows of *Dumbo,* natives in *The Jungle Book,* or Indians of *Peter Pan,* Jews mostly avoided such treatment. Mark I. Pinsky points out in *The Gospel According to Disney* (2004):

> The one clearly Jewish character we've seen in a Disney picture—the Big Bad Wolf disguised as a hook-nosed, Yiddish-accented peddler in 1933's *The Three Little Pigs*—is problematic. When confronted about this, Walt's brother and partner, Roy Disney, protested, "We have a great many Jewish business associates and friends and certainly would avoid purposely demeaning the Jews or any other race or nationality." Sounds strangely familiar. (111)

The American Jewish Congress called it "vile" and "revolting" (Pinsky 111). After the Holocaust, the wolf was re-edited to become a Fuller Brush Man with an Irish accent, finding a different stereotype to exploit. There was also "The Opry House," during which Mickey Mouse dressed up and danced like a Hasidic Jew. Admittedly, such images were rare in the Disney universe, with other minorities getting a larger share of this treatment.

Douglas Brode in his *Multiculturalism and the Mouse* (2005) suggests that Mickey Mouse is meant to be Jewish much like the Stooges—"In early short subjects, he is always the immigrant-outsider, trying to win a place in society, often by working as a street peddler" (105). Some saw him as a tiny David battling massive Goliaths. "Hitler himself was horrified by the image and concept of Mickey, considering the Mouse to be the most degenerate piece of pro-Jewish propaganda ever to come out of America" (105–106). In his mind, Jews were vermin, and Disney was reclaiming and flipping this image into a positive light.

Early Disney feature films include Jewish author Felix Salten's *Bambi* (admittedly with the intolerance allegory removed) and also Salten's *The Hound of Florence,* formally credited as inspiring *The Shaggy Dog.* "This semi-autobiographical novel tells the story of an artist who must spend every other day in aristocratic society as a dog. A central theme of the novel (and needless to say entirely lost in the Disney films) is the outsider as abject insider" (Reitter 2014). Removing the messages weakens the texts, but they did go on to entertain children with their Jewish sensibility.

Mr. Disney created anti-Nazi films during the war, including *Education for Death: The Making of a Nazi* and *Der Fuehrer's Face*, originally titled *Donald Duck in Nutzi Land* (Kinney 1943). In the latter, Donald must eat stale bread with a single coffee bean and work his 48-hour shift on an assembly line, saluting whenever Hitler's portrait slides along. Thus, Hitler's treatment of his own people is satirized, but not his racism.

While there's mixed evidence of Disney's own beliefs, many of his actions are suggestive. Disney was a founding member of the Motion Picture Alliance for the Preservation of American Ideals, a known anti-Semitic group, and supported racist industry lobbying groups. He personally hosted Nazi filmmaker Leni Riefenstahl a month after Kristallnacht, and Riefenstahl even commented that it was "gratifying to learn how thoroughly proper Americans distance themselves from the smear campaigns of the Jews" (Beitler 2017). His pet project EPCOT was intended as a city of the future but a strikingly Fascist one with everyone renting from the government and fully employed, with no slums permitted. "Unions would be prohibited, democracy non-existent, and social security merely a laughable notion" (Beitler).

At best, Disney could be seen as a Nazi-sympathizer. Famed Disney animator Art Babbitt, who worked closely with Disney, once claimed—as quoted in Peter Fotis Kapnistos'[s] book *Hitler's Doubles*—that "[i]n the immediate years before we entered the War there was a small, but fiercely loyal, I suppose legal, following of the Nazi party. . . . There were open meetings, anybody could attend and I wanted to see what was going on myself. On more than one I occasion I observed Walt Disney and Gunther Lessing [Disney's lawyer] there, along with a lot of prominent Nazi-afflicted Hollywood personalities. Disney was going to these meetings all the time." They were none other than the meetings of the German American Bund, or the American Nazi Party. (Beitler)

Still, composer Richard Sherman (of *Mary Poppins* and *The Jungle Book*) and the son of Jewish immigrants says, "It's absolutely preposterous to call him anti-Semitic," and describes his constant kind treatment (quoted in Elber 2015). "I saw no evidence other than the casual anti-Semitism that was common to non-Jews during Disney's 20th-century era," Gabler adds (quoted in Elber). By this point, most information is secondhand and speculative, leaving critics to make their own determinations. Brode (2005) notes that there are no Jewish characters in any Disney-era films and thus, "the worst charge that could be leveled against him is benign neglect" (103). As he continues:

There are, though, numerous characters, all of a highly positive nature, played by Jewish actors, in particular, Ed Wynn. Disney revived the faded career of radio's onetime "perfect fool," awarding Wynn (who otherwise would have had difficulty finding work at this time) some of the best supporting roles in the studio's canon. These include the fire chief in *The Absent-Minded Professor*, the Toymaker in *Babes in Toyland* (essentially, a Jewish actor cast as a thinly disguised Santa Claus, something of a first), the agriculture commissioner in *Son of Flubber*, and the lovable Uncle Albert (inspiring a Paul McCartney tune) in *Mary Poppins*. In *Those Calloways*, concerning big city money men who threaten a small town's integrity, both villains are played by Anglo actors, Philip Abbott and Roy Roberts. Wynn is cast as one of the old townsfolk, sitting around the proverbial cracker barrel. In Disney's vision, the Jewish actor (and, by implication, Jewish character) is fully assimilated into mainstream America.

Other Jewish actors who are cast in nonstereotypical roles include the stalwart heroes of *20,000 Leagues under the Sea*. There's also Jack Albertson as a friendly journalist in *The Shaggy Dog*, Lilli Palmer the dedicated owner of an Austrian horse team in *The Miracle of the White Stallions*, all-American wife Suzanne Pleshette in *The Ugly Dachshund* and playing a Western heroine in *The Adventures of Bullwhip Griffin*. Jewish actors thus found a variety of roles, though overt, and mainly covert, Jewish characters themselves were absent from the films.

Chapter 9

More Golden Ages

Superman, Captain America, Dr. Seuss

GOLDEN AGE SUPERHEROES

Pre–World War II, Jews were not only known for impacting the emerging industry of film but another almost as significant to American pop culture— comic books. In *From Krakow to Krypton: Jews and Comic Books,* Arie Kaplan (2008) observes how logically they're linked:

> Jews can't claim an oral tradition solely their own, but [storytelling became] certainly a part of Jewish tradition. And the comics were sort of coming through with pictures and a tradition of storytelling. Things like the Golem and a lot of that kind of lore, I think it's engrained in the Jewish culture. Also, it comes from mythology in general, because superheroes were coming out of Greek mythology and Norse mythology. But again, it's the attraction to that storytelling tradition that figures into Judaism.

In fact, with a long tradition against painting animals or human figures (deemed near to idol worship), Jews were encouraged to use their art to illustrate books like Haggadot, and thus channeled their art in this direction. There was also the question of job availability. Al Jaffee, later of *Mad Magazine,* comments, "We couldn't get into newspaper strips or advertising: ad agencies wouldn't hire a Jew. One of the reasons we Jews drifted into the comic-book business is that most of the comic-book publishers were Jewish. So there was no discrimination there" (quoted in Brod 2012, 2).

The Yiddish comic strip began early: Samuel Zagat launched *Abie's Moving Pictures* (1912–1913) with humor based around the Jews of New York, including his Gimpl Benish the unsuccessful matchmaker. Rube Goldberg's silly machine drawings appeared in 1912 as well. This launched a 72-year career, with over 50,000 drawings and thousands of comic strips. Further, Goldberg also drew anti-fascism cartoons in the thirties and won a Pulitzer Prize for his forties cartoon about the danger of nuclear war (Wilson). There was also Zuni Maud's satirical magazine, *Der Kibitzer* and his strip *Tsharli, Vas 'maskhste* (Charlie, What Are You Up To) on the immigrant experience. "But his character Tsharli, like the paper itself, seemed to cling to the existence of an identity endangered by assimilation" (Buhle 2008, 21). The Yiddish comic had very few text bubbles, increasing universality and comprehension beyond words. "Yet its lively characters and their actions were very American. It may be said to be the metaphorical zeyde, or grandfather, of the Jewish comic artist's emergence" (Buhle 22).

Comics historians offer other theories linking the predominance of Jews in the early comics industry to the Jewish attraction to communicative media more generally. Gerald Jones notes that of all the immigrant cultures of the period, the Jews were the most literate population. Trina Robbins attributes Jewish communicative skills to the need to be able to talk yourself out of getting beaten up. Journalist Jay Schwartz writes of the founding generation of comics creators: "They came from homes where Yiddish was shouted across the dining room table, along with at least one other language. That—plus English lessons outside the home and Hebrew to boot—made for multilingual youngsters keen on the Sock! Zoom! Bam! power of language." (Brod 2012, 3)

The first comics from Caniff's *Terry and the Pirates* to Gould's *Dick Tracy* appeared in newspapers, but this changed in 1933. An unemployed former teacher named Maxwell Charles "Charlie" Gaines (born Max Ginsberg) had a family to feed. After trying many get-rich-quick schemes and moving back in with his mother in the Bronx, he got the idea to reprint the most popular newspaper comics in books. In February 1934, ECP published *Famous Funnies* #1, the first American retail comic book, distributed free as a free promotion. It was a hit. By 1939, it was selling 400,000 copies a month. "By the Great Depression's end in 1941 the industry had hit its stride: by then, there were over 30 comic-book publishers producing 150 different comic books per month, with combined sales of 15 million copies a month, and a readership of 60 million" (Kaplan 2008,). Gaines was co-publisher of All-American Comics, which, before he sold it to DC in 1944, introduced Green Lantern, Wonder Woman and Hawkman.

Bible comics were popular, with many specifically Jewish adaptations of Old Testament stories. Eventually, Gaines published the still-popular collection *Picture Stories from the Bible: The Old Testament*. J. T. Waldman and Yehudi Mercado adapted the Scroll of Esther as well. Russian Jewish immigrant Albert Kanter launched *Classics Illustrated* in 1941. Will Eisner's

A Contract with God (1978), which featured Orthodox Jews, became the first graphic novel. Jews even put on the first Comic-Con.

DC Comics, meanwhile, was created by Jewish publishers Harry Donenfeld and Jack Liebowitz. Their *Detective Comics* (1937)—the first comic book of all-new material built around a single genre—was instantly popular, while their 1938 *Action Comics* debuted Superman and Batman. Gaines's assistant Sheldon Mayer mentored all the young artists while also influencing the creation of most staple DC heroes. Art Spiegelman (2019), creator of *Maus* adds:

> The pioneers behind this embryonic medium based in New York were predominantly Jewish and from ethnic minority backgrounds. It wasn't just Siegel and Shuster, but a whole generation of recent immigrants and their children—those most vulnerable to the ravages of the great depression—who were especially attuned to the rise of virulent antisemitism in Germany. They created the American *Übermenschen* who fought for a nation that would at least nominally welcome "your tired, your poor, your huddled masses yearning to breathe free."

Superman Begins

Superman himself was famously the creation of two Jewish boys, Jerome Siegel and Joe Shuster. The 23-year-old pair found that their idea was just too different for most publishers to get onboard. Gaines and Mayer took on the comic, which they published in *Action Comics* in June 1938. Siegel and Shuster, meanwhile, found themselves steadily producing strips on their increasingly beloved creation, whom they resembled more than a little.

> The two were ardent science-fiction fans with a shared love of magazines like *Amazing Stories* and *Weird Tales*, as well as newspaper strips like Dick Calkins's Buck Rogers and Hal Foster's version of Tarzan. The pulpy tales of space fantasy and jungle intrigue fueled the young duo's imagination, and they hoped to use their artistic talents to rise above their unfortunate economic status. Bespectacled, nerdy kids who were slight of build and shy around girls, Siegel and Shuster clung to each other as blood brothers. (Kaplan 2008)

He became the first superhero (basically speaking) and set many aspects of the genre, from nemesis to secret identity to big city living. Thus, Jewish writers and producers helped birth this distinctly American form that contained traces of their heritage. While Superman is immensely powerful—the ultimate fantasy—his everyday persona, the one he must use to get by in the workplace—is Clark Kent—"a timid, socially inept, physically weak, clumsy, sexually ineffectual quasi intellectual who wore glasses and apparently owned only one blue suit. In other words, the classic Jewish *nebbish* (roughly, nerd)" (Brod 2012, 6).

Editor Zeddy Lawrence comments, "It may not be true in all cases, but it's a pretty good rule of thumb. If the word 'man' appears at the end of someone's name, you can draw one of two conclusions: a) they're Jewish, as in Goldman, Feldman, or Lipman; or b) they're a superhero, as in Superman, Batman, or Spider-Man" (quoted in Brod 2012, 9). These stories blend the shadow possession of the dybbuk and traditions of human saviors who act through moral laws to create a new highly appealing epic mythology for a new secular audience. Shuster says in a novelization of his life that Jews came "from pogroms and persecution" to a world of hope. "Our dreams of heroes come from that, I think. Our Americans heroes are the wish-fulfillment of immigrants, dazzled by the brashness and the color of this new world, by its sheer size. We needed larger-than-life heroes, masked heroes to show us that they were the fantasy within each and every one of us" (Tidhar 2013, 246). Critic Adam Nemett (2018) notes:

> The first Superman was evil. In the 1933 comic, "The Reign of the Superman," two Cleveland Jews, Jerry Siegel and Joe Shuster, envisioned their initial Superman as a bum plucked from the breadline and transformed into a telepathic supervillain. But, according to Siegel, once he saw the plight of Jews in Nazi Germany, he decided he wanted to "help the masses, somehow." So, Superman was transformed from an evil tyrant to a savior. Born with the distinctly Jewish-sounding name Kal-El, he was sent into space from dying Krypton as part of a planetary pogrom and adopted by kindly Midwesterners—Moses in the reeds. By February 1940, Superman was dragging Hitler and Stalin to the international courts, with a feature in LOOK magazine depicting the two "power-mad scoundrels" being convicted of "modern history's greatest crime—unprovoked aggression against defenseless countries."

Nemett goes on to describe the inspiration for this hero: "Iron King," the "Strongest Man in the World," the "Superman of the Ages": Siegmund Breitbart. This Polish Jew was a popular circus star even amid the rising anti-Semitism of 1920s Austria. His costumes (cowboy, gladiator, and Tarzan as well as the Talmudic defender Bar Kochba) may have helped spark the superhero concept.

In fact, co-creator Jerome Siegel explains, "I am lying in bed counting sheep when all of a sudden it hits me. I conceive a character like Samson, Hercules, and all the strong men I ever heard of rolled into one. Only more so" (quoted in Goulart 1986, 84). He adds, "You see, Clark Kent grew not only out of my private life, but also out of Joe's. . . . As a high school student, I thought that some day I might become a reporter and I had crushes on several attractive girls who either didn't know I existed or didn't care I existed. It occurred to me: what if I was real terrific? What if I had something special going for me, like jumping over buildings or throwing cars around or something like that? Maybe then they would notice me" (quoted in Goulart 84–85). Cartoonist Jules Feiffer explains, "Superman was the ultimate assimilationist fantasy. the mild manners and glasses that signified a class of nerdy Clark Kents was in no way our real truth. Underneath the shmucky facade there lived Men of Steel! Jerry Siegel's accomplishment was to chronicle the smart Jewish boy's American dream. . . . It wasn't Krypton that Superman really came from: it was the planet Minsk or Lodz or Vilna or Warsaw" (quoted in Levitz 2013, 97). The creators often felt like aliens from a different planet, speaking Yiddish at home and balancing their parents' old ways with a new America.

Feiffer calls Superman the "ultimate assimilationist fantasy" of the foreigner who becomes a successful American, leaving most of his Kryptonian identity behind. He discards his ethnic name for the Americanized Clark Kent and acts generically nice and polite as an archetypal WASP, and then gets a good job as reporter. As Chabon ([2000] 2012) quips in his novel, "Superman, you don't think he's Jewish? Coming over from the old country, changing his name like that. Clark Kent, only a Jew would pick a name like that for himself" (585).

"When Jewish superhero creators imagined themselves as heroes, then, they imagined themselves as non-Jewish heroes. Whether this was because of social prejudice or personal preference, the fact remains that superheroes are rarely Jewish. To be heroic, Jews are supposed to lose their Jewishness, and become something else" (Bertlasky 2017). The Superman/Clark Kent dual identity symbolizes "passing" or assimilation, since the hero's "true" identity must ever remain "secret." The true self, of course, is magical. Superheroes' secret identities with two sets of names and abilities feel quite Jewish. The Clark Kent persona is chosen so the alien or exotic princess can assimilate and blend in with American culture. Frequently, there's ambiguity in the hero's "otherness" as the hero wishes to lose this difference, then finally takes pride in it.

Further, Superman has been repeatedly compared to Moses for his origin story, as his parents enclosed their baby in a tiny ship and sent him away to foreigners for safety. He's the outsider, come to practice the Jewish value of repairing the world. "Even before Superman strikes his first punch, when he still wears diapers, he is an alien immigrant who is granted asylum at a time when Jews are denied entry to America. Moreover, he is coddled and cuddled by the Kents, and accepted as one of their own." (Packer 2010, 94). The planet "Krypton" hints at a "crypto-Jew" identity. Meanwhile, his family, the House of El, is actually Hebrew for the House of God. His Hebrew name of

Kal-El means "All is God" or "All that God is" or "All for God" (Brod 2012, 5). "Is it just chance that he is sent from an old world, Krypton, that is about to explode, to a new one, Earth (which could readily be seen as standing for Europe, on the verge of self-destruction, and America, with its promise of new life)" (Brod 2012, 5).

He's not only Clark Kent the geek but a messianic figure—and more, a Jewish one like Bar Kochba: "The uniquely Christian vision of the Messiah is the supernal empowered 'chosen one' who surrenders and sacrifices himself and dies for the good of humanity. The Jewish Messiah, by contrast, is the empowered 'chosen one' who strives and struggles, who lives for the good of humanity, ultimately to triumph over adversity and evil, but without losing himself" (Dennis and Dennis 2014, 74). Indeed, Superman used his powers to aid the "little guy"—exposing corrupt politicians or thwarting greedy landlords and businessmen. There are also ties to the Golem, super-strong protector of the Jewish people. The word "truth" was inscribed to bring it to life and enlist it in the cause for justice. In fact, "truth and justice" were Superman's watchwords, with "and the American way" added by the radio show during wartime.

Superhero comics were American Jews' way of fighting the rising Nazism of Europe. Indeed, Will Eisner edited *Military Comics*, starring his creation Blackhawk, who led a paramilitary group against Nazi Germany. In a different spirit, the comic book hero The Spectre by Jerry Siegel and Bernard Baily (1940) was returned to earth after death with a mission from God to battle crime on earth. Sheldon Mayer united many heroes into the Justice Society of America—Sandman, the Atom, the Spectre, the Flash, Hawkman, Dr. Fate, Green Lantern, and Hourman. They soon went off to war.

> With the Japanese bombing Pearl Harbor and Hitler massacring Jews overseas, it suddenly became impossible for American comic-book publishers to ignore putting wartime themes into their work. Comic books became practically regulation army equipment, as millions of American boys shipped out with a stack of four-color propaganda pamphlets featuring various superheroes putting the smackdown on Axis forces. "As comics writers," Stan Lee said, "we had to have villains in our stories. And once World War II started, the Nazis gave us the greatest villains in the world to fight against. It was a slamdunk." (Kaplan 2008)

In fact, superheroes quickly gained reputations as defenders of the free world from the Nazis. "Superman gave such a pounding to Nazi agents from 1941 to 1945 that according to legend, the Nazi minister of propaganda, Joseph Goebbels, jumped up in the midst of a Reichstag meeting holding up a Superman comic book and denouncing the Man of Steel as a Jew" (Kaplan 2008). Also notable is the 1944 comic book series "Jewish War Heroes."

Post-war, as other writers took over Superman, the assimilation metaphor continued. Editor Mort Weisinger added many famous components to the Man of Tomorrow's story—the Phantom Zone, Bizarro, red kryptonite, and the what if stories. He describes his job as striving "to keep Superman popular. If he dies, I'd be out of a job. I think of practically all the plots, but I only write in an emergency" (quoted in Goulart 276). Despite this lightness, there was a new troubled side to the hero. "Like the Jewish people for nearly 2000 years, Superman was in mourning over the destruction of his ancient homeland; and like the Jewish people since the Holocaust, he mourned his entire community, expressing constant devotion to his lost culture, in part because it was his job to carry on as the sole survivor of the planet Krypton" (Oirich).

In 1956, Supergirl arrived—an orphan refugee packed off to her proverbial "cousin in America"—Superman. This origin story echoes the kindertransports that sent Jewish children to safety. Siegel also considered this Holocaust metaphor in the 1962 Superman story "One Minute of Doom," about the Krypton Memorial Day. Some comics observed the pair, who recognized themselves as "strangers in a strange land," celebrating peculiar Kryptonian holidays together. Even Kandor—a city of their lost homeland, preserved in a bottle, works well as metaphor here.

> This entire situation can be viewed as extremely Jewish. All of a sudden—like American Jews—Superman and Supergirl had a small homeland that they felt was dependent on them for its protection from those who held it for a while and wanted to regain it from the original and rightful owners. It was a miraculous, thriving remnant of a once-great culture, and the two could visit ancient archeological sites and the remains of their ancestral homeland, speak their ancestral language, be called by their real (Kryptonian) names, track down distant relatives and friends of their parents and even meet the occasional potential marriage partner of "a similar background." (Oirich)

These brief trips to their lost culture echo celebrating holidays in temple or trying a summer program in Israel.

Siegel and Shuster also tried to recreate the magic. Though superhero popularity was dwindling, Siegel and Shuster's Funnyman (2010) lasted six issues in the late forties with some additional newspaper strips. He resembles Danny Kaye and keeps up the quips. Larry Davis, a nightclub comedian, dons a clown costume and fake nose to devastate criminals with his quips. With the big fake nose and red hair, he's leaning into the stereotype though only as a persona, beneath which he looks more assimilated. Even his clownish car has its own fake nose. Specifically Jewish jokes appear too. He dodges a sexy robot wielding a mallet because he has a metal skull-cap under his wig and proposes a film with Pierre Blintz and Lucille Schlemiel. Villains include Noodnik Nogoodnik and other insider wordplay.

In 1956, DC editor Julius Schwartz revived many Golden Age characters, reinventing The Flash and Green Lantern. With them, Aquaman, Martian Manhunter, Green Arrow, and the "big three" (Superman, Batman, and Wonder Woman), he created the Justice League. Of course, this legacy lasted through the decades as the ultimate team-up.

Captain America

Just after their creation, Superman and DC had found competition. Martin (birth name Moe) Goodman, son of Russian Jewish immigrants, also jumped on the superhero bandwagon. He contracted with newly formed comic-book "packager" Funnies, Inc. to supply material for Marvel Comics #1 (October 1939), published by his new Timely Publications (later rebranded as Marvel Comics). Carl Burgos (born Max Finkelstein) created the lead feature in Marvel Comics #1, *The Human Torch*. This first issue sold out of 80,000 copies, so the next month, Goodman printed 800,000 more. He quickly assembled an in-house staff including his wife's cousin, Stan Lee. There, his first original character the Destroyer fought the Third Reich, and he soon joined the army, where he made propaganda videos.

Alex Schomburg was known for his covers for *Thrilling, Exciting*, and *Startling*, for which he wrote about Einstein, Hitler, and other heroes and villains of his day. Under his pen, Timely Comics' covers showed the Human Torch and Sub-Mariner battling Nazis early in 1940. Comics, unlike novels, had no reputation to ruin, and eagerly threw themselves into the fight.

Namor the Sub-Mariner is another anti-Nazi superhero who preceded Captain America. Namor appeared in 1939, the year when Europe declared war and the year when the steamship St. Louis was turned away from the Miami port, even though American authorities knew that the refugee Jews aboard risked death if returned to Nazi-controlled Europe. Namor's undersea origins, and the destruction endured by his mermen people, parallel the public indifference to the European Jewish plight in 1939. . . . He lives beneath the sea and captures Nazi submarines. After his fellow mermen people are destroyed by surface dwellers, he displaces his hostilities onto Nazis. Namor is more morally ambiguous than other early superheroes. He gets in fights with other superheroes and engages in overt acts of terrorism, but his pro-American patriotism and anti-Nazi attitudes are beyond reproach. (Packer 2010, 33)

Funnies, Inc. writer-artist Joe Simon (born Hymie Simon) and Jack Kirby (born Jacob Kurtzberg) teamed up on many projects, beginning with the

Blue Bolt in 1940. At Timely, Simon became its first editor and Kirby the art director. Their most enduring creation was Captain America, who constantly battled the Nazi agent the Red Skull. "Two Jews created this weak little guy named Steve Rogers who gets shot in the arm and, by way of a 'secret serum, 'becomes this super-strong hero who starts destroying Nazis," says comic book artist Peter Kuper. "What a distinctly empowering image!" (quoted in Kaplan 2008).

Within six months of Captain America's debut, there were two dozen imitators. American Jewish creators, suffering from isolationist guilt, could at least send fictional heroes into battle. Famously, Cap punched Hitler in the face on an early cover, before America had entered the war. Spiegelman (2019) adds:

> Captain America was a recruiting poster, battling against the real Nazi super-villains while Superman was still fighting cheap gunsels, strike breakers, greedy landlords and Lex Luthor—and America was still equivocating about entering the conflict at all. No wonder Simon and Kirby's comic book became an enormous hit, selling close to a million copies a month throughout the war. But not everyone was a fan in 1941—according to Simon, the German American Bund and America Firsters bombarded the publisher's offices with hate mail and obscene phone calls that screamed "Death to the Jews!" Mayor Fiorello La Guardia, a real-life superhero, called to reassure him, saying: "The city of New York will see that no harm comes to you."

On one occasion, Kirby answered the phone, and a voice said three men were waiting in the lobby for the guy who "does this disgusting comic book" to show him what real Nazis would do to the Sentinel of Liberty. To the shock of his fellow artists, Kirby rolled up his sleeves and headed downstairs. Fortunately for everyone, the callers were no longer there (Evanier 2008, 55). Later, Simon and Kirby struggled to create a backlog of material during the draft for World War II, as Kirby explained that their goal was "to get enough work backlogged that I could go into the Army, kill Hitler, and get back before the readers missed us" (Evanier 2008, 66). Kirby saw combat with Company F of eleventh Infantry under Patton and indeed returned to continue drawing.

In their story, Steve Rogers is transformed via the chemical genius of Dr. Reinstein (a thinly veiled reference to Einstein). "The story's message is clear: The Jewish boys from the Lower East Side are ready to defend America" (Weinstein 2006, 42). Kirby comments, "Captain America was created for a time that needed noble figures. . . . We weren't at war yet, but everyone knew it was coming. That's why Captain America was born; America needed a superpatriot" (quoted in Goulart 1986, 154). The character did indeed recruit Americans into the military. "The comic book character gave soldiers and sailors psychological strength as they sat in submarines and bunkers. Thinking that a sickly soldier would be willing to do whatever it took to aid the war effort was enough to convince unlikely heroes to join the effort" (Packer 2010, 106).

Cap wasn't overtly Jewish, but there were suggestive moments besides his hailing from Brooklyn. Bernie Rosenthal was Cap's Jewish girlfriend. Further, *Captain America* #8 (Simon and Kirby 1941a) harkens back to Jewish slavery in ancient Egypt. The magical Ruby of the Nile brings the mummified Pharaoh back to life, and like a modern-day Moses, Captain America is sent to destroy him. "The Exodus was a favorite theme of Kirby's, one he returned to again and again in his work" (Weinstein 42).

The concentration camps and rather fantastical images of the Nazi machinery of death did appear in American comics of the 1940s: On the cover of *Captain America* #46 (Alascia 1945), "Invitation to Murder," Cap swoops through a maze of pipes and brickwork while ragged refugees stand in lines behind him. Nazis sitting around a bearded corpse are shocked as Cap and Bucky leap down on top of them. During the war, comics focused on America's victory over Nazism and her status as a liberator of Europe. "The Jewish victims of the Holocaust were categorized as refugees and were regarded with a mixture of shame and contempt by their American co-religionists intent upon taking advantage of new possibilities for upward mobility in post-war American society" (Bower 2004, 183). Meanwhile, muscled hero Captain America wanted to save the downtrodden but certainly not become identified with them. His sidekick Bucky was more flexible, and in *Captain America* #4 (1941b), he's strapped to an operating table, held captive at the "Horror Hospital" at the mercy of a Dr. Mengele stand-in.

More Heroes

The Shield bears a grudge against Germany that dates back to World War I. He is chemist Joe Higgins, whose father was slain by a German saboteur during the Black Tom explosion, which damaged the Statue of Liberty in this story. Further, Joe's father was blamed for the attack. As Joe seeks revenge and justice, he's the perfect warrior for the new crisis.

Daredevil (a different character from Stan Lee's blind acrobat) was a 1941 creation by Arthur Bernhard. Like Captain America, this Daredevil punched out Hitler. "Bernhard says this was one more expression of his antifascist, anti-Hitler activities, His views were shared by Lev Gleason, who became his partner at about this time" (Goulart 228). None of these characters were literally Jewish. "Identifiably Jewish superheroes would not have been an option for wartime comics, and neither artists, writers, nor publishers seemed even to contemplate them" (Buhle 57). Still, for those who knew the code, it was obvious. Other Jewish artists and writers of the time—Emanuel (Mac) Raboy, Fred Ray, Jerry Robinson, Alex Schomburg, Irwin Hasen, Lou Fine—drew assimilationist power fantasies like Captain Marvel (later remarketed as Shazam) and Batman, war comics, secret agent comics, and of course all the characters of the Justice Society of America.

Another breakout early comic's character was Sheena, Queen of the Jungle, originally published by Fiction House in 1937 and amazingly popular with soldiers. She pioneered an entire genre of Jungle Girl comics with dozens of competitors. She was invented by Samuel Maxwell "Jerry" Iger (a Jewish writer who partnered with Will Eisner) with art by Mort Meskin. Some see her name as coming from H. Rider Haggard's character "She," while others believe it came from the ethnic slur "sheeny" or the word for pretty, "shayna."

Green Lantern's creator, Martin Nodell, was the New York son of Jewish immigrants like so many others. Inspired by a lantern-wielding subway worker, Nodell planted the seeds of what became an extensive mythology. Further, Aladdin with his magic ring was an influence, allowing the story to branch out beyond western culture. Notably, Green Lantern Alan Scott had as much of an insider name as Clark Kent. Brooklyn sidekick Doiby Dickles was more relatable for the creators—he was Irish but made a good stand-in for other kinds of minorities. Scott and Dickles fought Nazis too, until Dickles married a space princess and became an insider. Nodell and Bill Finger published Green Lantern for seven years. The character also featured in a number of crossover adventures, which led to the Justice Society of America.

Batman was created by the Jewish team Bob Kane (né Kahn) and Milton "Bill" Finger. The Joker, Catwoman, and many more staple characters were likewise their creations. However, if Superman is a symbolic Jew, Batman "was a Jewish parent's ultimate assimilationist nightmare" and a common image of the wicked son in the Haggadah—a self-indulgent rich playboy (Brod 2012, 12). While Superman rescued the little guy, Batman showed off his cool gadgets and foiled jewel heists.

> Most artists of the era would agree: they were creating a product for general audiences and didn't try to sneak any sort of subtext, Jewish or not, into their work. If any Jewish symbolism did seep out, it was purely subconscious on the part of the cartoonist/writer involved. In fact, most comics professionals during the Golden Age of comics just saw comics as a way to pay the bills. They were trying to make a living, and it never occurred to them to layer their stories with any sort of symbolism or subtext. (Kaplan 2008)

At the same time, Batman was of course morality embodied. In a particularly anti-fascist story, "Swastika over the White House" (Cameron and Robinson

1943), Batman and Robin defeat a Nazi mob in America, entrapping it in its own giant swastika. Robin was also a character in which the creators could see themselves. Bob Kane explained, "In my subconscious mind, I longed to be like Robin when I was his age, fighting alongside his idol Batman (or in my case, Doug Fairbanks, Sr.) I figured Robin would appeal to all children of his age group as an identifiable person for their inner fantasies" (quoted in Goulart 1986, 111). Moreover, Batman's everyday persona, like Clark Kent's, is a bit too exaggerated, too perfect. Both are success stories of the ultimate insider, dreamed up by writers who hoped to get there soon—ones who concealed their identities and did their best to conceal the superhero within.

Will Eisner's The Spirit, Denny Colt, was a masked vigilante from 1940 to 1952. As Jules Feiffer, who helped write it, observed, the characters looked like very recent immigrants and as for the Spirit, "We all knew he was Jewish!" (quoted in Brod 2012, 110). Eisner went on to write the realistic historical collection of Jewish tenement comics called *A Contract with God.* In later years, Eisner openly and seriously explored his Jewish identity through his craft. "Although we may have thought we were creating Aryan characters, with non-Jewish names like Bruce Wayne, Clark Kent and my own Denny Colt," Eisner explained, "I think we were responding to an inner neshama [Jewish soul] that responds to forces around us—just like the story of the Golem in Jewish lore" (quoted in Weinstein 2006, 41).

Eisner's *Life in Pictures* (2007) is an autobiography of growing up in America with communism and Nazism warring for public approval. His girlfriend's father tells him, "In the end, the communists and Nazis will fight for power and control of Germany. It will be a bloody fight! If the Nazis win . . . that will be the end for the Jews there . . . you'll see" (131). As the people of his neighborhood war between these ideologies, he tells stories of his family's leaving the old country and dealing with anti-Semitism there and in America. "To the Heart of the Storm" and "The Name of the Game" both explore his family history—the latter presents it through something of a fairytale lens. "We were better than our neighbors, so we accepted that the only way up was by marriage. And why not? All the stories we grew up with told us this. Whether it was history, Bible stories, or fairy tales, it was always the same" (315). "The Dreamer" shows his start in the comics industry alongside Kirby, Kane, and more—but they all change their Jewish names to avoid harassment "Y'need a classy name t'get ahead," one explains simply (80).

After the Golden Age, with the war concluded, the heroic stories lost much of their point. Horror and romance took their place and superheroes faded. Finally, Friedrich Wertheimer, a German Jew who changed his name to Dr. Fredrick Wertham when he moved to New York, wrote a homophobic, sexist book in 1954 that fiercely censured how comics were harming children, which he called *Seduction of the Innocent.* His disagreements with the children of East European immigrants "echo those of generations of middle- and upper-class assimilated Western European Jews looking down on the primitive products of the culture of the Eastern European small towns and villages, the shtetls, with the Eastern Europeans Jews thumbing their noses right back at them" (Brod 78). As one side fought to depict violence while the other fought for censorship, "when the Jews of both sides of the argument looked at the other side, they saw Nazis" (Brod 79). Instead of banding together, both sides destroyed the new industry. The industry finally decided to self-censor with the Comic Books Code, and comics became much more prim and family-friendly. Batman and Robin even got girlfriends. Most superheroes, however, had been set aside for horror, science fiction, and romance comics as the genre moved on. With this, the Golden Age closed.

PICTURE BOOKS

Curious George

As critic Mary Galbraith (2000b) notes, children's books from interwar Europe repeat a trend: "A child figure is confronted by murderous, abandoning, interrogating, or dismissive adults and must make a profound decision: what needs must I sacrifice in order to keep my (original or adoptive) mother or father(land)? In five of these books—*Millions of Cats, The Story of Babar, The Story about Ping, The Story of Ferdinand,* and *Curious George*—the child must decide what to sacrifice in order to avoid being killed; a sixth, *Madeline,* can also be interpreted in this light" (338). All these stories framed a Europe being torn apart by war. "These picture books capture in uniquely effective ways the frightening predicaments children face and the unspeakable decisions they must make when adults behave strangely and dangerously" (Galbraith 2000b, 339).

Curious George has subtle but distinct ties to the rising racism of the thirties. As the book begins, simply by his trying on the yellow hat, left out by its owner as bait, the curious monkey is taken prisoner. The man tells him, "George, I am going to take you to a big Zoo in a big city. You will like it there." (This story has also been compared to slavery and colonialism.) At the same time, George's struggle to follow society's rules, combined with the possibly autobiographical tale of George's creators, gives the story another spin.

> In George's narrative universe, there is no attunement, no critique of abuse, and no strategy which does not put him in a double bind. When he acts like a normal monkey, he gets kidnapped. After being kidnapped, he must fend for himself,

but without getting into trouble. He is not loved, but he must obey without being supervised. When he acts from ignorance, he is punished, and when he presumes to be a human, he is punished. (Galbraith 2000a 129–130)

Curious George is let loose on a ship, where his lack of understanding of the place leads him to try to fly like a seagull and fall overboard. On land, much later, he imitates the Man in the Yellow Hat and plays with the phone. This calls the fire department and the firefighters arrest him for doing so, with George mute and unable to defend himself. Calling him a "naughty little monkey," they insist, "We will have to shut you up where you can't do any more harm." He springs out the door and up the telephone wires, using his agile monkey powers to escape. "He is a curious monkey who, through his curiosity, gets himself into trouble and, through his own ingenuity, gets himself out of trouble," Margaret Rey, his female creator, says (Yamazaki 2017). However, he ends the story locked in the zoo. "What a nice place for George to live!" the book cheerfully concludes.

Galbraith explains, "Like Hans Christian Andersen, Wanda Gág [author-illustrator of *Millions of Cats*] borrowed European folktale motifs to create powerful allegories of her own childhood experience. The child self for both Andersen and Gág is embodied in a nonhuman figure (duckling, mermaid, cat, invisible dog) who struggles to survive, be accepted, and find happiness among humans" (2000b, 354). The Reys' use of a monkey protagonist repeats the trope. At the same time, his status as a monkey works as a metaphor for the lower form of life label Nazis placed on Jews. "In this reading, George's identity is linked to virulent forms of life which must be ghettoized and marked—in this case, weirdly, in a festive zoo with balloons" (Galbraith 2000a, 130). George is indeed consigned there, to the perky-looking animal jail. Galbraith continues by noting that the author, H. A. Rey, had been a German solider during World War I and yet as a Jew was accused of losing the war. "This fits with George's themes of struggling for an identity that is continually being jerked away, and being blamed for things he doesn't know about, and being alternately hailed as a hero and chased as an enemy by the same people" (2000a, 132).

H. A. and Margret Rey, the creators, have a biography directly tied to the Holocaust. Hans Augusto Reyersbach grew up in Hamburg, as did Margarete Waldstein. Reyersbach fought for the Germans in World War I and finally moved to Brazil seeking work as an artist. When Hitler came to power, Margret moved to London. Then she sailed to Brazil to see her good friend and announced they were going to team up as artists. There, they shortened their names to a more pronounceable H. A. and Margret Rey. "It was much easier for clients in his new country. And it was a name to remember" (Borden 2005, 15). They got married in Brazil and then honeymooned in 1937 Paris.

Adoring the artistic community, they stayed there for four years. Hans's animal drawings became their first children's book *Whiteblack the Penguin.* Their second book, then called *The Adventures of Fifi*, focused on the youngest monkey. Margret recalls being German Jews with Brazilian passports in France after the war broke out—assumed by many to be spies. She describes watching two big policemen digging through their luggage for hours, until they found the children's books at the bottom. "At that moment, the whole atmosphere changed, y'know? The heat was off. They let us go. I'm pretty damn sure it was George who saved us there" (Yamazaki 2017).

Jews were shocked when the Nazis conquered France in June 1940, as they'd been told it could never happen. The Reys wanted to head for Brazil, though they had no car and trains weren't running. "Bicycles were the only way to get out of Paris," Margret adds (Yamazaki 2017). At the store, only a tandem remained. They rode it so badly that Hans went back for parts and assembled the tandem into two bicycles. With an advance from their publisher for the three picture books planned, they had enough to escape. At five in the morning, they could hear the German tanks rolling in as they biked away. "They traveled light—a few clothes, their winter coats, some bread, cheese, meat, water, an umbrella, and Hans's pipe. More than five million people were on the roads that day, fleeing France" (Borden 2005).

> Strapped to their bike racks to be smuggled out of the country were the also the watercolors for and draft of *Curious George*, still tentatively titled *Fifi*, Hans making sure to keep his artwork dry in the basket covered by his winter coat. With them were four other manuscripts, including the draft for *Whiteblack the Penguin Sees the World,* which didn't see publication until 2000 (though it had initially been planned for publication in 1943 and had at one time been in the hands of legendary editor Ursula Nordstrom). (Borden)

They biked 120 kilometers to Orleans. From there, they were lucky enough to catch a train to Bordeaux, then Lisbon. "After a very adventurous trip from Paris on bicycles, we have arrived safely," Hans wrote to his contacts (Yamazaki 2017). In July, they got their travel papers for Brazil. After a few months, their US visa was granted. On October 14, 1941, they reached New York.

Dr. Seuss

Other European immigrant families were clearly marked by their experiences. Theodor Geisel, known to his readers as Dr. Seuss, was born in 1904. His grandfather and namesake had emigrated to the United States from Germany, so growing up during World War I and Prohibition (his family were brewers), he encountered bullying and harassment, though he was not Jewish (Galbraith 2000a, 126–127).

Dr. Seuss's *To Think that I Saw it on Mulberry Street* was published in 1937, written on the journey home after touring an increasingly volatile Europe during the 1936 Berlin Olympics. Galbraith explains that Mulberry Street's parade recalls the "parade of nations" presented in Leni Riefenstahl's *Olympia* (1938): in Mulberry Street, the "Mayor's small moustache and raised arm evoke Hitler, while the brass band and international cast of characters evoke the parade of nations at the opening of the games" (2000a, 128). The book's "simple horse and wagon—which evokes the peaceful Germans of Geisel's hometown and thus the everyday, nonthreatening behavior of Germany—will transform itself gradually into a military monolith . . . marching down the main street as an airplane drops confetti" (128). As Galbraith concludes, "This is the key question of the book: should a child who sees whales try to tell the truth to a parent who admits to seeing only minnows?" (2000a, 129). Geisel was certain that he saw a threat in Hitler, while European leaders were still busy appeasing him.

Another story from Mulberry Street, written in 1950 and recently republished, has Officer Pat explain that when he sees a gnat bothering a cat, he must intervene. If he does not, things will escalate until the town will be blown to bits. This is "How Officer Pat Saved the Whole Town," ([1950] 2014). The story works as an analogy for Hitler's rise, which could have been stopped decades before.

The King's Stilts ([1939] 2016) is the only prewar Seuss book in which a king's behavior pointedly affects his entire country. The book has King Birtram, depressed by the theft of his stilts, failing to protect his kingdom from the Nizzards, who gnaw at the Dike Trees' roots that protect the island nation. Written on the eve of the war, the book registers Seuss's anxieties about the growing global crisis. "As a leader who has grown lazy about the potential dangers to his country, King Birtam could represent isolationists' influence in both America and Great Britain" (Nel 2004, 48). Reviewing *The King's Stilts* for the Dartmouth Alumni Magazine, Seuss's classmate Alexander Laing explains, "the Dr. may not have meant it, but to me those contemptible Nizzards are bombing planes" (quoted in Nel 48).

Back in the United States, as he read of the Nazi march on Paris, Seuss put *Horton Hatches the Egg* ([1940] 1968) on hold to concentrate on anti-Hitler political cartoons. "I didn't know how to end the book anyway, so I began drawing savage cartoons," Seuss said. "I had no great causes or interest in social issues until Hitler" (quoted in Morgan 1996, 98). Meanwhile, *Horton* was a resounding success (with his wife providing the ending) and the author knew at last how he wanted to spend his life. Notably, *Horton* was his first book with a strong moral angle, as Horton devotes himself to faith and duty and successfully hatches the egg.

Seuss offered an editorial cartoon to the tabloid *PM*. In a letter to the editor, he named himself the world's most outstanding writer of fantasy and called Italian Fascist propaganda writer Virginio Gayda the runner-up (Morgan 100). The editor requested more, and Seuss didn't write another children's book for seven years. In fact, he published over 400 cartoons between April 1941 and January 1943 (Nel 2004, 39). Seuss recalls, "While Paris was being occupied by the clanking tanks of the Nazis and I was listening on my radio, I found I could no longer keep my mind on drawing pictures of Horton the Elephant. I found myself instead drawing pictures of Lindbergh the ostrich [with his head in the sand]" (Nel 39). His September 22, 1941 cartoon has a star-hatted bird locked in the stocks, a sign hanging from his beak: "I AM PART JEWISH," it says. Leaning against the stocks, a placard states, "PUBLIK NOTICE: THIS BIRD IS POSSESSED OF AN EVIL DEMON!" and has been signed by "Sheriffs" Lindbergh and Nye. The hat clearly identifies the bird as American, beseeching sympathy, while the misspelling of "PUBLIK" and the phrase "EVIL DEMON," along with the bird's treatment, make the "Sheriffs" look uneducated and particularly cruel.

He went on to satirize Hitler alongside all the American politicians who preached noninterference. Seuss often depicted Hitler as a tyrannical baby, especially in the series "Mein Early Kampf," where Hitler appears as an infant "giv[ing] the hotfoot to" a stork delivering him (January 20, 1942), "reject[ing] milk from Holstein cows as Non-Aryan" (January 21, 1942), and taking a bite out of a bust of Bismarck (January 29, 1942) (Nel 48). Other cartoons predicted a Japanese attack.

> Ted's cartoons grew savagely eloquent and often very funny, displaying his gift for derision. Set in a men's club, "The Battle of the Easy Chair" portrayed a member telling his valet, "Wake me, Judkins, when the Victory Parade comes by!" Australia became a boxing kangaroo, its tail being devoured by the Japanese. The French puppet Pierre Laval was a louse on Hitler's finger. Nazis were low-slung dachshunds—until American dachshund owners rose in protest. A favorite Seussian device of long, intertwining bears made Siamese twins of the Nazi party and the America First Committee. In February 1942 *Newsweek* called Ted's satire "razor-keen" and noted that he was stirring "hornet's nests" with drawings so unflattering that even the United States had become "a scrawny eagle with Uncle Sam whiskers and a star-spangled topper." (Morgan 104–105)

Too old for the draft, he joined Frank Capra's Signal Corps unit in Hollywood and made propaganda films. When he left the service in 1946, he received the Legion of Merit for his war cartoons. He continued at Hollywood afterward, making short films and documentaries, but finally returned to picture books. Many were influenced by the war, as *Bartholomew and the Oobleck* ([1949] 1976) was based on a memory of a journey to Belgium, in which he was unexpectedly trapped by the Battle of the Bulge. American soldiers had been complaining, "Rain, always rain! Why can't we have something different for a change?" and thus the book was born (Morgan 122). Also notable are the king's blunders. "In this postwar work, dictatorial blundering affects not just Bartholomew but the entire nation" (Nel 47). This was part of a larger trend, of course. "What we might call Seuss's 'message books' are a distinctly postwar phenomenon, beginning in 1949 with the publication of *Bartholomew and the Oobleck*" (Nel 47). The king ends his foolishness by saying "I'm sorry" and "It is all my fault" though for most of the book he insists he won't, adding, "Kings never say 'I'm sorry! And I am the mightiest king in all the world." While this is apparently the same character as in *The King's Stilts*, he's much closer to the tantrum-throwing Hitler than these earlier kings.

The newly published "Horton and the Kwuggerbug" ([1951] 2014) has, in Aesop's fable style, the two animals making a partnership to gather nuts and then share them. The deal gets worse and worse, with the bug insisting each time, "A deal is a deal." At last, he takes all the nuts and stuffs the shells (Horton's half) in his trunk. In response, Horton blasts the Kwuggerbug out his trunk, so far that it takes him a whole month to arrive. The beginning of this story suggests Hitler's endlessly caving on his treaties, until, in this story, Horton stands up for himself and seeks justice. Presumably after the war, Seuss felt free to lambast Hitler while trying to prevent a similar dictator.

For instance, Yertle the Turtle is a self-aggrandizing tyrant who insists on standing on the backs of his servants, and early versions showed him with a moustache as a Hitler stand-in. *Yertle the Turtle* ([1950] 1986), Seuss has said "was modeled on the rise of Hitler" (quoted in Cott 1983, 30). Like the king of *Bartholomew and the Oobleck*, Yertle is dangerously ambitious, desperate to control the uncontrollable. Yertle insists, "I am the ruler of all that I see," a premise that's arrogant to the point of idiocy. The turtles live comfortable, happy lives, in which "It was clean. It was neat. The water was warm. There was plenty to eat." Still, he's endlessly greedy, and builds a tower of his unhappy subjects to stand on until his arrogance finally brings his literal downfall.

Soon after the war came *Horton Hears a Who* ([1954] 1982), in which victims will be snuffed out in a worldwide apocalypse, even as well-meaning strangers are blind to their plight. Horton's neighbors mistreat him horribly for standing up for the tiny people only he can hear with his extra sensitivity. Even as his neighbors beat him and maul him, he tells his friends, "You very small persons will not have to die/If you make yourselves heard! So come on,

now, and TRY!" A parallel with the war victims and the necessity of their getting world press was clear. In this story, Horton has expanded from his prewar
care of a single egg to saving an entire civilization. Seuss dedicated the book
to to "My Great Friend, Mitsugi Nakamura," a Kyoto University professor
he met on his tour of Japan, in yet another plea for tolerance and compassion
(Morgan 1996, 151). "Significantly, Seuss wrote the book directly after his
return from Japan: he visited that nation in 1953 to see how the American
occupation had changed the ideas of young people, learning that they were
less interested in militarism and more interested in the West" (Nel 53).

Soon came *The Sneeches* ([1961] 1989), a book about discrimination
between the group with stars on their bellies and the group without, which
Seuss considered abandoning because of criticism that it was anti-Semitic
(Morgan 173). In fact, Seuss intended the book to combat anti-Semitism
(Cott 1983, 30). The stars emphasize the arbitrariness of prejudice as the
book insists, "You might think such a thing wouldn't matter at all." On every
page, miserable-looking Sneeches emphasize how it feels to be excluded. The
fact that when the plain-bellied Sneeches get stars, the starred ones want to
go plain once again emphasizes how arbitrary racial or any other divide is.
In a happy ending, signaling that cartoon critters can be smarter than racists,
the Sneeches all give up on the phony divides and make peace. *The Butter
Battle Book*, where nuclear destruction threatens in a war based on whether
the people eat bread butter side up or butter side down, has a similar message.

More books followed, all tied to children's humor but also his personal
experiences. Like Seuss's political cartoons, his children's books often end
by asking the child to consider the deeper message and the moral themes
within. *The Lorax* and *The Butter Battle Book* encourage readers to get
involved and fix their world, much as his cartoons once did. All in all, the
books drew readers not only through the humor and rhyme, but through the
insistence that they join in repairing the world torn apart by prejudice and
neglect. What horrified Seuss about fascism was the indoctrination through
racist, manipulative education. In his children's books, Seuss thus tried guid-
ing children to become thoughtful and kind. As Seuss writes in an essay
published in 1960, "Children's reading and children's thinking are the rock
bottom base upon which the future of this country will rise. Or not rise." He
continues, "In these days of tension and confusion, writers are beginning to
realize that books for children have a greater potential for good or evil than
any other form of literature on earth" (quoted in Nel 61).

K'tonton

K'tonton, the hero of the 1935 (1964) classic, *The Adventures of K'tonton*, is
the original Jewish Tom Thumb (the name means "very small" in Hebrew).

Written by Sadie Rose Weilerstein, daughter of immigrants and the wife of
a conservative rabbi, the book was actually the first Jewish children's book
written in English.

At first she wrote stories only for her children. But her mother, behaving like the
stereotype of a Jewish mother, marched a handful of her daughter's stories over
to the New York Public Library, demanding to know if they were any good. A
Jewish librarian there directed her to Bloch, an educational Jewish publishing
house that wound up putting out Weilerstein's first book, *What Danny Did,* in
1928. *Outlook,* the National Women's League of United Synagogue's magazine, published the first K'tonton story in 1930. (Ingall 2010)

K'tonton's mother wishes for any child, even a tiny one, and is told to bite
the end off the etrog (a citron, shaken ceremonially on Sukkot). She does,
and when her tiny son is born, she makes the etrog-box into his cradle. The
preface explains, "The background of the K'tonton stories is drawn from the
wide field of Jewish tradition and folk-lore. K'tonton is unique only in his
size and his precocity. His dreams and ambitions, the festivals he celebrates,
the ceremonials he delights in, are shared in varying degree by Jewish children everywhere."

His adventures over a collection of holiday stories take obvious courses for
a tiny hero: Riding the fish-chopping knife during Shabbat preparations and
dancing in the cored apple on a flag for Simchat Torah, perching on the palm
fronds at Sukkot, getting closed in a hamentaschen.

In "K'tonton Takes a Ride on a Runaway Trendel" (an alternate Yiddish
word for dreidel, updated to dreidel in later editions), K'tonton is disap-
pointed because his relatives have forgotten to give him gelt that he might
donate to fill up his Palestine Box "to buy land, you know—for the Jewish
farmers, the Halutzim" (28) as Israel has not yet been established. His uncle
lets him ride the dreidel, but it rolls away into the street. The whole family
chases it, and they call to a policeman to stop him, but the policeman doesn't
know what a dreidel is. Eventually, K'tonton comes to rest beside an "A BIG
ROUND SHINING QUARTER!" (31). With this reminder, they all have a
happy holiday as they donate money as a family.

Of course, American Jewish stories are often filled with ambivalence over
the tension of being both Jewish and American. The K'tonton stories resolve
it cheerfully. "On the one hand, K'tonton is ritually observant, a good little
Jewish boy," points out Jonathan Krasner, assistant professor of the American
Jewish Experience at Hebrew Union College. "But he's also completely
acculturated. In the 1930s American Jews were eager to present themselves
as Americans and to minimize the differences between them and their com-
patriots. And in the illustrations, K'tonton *looks* American. He's a fun-loving,

spunky, energetic, curious kid who gets in trouble. He's not a stereotype of a kid in *cheder* bent over his books. He reflects a more American ideal of what a kid is. Weilerstein managed to create a perfect synthesis" (quoted in Ingall 2010).

> K'tonton is small and seemingly powerless—a stand-in for 5-year-olds everywhere—but the little guy has agency. He gets out of every scrape; he does mitzvot; he sees the world. He takes huge risks, like shinnying up a giant lulav and stowing away in a carry-on on a trip to Israel, but everything always comes out OK. What could be more enticing to a young reader? (Ingall)

Some of his heroic deeds besides giving charity can be imitated by young readers— K'tonton finds the critical last bit of leaven before Passover. In a sweet Shavuot story, he stays up all night to make a wish that he instantly be a great scholar and make his mother proud, but confronted by a moment of animal cruelty, sweetly wishes "that the little calf could be with its mother this minute" (69). The wish is granted, and he does not become a scholar on the spot, but has shown compassion by releasing a suffering animal.

Along with all this altruism, God and a spiritual element are present throughout. K'tonton climbs into a shofar and actually drives out Satan by crying out the Sh'ma, while on Shmini Atzeret, he prays for rain and it comes. In the sukkah, he greets the holy guests and receives blessings from each. On Yom Kippur, his fasting makes him realize how cruel he was for scapegoating a kitten, which his mother no longer feeds, so he confesses his small sin.

> K'tonton's lightness and brightness was inspired by earlier, darker tales. Weilerstein didn't draw just from Tom Thumb and Thumbelina, but also from S. Y. Agnon's *The Story of Rabbi Gadiel the Baby,* about a miniature medieval rabbi who saves Jews from a blood libel. Weilerstein's 5-year-old son overheard her and her husband discussing the story and asked what they were talking about. Weilerstein, preferring not to share the details of vampiric murder accusations and pogroms with her small child, wound up spinning the tale into K'tonton. (Ingall)

The book is out of print, like its sequels, but there is *The Best of K'tonton* (1980), a compilation of sixteen tales from three early K'tonton books: *The Adventures of K'tonton*, *K'tonton in Israel*, and *K'tonton on an Island in the Sea.*

In this last, the hero goes more afield. Stranded on in "Sabbath on the Island," K'tonton misses home but then quotes from the Talmud: "You are not obliged to finish the task, but neither are you excused from beginning it" (47). With this, he washes his shirt, sweeps the floor, builds a Shabbat table of driftwood with a leaf cover, gathers raisins, and makes hallahs from pounded seeds. Of course, all this is relatable to children making fake foods playing in the yard. When he sings "Lecha Dodi," a miracle comes to him and his clumsy substitute foods taste like real Shabbat dishes. A pair of fireflies lights his candles and he knows "the Sabbath Queen had found him in this strange, far-off place. Maybe his mother and father would find him too." This sweet and spiritual story indeed results in a happy ending.

Continuing his island adventures, he holds a Shavuot party for the mice, birds, and turtles, generously sharing the best treats, even as he prays each night to return home. When his pants wear out, he considers living in a hole in the ground like Simeon Bar Yochai from the Talmud. At last, he floats back to his parents on the traditional Shabbat of Comfort after Tisha B'Av.

In the other collection, he stows away in a suitcase bound for Israel. He's determined to observe the mitzvah of making aliyah, though he makes sure to leave his parents a note. They're actually delighted enough that they join him there. When he arrives, he's thrilled to see the Jewish National Fund trees that he helped contribute to plant. A friendly driver invites him to a Passover seder, where, as the littlest and most curious, he sings the Four Questions. In Jerusalem, he entertains children in the hospital. Visiting Haifa, he enters the Technion, where he asks a scientist to use his microscope to make him big. Mr. Carl must tell him that microscopes don't work that way. However, he tells K'tonton to find Israel on a map. When he suggests little Israel can't possibly be important, because "It's just a speck on a map," K'tonton disagrees and thus finally accepts that for him and the State of Israel, "size isn't everything" (89).

Weilerstein has other Jewish children's books, like the Rosh Hashana exploration *What the Moon Brought* (1942). After two sisters celebrate the holiday, they visit their grandparents. On discovering their garden is dying, the girls save the area with watering cans, and then the bees are filled with gratitude. They generate so much honey that they call a meeting to decide how to use the surplus and decide to send it to Ruth and Debby to sweeten their holiday.

Weilerstein was twice awarded the annual Juvenile Award of the Jewish Book Council of America. She set the stage for Jewish picture books in English, ones that merge assimilated children with the world of holidays and good deeds. Today, such industries are thriving, but, as with all genre works, someone had to start it all.

Conclusion

French film theorist Christian Metzetz posited that genres go through a cycle of four stages during their lifetime: experimental, classic, parody, and deconstruction. Whether it's the Western or the superhero story, the genre takes time to come together into an iconic pattern, establishing conventions for future generations. Before this come more primitive works that are testing out the best pattern to follow, finding a voice, incorporating older patterns, and choosing their most useful elements.

In context of the theory of genre, the first Yiddish novels and short stories were still in the experimental stage before the loss of Yiddish culture halted the production of more. Most readers, when asked to identify the great Jewish novels and memoirs, point to Philip Roth, Primo Levi, Saul Bellow, Claude Lévi-Strauss, Elie Wiesel, Chaim Potok—writers from the post-Holocaust era. Jewish films too, were most notable for the absence of overt Jewishness at this point in history. More people have seen *Fiddler on the Roof* than read Sholem Aleichem's tales of Tevye the Dairyman, and *Fiddler*, like *Annie Hall*, *Funny Girl*, *Exodus*, and *Yentl*, defined Jewishness for a postwar audience. Nonetheless, the Catskills culture trained early humorists like the Three Stooges as well as filmmakers who would go on to entertain the next generation.

In the thirties and forties, comic books were similarly forming the super-hero genre—mixing spies, magicians, and fairytale characters with its Superman and Captain America. Science fiction was likewise in its early years. From the late nineteenth century through the 1930s, it was still mixed with gothic, lost world, and other "weird fiction." Kafka's stories fall more under this last category than under formal science fiction. He and those like him found power through this new genre to protest intolerance and battle for understanding.

The American first golden age of science fiction is generally recognized as the period from 1938 to 1946, when John W. Campbell became a ground-breaking editor. (Others stretch the end date to the fifties, with the boom in science fiction novels.) These stories offered few overt Jews but many metaphoric ones. Nonetheless, Jews left their mark in the formative years of the genre, not only through Gernsback and the other magazine editors, but with the authors pioneering concepts like first contact stories and space opera.

Those in a darkening Europe wrote fiction and poetry with imagery of shunned werewolves and abused robots to criticize fascism and prejudice. In America, things were more hopeful, though the second-generation young people were struggling to fit in. The theme for this era was that of the foreigner—an outsider but one determined to succeed.

Works Cited

Abramovich, Sholem Yakov. 1873. "The Mare." Translated by Joachim Neugroschel. In *The Great Works of Jewish Fantasy and the Occult.* 545–663. New York: Overlook.

Abrams, Nathan. 2018. *Stanley Kubrick: New York Jewish Intellectual.* New Jersey: Rutgers University Press.

Adams, Jenni. 2011. *Magic Realism in Holocaust Literature: Troping the Traumatic Real.* London: Palgrave Macmillan.

Agnon, S. Y. (1939) 1968. *A Guest for the Night.* Translated by Misha Louvish. New York: Schocken Books.

———. (1943) 1975. "The Lady and the Peddler." In *Modern Hebrew Literature,* edited by Robert Alter. 201–212. Springfield, NJ: Behrman House.

———. 1947. *In the Heart of the Seas.* New York: Schocken Books.

———. (1951) 1975. "At the Outset of the Day." In *Modern Hebrew Literature,* edited by Robert Alter. 218–224. Springfield, NJ: Behrman House.

———. 1966. "Three Stories: Fable of the Goat: A Story." Translated by Barney Rubin. *Commentary Magazine,* December 1966. https://www.commentarymagazine.com/articles/three-stories-fable-of-the-goat.

Alascia, Vince. 1945. "Invitation to Murder." In *Captain America* #46. New York: Timely.

Allen, Irwin, dir. (1957) 2009. *The Story of Mankind.* Burbank, CA: Warner Brothers.

Ansky, S. (1926) 1971. *The Dybbuk: A Play in Four Acts.* Translated by Henry G. Alsberg and Winifred Katzin. New York: Liveright.

Aronin, Ben. 1934. *The Lost Tribe: Being the Strange Adventures of Raphael Drale in Search of the Lost Tribes of Israel.* New York: Simons Press.

———. 1943. *Cavern of Destiny.* Springfield, NJ: Behrman's Jewish Book House Publishers.

Ashliman, D. L., ed. and trans. 2005. "Anti-Semitic Legends." *Folktexts.* https://www.pitt.edu/~dash/antisemitic.html.

Asimov, Isaac. (1941) 2003. "Nightfall." In *The Science Fiction Hall of Fame, Vol. 1 1929–1964*, edited by Robert Silverberg. 113–144. New York: Tor.

———. (1950) 1979. "Darwinian Pool Room." In *The End of Summer: Science Fiction of the Fifties*, edited by Barry N. Malzberg and Bill Pronzini. 15–24. New York: Ace.

———. (1950) 2017. *Pebble in the Sky*. New York: Tor.

———. (1952) 2008. *Foundation and Empire*. New York: Bantam Spectra.

———. (1956) 2000. "The Last Question." In *The SFWA Grand Masters Vol. 2*, edited by Frederik Pohl. 210–223. New York: Tor.

———. (1957) 1978. "A Loint of Paw." In *100 Great Science Fiction Short Short Stories*, edited by Isaac Asimov, Martin Harry Greenberg and Joseph D. Olander. 1–2. New York: Doubleday.

———. (1959) 1969. "Unto the Fourth Generation." In *Nightfall and Other Stories*, edited by Isaac Asimov. 299–306. New York: Doubleday.

———. (1962) 1969. "My Son, the Physicist." In *Nightfall and Other Stories*, edited by Isaac Asimov. 329–332. New York: Doubleday.

———. 1974. "Why Me?" In *Wandering Stars*, edited by Jack Dann. 1–6. New York: Harper & Row.

———. 1975. "How Easy to See the Future!" *Natural History*. 62–66.

———. 1988. "The Two-Centimeter Demon." In *Azazel*, edited by Isaac Asimov. 1–11. New York: Doubleday.

———. 1994. *I, Asimov*. New York: Doubleday.

Baioni, Giuliano. 1989. "Zionism, Literature, and the Yiddish Theater." In *Reading Kafka*, edited by Mark Anderson. 95–115. New York: Schocken Books.

Barnett, David. 2014. "Meyrink's The Golem: Where Fact and Fiction Collide." *The Guardian*, January 30, 2014. https://www.theguardian.com/books/booksblog/2014/jan/30/the-golem-gustav-meyrink-books.

Barzilai, Maya. 2016. *Golem: Modern Wars and their Monsters*. New York: New York University Press.

Baum, Alwin L. 1986. "Parable as Paradox in Kafka's Stories." In *Modern Critical Views: Franz Kafka*, edited by Harold Bloom. 151–168. New York: Chelsea House.

Beitler, Ryan. 2017. "Walt the Quasi-Nazi: The Fascist History of Disney is Still Influencing American Life." *Paste*, June 16, 2017.

Bell, Sita. 2009. *Anti-Semitic Folklore Motif Index*. Master's Thesis. Utah State University. https://digitalcommons.usu.edu/etd/299.

Bernardi, Daniel, Murray Pomerance and Hava Tirosh-Samuelson. 2012. "Introduction: The Hollywood Question." In *Hollywood's Chosen People: The Jewish Experience in American Cinema*, edited by Daniel Bernardi, Murray Pomerance and Hava Tirosh-Samuelson. 1–18. Detroit, MI: Wayne State University Press.

Bernds, Edward, dir. (1962) 2014. *The Three Stooges Meet Hercules*. The Three Stooges Collection. Minnetonka, MN: Mill Creek Ent. DVD.

———. (1963) 2003. *The Three Stooges in Orbit*. Culver City, CA: Sony. DVD.

Bertman, Stephen. 2015. "The Role of the Golem in the Making of Frankenstein." *The Keats-Shelley Review* 29: 42–50. 10.1179/0952414215Z.00000000056.

Bester, Alfred. (1941) 1997. "Adam and No Eve." In *Virtual Unrealities*, edited by Robert Silverberg, Byron Preiss, and Keith R.A. DeCandido. 273–286. New York: Vintage.

Biale, David. 2007. *Blood and Belief: The Circulation of a Symbol between Jews and Christians*. Berkeley: University of California Press.

Blunden, Allan. 1980. "A Chronology of Kafka's Life." In *The World of Franz Kafka*, edited by J. P. Stern. 11–29. New York: Holt, Rinehart and Winston.

Blutinger, Jeffrey C. 2010. "Creatures from Before the Flood: Reconciling Science and Genesis in the Pages of a Nineteenth-Century Hebrew Newspaper." *Jewish Social Studies: History, Culture, Society* 16, no. 2 (Winter): 67–92.

Borden, Louise. 2005. *The Journey that Saved Curious George: The True Wartime Escape of Margret and H. A. Rey*. Illustrated by Allan Drummond. New York: Houghton Mifflin.

Borges, Jorge Luis. (1940) 1967. "The Circular Ruins." Translated by Anthony Kerrigan. In *A Personal Anthology by Jorge Luis Borges*. 68–74. New York: Grove Press.

———. (1941) 2007. "The Library of Babel." Translated by J. E. I. In *Labyrinths: Selected Stories & Other Writings*. 51–58. New York: New Directions.

———. (1942) 2007. "Death and the Compass." Translated by D. A. Y. In *Labyrinths: Selected Stories & Other Writings*. 76–87. New York: New Directions.

———. (1943) 2007. "The Secret Miracle." Translated by Harriet de Onís. In *Labyrinths: Selected Stories & Other Writings*. 88–94. New York: New Directions.

———. (1949) 1967. "The Aleph." Translated by Anthony Kerrigan. In *A Personal Anthology by Jorge Luis Borges*. 138–154. New York: Grove Press.

———. (1949) 2007. "The God's Script." Translated by L. A. Murillo. In *Labyrinths: Selected Stories & Other Writings*. 169–173. New York: New Directions.

———. (1964) 1967. "The Golem." Translated by Anthony Kerrigan. In *A Personal Anthology by Jorge Luis Borges*. 77–79. New York: Grove Press.

Bower, Kathrin M. "Holocaust Avengers: From 'The Master Race' to Magneto." *International Journal of Comic Art* 6, no. 2 (2004): 182–194.

Broches, Rochel. (1940) 2007. "Little Abrahams." Translated by Arnice Pollock. In *Arguing with the Storm: Stories by Yiddish Women Writers*, edited by Rhea Tregebov. 91–102. New York: Feminist Press.

Brod, Harry. 2012. *Superman is Jewish?* New York: Free Press.

Brode, Douglas. 2005. *Multiculturalism and the Mouse: Race and Sex in Disney Entertainment*. Austin, TX: University of Texas Press.

Bruce, Iris. 2016. "What if Franz Kafka Had Immigrated to Palestine?" In *What Ifs of Jewish History from Abraham to Zionism*, edited by Gavriel D. Rosenfeld. 187–214. Cambridge: Cambridge University Press.

Budick, Emily Miller. 2015. *The Subject of Holocaust Fiction*. Indiana: Indiana University Press.

Buhle, Paul. 2008. *Jews and American Comics*. New York: New Press.

Burroughs, Edgar Rice. (1925) 2015. *The Moon Men*. New York: A. C. McClurg & Co. Project Gutenberg. http://gutenberg.net.au/ebooks05/0500221h.html.

Burton, Richard D. E. 2013. *Prague: A Cultural History*. Northampton, MA: Interlink Pub Group.

Butler, Samuel. (1872) 2002. *Erewhon*. Mineola, NY: Dover Publications.

Cameron, Don (w) and Jerry Robinson (a). 1943. "Swastika over the White House." In *Batman* #14. New York: DC Comics.

Canetti, Elias. (1977) 2005. "From *The Tongue Set Free*." *The New York: Schocken Book of Modern Sephardic Literature*, edited by Ilan Stavans. 73–87. New York: Schocken.

Cantor, Jay. 2014. *Forgiving the Angel: Four Stories for Franz Kafka*. New York, Alfred A. New York: Knopf.

Čapek, Brothers. (1923) 1987. "R. U. R." In *R. U. R. and the Insect Play*, adapted by Nigel Playfair and translated by P. Selver. 1–104. Oxford: Oxford University Press.

Čapek, Karl. (1927) 2019. *The Absolute at Large*. Translated by Thomas Mark. Mineola, NY: Dover.

———. 1929. *Adam the Creator*. Translated by Dora Round. New York: Allen & Unwin/Smith.

———. (1936) 1985. *War with the Newts*. Translated by Ewald Osers. Highland Park, NJ: Catbird Press.

———. 1938. *Power and Glory*. Translated by Paul Selver and Ralph Neale. London: George Allen & Unwin.

Caplan, Marc. "Science Fiction in the Age of Jewish Enlightenment." *Prooftexts* 19, no. 1 (1999): 93–100. Accessed August 10, 2020. www.jstor.org/stable /20689537.

Carpenter, Humphrey, ed. with Christopher Tolkien. 1981. *The Letters of J. R. R. Tolkien*. Boston: Houghton Mifflin Company.

Chabon, Michael. (2000) 2012. *The Amazing Adventures of Kavalier and Clay*. New York: Random House.

Chaplin, Charlie, dir. 1940. *The Great Dictator*. Burbank, CA: Criterion Collection. Prime Video.

Charles, R. H., ed. (1913) 2004. *The Apocrypha and Pseudepigrapha of the Old Testament*. Oxford: The Clarendon Press.

"Children's Literature: Polish Literature." 2010. *The Yivo Encyclopedia of Jews in Eastern Europe*. http://www.yivoencyclopedia.org/article.aspx/Childrens_ Literature/Polish_Literature.

Cott, Jonathan. 1983. *Pipers at the Gates of Dawn: The Wisdom of Children's Literature*. New York: Random House.

Cramer, Zak. 2011. "The Hebrew and Elvish Languages: Why Do So Many Elves Have Jewish Names?" *Mythprint* 48, no. 7 (July): 3.

———. 2006. "Jewish Influences in Middle-Earth." *Mallorn* 44 (August): 9–16.

Crumb, Robert and David Zane Mairowitz. 2007. *Kafka*. Seattle, WA: Fantagraphics.

Dauber, Jeremy. 2010. *In the Demon's Bedroom*. New York: Yale University Press.

Davin, Eric Leif. 2006. *Partners in Wonder: Women and the Birth of Science Fiction, 1926–1965*. Lanham, MD: Lexington Books.

Davis, John Curran. 2012. "Interview: Translator John Curran Davis on Polish Writer Bruno Schulz." *Weird Fiction Review*, January 23, 2012. https://weirdfictionreview .com/2012/01/interview-translator-john-curran-davis-on-polish-writer-bruno-schulz.

Dennis, Geoffrey and Avi S. Dennis. 2014. "Vampires and Witches and Commandos, Oy Vey: Comic Book Appropriations of Lilith." *Shofar: An Interdisciplinary Journal of Jewish Studies* 32, no. 3 (Spring): 72–101. EBSCOhost, doi:10.1353/sho.2014.0031.

Di Filippo, Paul. 2013. "The Jackdaw's Last Case." In *Super Stories of Heroes & Villains*, edited by Claude Lalumière. 253–276. San Francisco: Tachyon.

Disraeli, Benjamin. (1845) 2006. *Alroy: The Prince of the Captivity*. London: Walter Dunne. Project Gutenberg. http://www.gutenberg.org/files/20002/20002-h/20002-h.htm.

Donnelly, Ignatius. (1890) 2012. *Caesar's Colum: A Story of the Twentieth Century*. Chicago: F. J. Shulte & Co. Project Gutenberg. https://www.gutenberg.org/files/5155/5155-h/5155-h.htm.

du Maurier, George. 1894. *Trilby*. New York: Harper and Brothers.

Ebiri, Bilge. 2014. "The Interview Has Renewed Interest in Chaplin's *The Great Dictator*, Which Is a Great Thing." *Vulture*, December 19, 2014. https://www.vulture.com/2014/12/charlie-chaplin-great-dictator-history.html.

Edel, Leon. 1975. "Marginal Keri and Textual Chetiv: The Mystical Novel of A. M. Klein." In *The A. M. Klein Symposium*, edited by Seymour Mayne. 15–29. Ottawa, Canada: University of Ottawa Press.

Ehrenburg, Ilya. 1922. *The Extraordinary Adventures of Julio Jurenito and his Disciples*. Translated by Anna Bostock and Yvonne Kapp. London: MacGibbom & Kee.

Eisner, Will. 2007. *Life in Pictures*. New York: WW Norton and Co.

Elber, Lynn. 2015. "Walt Disney Experts Rebut Dogged Anti-Semitic Allegations." *AP Television Writer*, August 3, 2015. *Newspaper Source Plus*.

Elior, Rachel. 2008. *Dybbuks and Jewish Women: In Social History, Mysticism and Folklore*. Translated by Joel Linsider. Jerusalem, Israel: Urim.

Enright, D. J. 1980. "K. on the Moon." In *The World of Franz Kafka*, edited by J. P. Stern. 220–222. New York: Holt, Rinehart and Winston.

Erens, Patricia. 1984. *The Jew in American Cinema*. Bloomington: Indiana University Press.

Evanier, Mark. 2008. *Kirby: King of Comics*. New York: Abrams.

Ewers, Hanns Heinz. (1921) 1934. *Vampire*. Translated by Fritz Sallagar. New York: John Day.

Faber, Michael. 2010. "Tree of Codes by Jonathan Safran Foer—Review." *The Guardian*, December 18, 2010. https://www.theguardian.com/books/2010/dec/18/tree-codes-safran-foer-review.

Feierberg, M. Z. (1900) 1975. "In the Evening." In *Modern Hebrew Literature*, edited by Robert Alter. 68–84. Springfield, NJ: Behrman House.

Fingeroth, Danny. 2007. *Disguised as Clark Kent: Jews, Comics, and the Creation of the Superhero*. New York: Continuum.

Fishburn, Evelyn. 2013. "Jewish, Christian, and Gnostic Themes." In *The Cambridge Companion to Jorge Luis Borges*, edited by Edwin Williamson. 56–67. Cambridge: Cambridge University Press.

Fleischer, Max and Dave, dir. 1923. "Betty Boop's Ups and Downs." In *Betty Boop: Her Wildest Adventures*. Gaiam: 2004. DVD.

———. 1932. "Stopping the Show." In *Betty Boop—Vol. 1: 22 Cartoon Classics*. Prime Video: 2017.

Foer, Jonathan Safran. 2002. *Everything Is Illuminated*. New York: Houghton Mifflin.

———. 2010. *Tree of Codes*. London: Visual Editions.

Frankel, Ellen, ed. 1989a. "Rabbi Akiva's Daughter or the Jewish Snow White." In *The Classic Tales*. 579–583. Northvale, NJ: J. Aronson.

———. 1989b. "The Will of Heaven." In *The Classic Tales*. 365–369. Northvale, NJ: J. Aronson.

Fried, Lewis. 1988. *Handbook of American-Jewish Literature: An Analytical Guide to Topics, Themes, and Sources*. Westport, CT: Greenwood Press.

Friedlander, Saul. 2013. *Franz Kafka: The Poet of Shame and Guilt*. New York: Yale University Press.

Frug, Simon (1890) 2007. "Song." Translated by Alyssa Dinega Gillespe. In *An Anthology of Jewish-Russian Literature, Book One: Centuries of Dual Identity in Prose and Poetry*, edited by Maxim Shrayer. 88. Armonk, NY: Sharpe.

Gabler, Neal. 2006. *Walt Disney: The Triumph of the American Imagination*. New York: Vintage.

Galbraith, Mary. 2000a. "Agony in the Kindergarten: Indelible German Images in American Picture Books." In *Text, Culture and National Identity in Children's Literature*, edited by Jean Webb. 124–143. NORDINFO Publication 44.

———. 2000b. "What Must I Give Up in Order to Grow Up? The Great War and Childhood Survival Strategies in Transatlantic Picture Books." *The Lion and the Unicorn* 24, no. 3, (September): 337–359.

Gelman, Simkhe. (1936) 2020a. "The Birds Go on Strike." In *Honey on the Page: A Treasury of Yiddish Children's Literature*, edited and translated by Miriam Udel. 233–235. New York: NYU Press.

———. (1936) 2020b. "The Girl in the Mailbox." In *Honey on the Page: A Treasury of Yiddish Children's Literature*, edited and translated by Miriam Udel. 268–269. New York: NYU Press.

Gerrold, David. 1994. "Franz Kafka, Superhero." In *By Any Other Fame*, edited by Mike Resnick and Martin Greenberg. 114–129. New York: Daw.

Gibbon, Lewis Grassic. (1932) 2001. *The Lost Trumpet*. Edinburgh: Polygon.

Gibson, Arthur. 2000. "Philosophy of Psychotic Modernism: Wagner and Hitler." In *Christian-Jewish Relations Through the Centuries*, edited by Brook W. R. Pearson and Stanley E. Sheffield Porter. 351–386. Cambridge, MA: Academic Press.

Goff, Samuel. 2017. "Edenia: A Lost Yiddish Utopia for Ukraine and its Afterlife in Modern-day Kharkiv." *The Calvert Journal*, June 30, 2017. https://www. calvertjournal.com/articles/show/8498/edenia-lost-yiddish-utopia-ukraine-afterlife -modern-day-kharkiv.

Gold, Horace L. (1939) 1974. "Trouble with Water." In *Wandering Stars*, edited by Jack Dann. 103–126. New York: Harper & Row.

———. 1951. "Looking Forward." *Galaxy Science Fiction*, June 1951, 2.

Goldberg, Judith N. 1983. *Laughter through Tears: The Yiddish Cinema*. London: Associate University Presses.

Goldman, Albert. 1987. "Laughtermakers." In *Jewish Wry: Essays on Jewish Humor*, edited by Sarah Blacher Cohen. 80–88. Bloomington, IL: Indiana University Press.

Goldsmith, Arnold L. 1981. *The Golem Remembered, 1909–1980: Variations of a Jewish Legend*. Detroit, MI: Wayne State University Press.

Goulart, Ron. 1986. *Great History of Comic Books*. Chicago, IL: Contemporary Books.

Griffith, George. (1893) 2010. *The Angel of the Revolution: A Tale of the Coming Terror*. Edinburgh: Morrison & Gibb. Project Gutenberg. https://www.gutenberg.org/ebooks/31324.

Grossman, David. 1986. *See Under: Love*. Translated by Betsy Rosenberg. New York: Farrar, Straus and Giroux.

Grumberg, Karen. 2019. *Hebrew Gothic: History and the Poetics of Persecution*. Bloomington, IN: Indiana University Press.

Gunn, James. 1982. *Isaac Asimov: The Foundation of Science Fiction*. Oxford: Oxford University Press.

Guttenberg, Violet. 1904. *A Modern Exodus*. London: Greening.

Helfgott, Leonard M. 2011. "Groucho, Harpo, Chico, and Karl: Immigrant Humor and the Depression." In *Jews and Humor*, edited by Leonard Jay Greenspoon. 107–119. Lincoln, NE: Harris Center for Judaic Studies.

Heller, Erich. 1986. "The Castle." In *Modern Critical Views: Franz Kafka*, edited by Harold Bloom. 133–149. New York: Chelsea House.

Herzl, Theodor. (2018) 1916. *Altneuland*. Translated by Dr. D. S. Blondheim, Jewish Virtual Library. http://www.jewishvirtuallibrary.org/quot-altneuland-quot-theodor-herzl.

Horwitz, Daniel M., ed. 2016. "Magic." In *A Kabalah and Jewish Mysticism Reader*. 295–305. Lincoln, NE: University of Nebraska Press.

Howe, Irving. 1992. *Introduction to The Castle by Franz Kafka*. v–xxi. New York: Knopf.

Huxley, Aldous. (1920) 1970. "Farcical History of Richard Greenow." In *Limbo*. 1–115. London: London.

———. (1925) 1994. *Those Barren Leaves*. London: London.

———. (1930) 1957. "Chawdron." In *Collected Short Stories*. 302–336. New York: Harper & Brothers.

———. (1948) 1992. *Ape and Essence*. London: Elephant.

Ibn Ezra, Abraham. (1143) 1995. *The Secret of the Torah: A Translation of Abraham Ibn Ezra's Sefer yesod mora ve-sod ha-Torah*. Translated by H. N. Strickman. Lanham, MD: Jason Aronson, Inc.

Idel, Moshe. 1990. *Golem: Magical and Mystical Traditions on the Artificial Anthropoid*. New York: State University of New York Press.

Ingall, Marjorie. 2010. "K'TonTon Time." *Tablet Magazine*, October 4, 2010. https://www.tabletmag.com/jewish-life-and-religion/46184/k%e2%80%99tonton-time.

Jabotinsky, Vladimir. (1926) 1930. *Samson the Nazarite*. Translated by C Harry Brooks. London: M. Secker.

Jacobs, Joela. 2015. "Assimilating Aliens: Imagining National Identity in Oskar Panizza's Operated Jew and Salomo Friedlaender's Operated Goy." In *Alien*

Imaginations: Science Fiction and Tales of Transnationalism, edited by Ulrike Küchler, Silja Maehl and Graeme Stout. 57–71. New York: Bloomsbury Academy.

Jaret, Charles. 1985. "Jew and Jewish Themes in Science Fiction." *Journal of Popular Literature* 1, no. 2 (Fall/Winter): 126–144.

Jenkins, Philip. 1992. "Sticking up for Jews? Anti-Semitic Stereotypes in the English Novel." Pennsylvania State University. http://www.personal.psu.edu/faculty/j/p/jpj1/antisemitism.htm.

Kafka, Franz. (1912) 1981. "Description of a Struggle." Translated by Tania and James Stern. In *Franz Kafka: The Complete Stories*. 9–51. New York: Schocken Books.

———. (1912) 1993. "The Judgement." Translated by Willa and Edwin Muir. In *Franz Kafka Collected Stories*. 25–39. New York: Knopf.

———. (1915) 1971. "Blumfeld, an Elderly Bachelor." Translated by Tania and James Stern. In *Franz Kafka: The Complete Stories*. 183–205. New York: Schocken Books.

———. (1915) 1993. "The Metamorphosis." Translated by Willa and Edwin Muir. In *Franz Kafka Collected Stories*. 75–128. New York: Knopf.

———. (1917) 1993a. "A Report to the Academy." Translated by Willa and Edwin Muir. In *Franz Kafka Collected Stories*. 195–204. New York: Knopf.

———. (1917) 1993b. "Jackals and Arabs." Translated by Willa and Edwin Muir. In *Franz Kafka Collected Stories*. 175–182. New York: Knopf.

———. (1920) 1960. "The Animal in the Synagogue." Translated by Clement Greenberg. In *Parables and Paradoxes*, edited by Nahum N. Glatzer. New York: Schocken Books.

———. (1922) 1993. "The Married Couple." Translated by Willa and Edwin Muir. In *Franz Kafka Collected Stories*. 460–465. New York: Knopf.

———. (1924) 1993. "Josephine the Singer, or the Folk Mouse." Translated by Willa and Edwin Muir. In *Franz Kafka Collected Stories*. 233–250. New York: Knopf.

———. (1925) 1992. *The Trial*. New York: Knopf.

———. (1927) 1946. *Amerika*. Translated by Willa and Edwin Muir. New York: Schocken.

———. (1930) 1992. *The Castle*. Translated by Anthea Bell. New York: Knopf.

Kaplan, Arie. 2008. *From Krakow to Krypton: Jews and Comic Books*. The Jewish Publication Society. EBSCO.

King, Susan. 2010. "*Wolf Man* Writer Reflected Wartime Jewish Experience." *LA Times*, February 3, 2010. https://www.latimes.com/archives/la-xpm-2010-feb-03-la-et-classic-hollywood3-2010feb03-story.html.

Kinney, Jack. (1943) 2004. *Der Fuehrer's Face. Walt Disney Treasures*. Burbank, CA: Disney. DVD.

Kipnis, Levin. (1961) 2020. "Children of the Field." In *Honey on the Page: A Treasury of Yiddish Children's Literature*, edited and translated by Miriam Udel. 40–44. New York: NYU Press.

Kitchen, Denis and Paul Buhle. 2009. *The Art of Harvey Kurtzman: The Mad Genius of Comics*. New York: Abrams.

Klein, A. M. (1926) 1990. "The Shechinah of Shadows." In *A. M. Klein: Complete Poems*, edited by Zailig Pollock. 3–4. Toronto: University of Toronto Press.

———. (1930) 1983a. "The Chanukah Dreidel." In *A. M. Klein: Short Stories*, edited by M. W. Steinberg. 43–48. Toronto: University of Toronto Press.

———. (1930) 1983b. "The Lost Twins." In *A. M. Klein: Short Stories*, edited by M. W. Steinberg. 24–29. Toronto: University of Toronto Press.

———. (1930) 1983c. "Prophet in Our Midst: A Story for Passover." In *A. M. Klein: Short Stories*, edited by M. W. Steinberg. 14–17. Toronto: University of Toronto Press.

———. (1932) 1983a. "Master of the Horn." In *A. M. Klein: Short Stories*, edited by M. W. Steinberg. 62–67. Toronto: University of Toronto Press.

———. (1932) 1983b. "Once upon a Time." In *A. M. Klein: Short Stories*, edited by M. W. Steinberg. 83–88. Toronto: University of Toronto Press.

———. (1944) 1974. "The Hitleriad." In *The Collected Poems of A. M. Klein*, edited by Miriam Waddington. Toronto: McGrawHill Ryerson.

———. (1951) 1985. *The Second Scroll*. Marlboro, VT: The Marlboro Press.

Kornbluth, C. M. (1941) 1997. "Kazam Collects." In *His Share of Glory: The Complete Short Science Fiction of C. M. Kornbluth*, edited by Timothy Szczesuil. 361–371. Framingham, MA: NESFA Press.

———. (1950) 1976. "The Mindworm." In *The Best of C. M. Kornbluth*, edited by Fredrik Pohl. 176–189. New York: Taplinger.

———. (1951) 1997. "The Marching Morons." In *His Share of Glory: The Complete Short Science Fiction of C. M. Kornbluth*, edited by Timothy Szczesuil. 372–395. Framingham, MA: NESFA Press.

———. 1955. *Not This August*. New York: Doubleday.

Kraus, Karl. 1984. *The Last Days of Mankind*. In *In these Great Times*, edited by Harry Zohn. 159–258. Manchester: Carcanet.

Kreitman, Esther Singer. (1936) 2009. *The Dance of the Demons*. Translated by Maurice Carr. New York: The Feminist Press at CUNY.

Kulisher, Ruvim. (1849) 2007. "From *An Answer to the Slav*." Translated by Maxim D. Shrayer. In *An Anthology of Jewish-Russian Literature, Book One: Centuries of Dual Identity in Prose and Poetry*, edited by Maxim Shrayer. 28–32. Armonk, NY: Sharpe.

Kuttner, Henry and C. L. Moore. 1943. "Nothing but Gingerbread Left." *Astounding Stories*, January 1943.

Lacoue-Labarthe, Isabelle. 2016. "The Emergence of Jewish 'Feminist Consciousness': Europe, the United States, Palestine (1880–1930)." *Clio: Women, Gender, History* 44: 94–121.

Lebovic, Matt. 2013. "Are Tolkien's Dwarves an Allegory for the Jews?" *Times of Israel*, December 11, 2013. http://www.timesofisrael.com/are-tolkiens-dwarves-an-allegory-for-the-jews.

Lee, Malka. (1955) 1994. "Through the Eyes of Childhood." Translated by Sarah Silberman Swartz. In *Found Treasures: Stories by Yiddish Women Writers*, edited by Frieda Forman. 159–185. Toronto: Second Story Press.

Legutko, Agnieszka. 2010. "Feminist Dybbuks: Spirit Possession Motif in Post-Second Wave Jewish Women's Fiction." *Bridges: A Jewish Feminist Journal* 15, no. 1: 6–26.

Lethem, Jonathan and Carter Scholz. 2001. "Receding Horizons." In *Kafka Americana*, edited by Jonathan Lethem and Carter Scholz 23–50. New York: Norton.

Levinson, Rose L. 2013. *Death of a Holy Land: Reflections in Contemporary Israeli Fiction.* Lanham, MD: Lexington Books.

Levitz, Paul. 2013. *The Golden Age of DC Comics 1935–1956.* New York: DC Comics.

Linyetski, Y. Y. (1876) 2006. "The Hasidic Steam Engine." In *Radiant Days, Haunted Nights: Great Tales from the Treasury of Yiddish Literature*, edited by Joachim Neugroschel. 231–239. New York: Abrams.

Liptak, Andrew. 2013. "The Futurians and the 1939 World Science Fiction Convention." *Kirkus Reviews*, May 9, 2013. https://www.kirkusreviews.com/features/futurians-and-1939-world-science-fiction-conventio.

Lord, Del. 1943. "Higher than a Kite." *Three Stooges: The Complete DVD Collection.* Culver City, CA: Sony: 2016. DVD.

Louvish, Simon. 1999. *Monkey Business: The Lives and Legends of the Marx Brothers: Groucho, Chico, Harpo, Zeppo, With Added Gummo.* London: Faber & Faber.

Lovecraft, H. P. (1927) 2009. "Supernatural Horror in Literature." *HP Lovecraft.com*, October 20, 2009. http://www.hplovecraft.com/writings/texts/essays/shil.aspx.

Madison, Charles A. 1968. *Yiddish Literature.* New York: Frederrick Ungar.

Manger, Itzik. (1938) 1965. *The Book of Paradise: The Wonderful Adventures of Shmuel-Aba Abervo.* Translated by Leonard Wolf. New York: Hill and Wang.

Martin, Douglas. 2000. "Curt Siodmak Dies at 98; Created Modern Wolf Man." *The New York Times*, November 19, 2000. https://www.nytimes.com/2000/11/19/nyregion/curt-siodmak-dies-at-98-created-modern-wolf-man.html.

Mast, Gerald. "Woody Allen." In *Jewish Wry: Essays on Jewish Humor*, edited by Sarah Blacher Cohen. 125–140. Bloomington, IL: Indiana University Press.

Matza, Diane. 1992. "Tradition and History: Sephardic Contributions to American Literature." *American Jewish Archives* 44, no. 1 (1992): 379–409. http://americanjewisharchives.org/publications/journal/PDF/1992_44_01_00_matza.pdf.

Mayakovsky, Vladimir. (1929) 1970. "The Bedbug." In *The Bedbug and Selected Poetry*, edited by Patricia Blake, translated by Max Hayward and George Reavey. 241–303. New York: World Publishing Company.

Mayo, Archie, dir. 1946. *A Night in Casablanca.* Burbank, CA: Universal Studios. Prime Video.

Maze, Ida. (1970) 1994. "Dina." Translated by Ethel Raicus. In *Found Treasures: Stories by Yiddish Women Writers*, edited by Frieda Forman. 131–143. Toronto: Second Story Press.

McCarey, Leo, dir. 1933. *Duck Soup.* Burbank, CA: Universal Studios. Prime Video.

Meek, S. P. (1930). 2018. *The Drums of Tapajos, Illustrated Edition* (Lost World-Lost Race Classics) (Volume 15). Medford, OR: Armchair Fiction & Music.

———. 1931. "Giants on the Earth." *Astounding*, December 1931–January 1932.

Meyrink, Gustav. (1915) 2017. *The Golem.* Translated by Mike Mitchell. Great Britain: Dadalus, Ltd.

Miron, Dan. 2019. *Animal in the Synagogue: Franz Kafka's Jewishness.* Lanham, MD: Lexington Books.

Mitchell, J. Leslie. 1932. *The Lost Trumpet.* Indianapolis, IN: Bobbs-Merrill.

Moore, C. L. 1936. "Tryst in Time." *Astounding Stories,* December 1936.

———. (1936) 1975. "Tree of Life." In *The Fantastic Pulps,* edited by Peter Haining. 315–342. New York: St. Martin's.

———. (1940) 1998. "Fruit of Knowledge." In *The Fantasy Hall of Fame,* edited by Robert Silverberg. 47–75. New York: Harper Prism.

Morgan, Judith and Neil. 1996. *Dr. Seuss and Mr. Geisel.* Cambridge, MA: Da Capo.

Moss, Kenneth B. 2009. *Jewish Renaissance in the Russian Revolution.* Boston, MA: Harvard University Press.

Nadir, Moyshe. (1924) 2001. "The Man Who Slept through the End of the World." In *Jewish American Literature: A Norton Anthology,* edited by Jules Chametzky. 231–232. New York: Norton.

———. (1936) 2018. "In the Land of Happy Tears." Translated by David Stromberg. In *In the Land of Happy Tears,* edited by David Stromberg. 3–7. New York: Random House.

Nagarajan, Nadia Grosser, ed. 2005a. "The House on Back Street." In *Pomegranate Seeds: Latin American Jewish Tales.* 166–172. Albuquerque: University of New Mexico Press.

———. 2005b. "The Rabbi's Tomb." In *Pomegranate Seeds: Latin American Jewish Tales.* 85–90. Albuquerque: University of New Mexico Press.

———. 2005c. "Sea Monsters." In *Pomegranate Seeds: Latin American Jewish Tales.* 101–105. Albuquerque: University of New Mexico Press.

———. 2005d. "Where the Navel Is Buried." In *Pomegranate Seeds: Latin American Jewish Tales.* 154–161. Albuquerque: University of New Mexico Press.

Nathan, Robert. 1929. *There Is Another Heaven.* Indianapolis, IN: Bobbs-Merrill.

———. 1935. *Road of Ages.* New York: Knopf.

———. 1939. *Portrait of Jennie.* New York: Knopf.

———. 1947. *Mr. Whittle and the Morning Star.* New York: Knopf.

———. 1975. *Heaven and Hell and the Megas Factor.* New York: Delacorte.

Nel, Philip. 2004. *Dr. Seuss: American Icon.* New York: Continuum.

Neman, Y. 2012. "Astronomy in Israel: From Og's Circle to the Wise Observator." In *Cataclysmic Variables and Related Objects: Proceedings of the 72nd Colloquium of the International Astronomical Union Held in Haifa,* Israel, August 9–13, 1982. edited by M. Livio, G. Shaviv. Springer Science & Business Media.

Nemett, Adam. 2018. "Only We Can Save Us: A Brief History of Jewish Superheroes, Real and Fictional." *Jewish Book Council,* November 1, 2018. https://www.jewishbookcouncil.org/pb-daily/only-we-can-save-us-a-brief-history -of-jewish-superheroes-real-and-fictional.

Nesbit, E. (1899) 2006. *The Story of the Treasure Seekers.* San Francisco, CA: Chronicle Books.

———. (1906) 1996. *The Story of the Amulet.* New York: Puffin.

Nevala-Lee, Alec. 2018. *Astounding: John W. Campbell, Isaac Asimov, Robert A. Heinlein, L. Ron Hubbard, and the Golden Age of Science Fiction.* New York: Dey St.

Oirich, Alan E. 2006. "SuperMensch" *Aish*, June 28, 2006. http://www.aish.com/ci /a/48949071.html.

Oişteanu, Andrei. 2009. *Inventing the Jew. Antisemitic Stereotypes in Romanian and Other Central East-European Cultures.* Lincoln, NE: University of Nebraska Press.

Olesha, Yuri. (1927) 2004. *Envy.* Translated by Marian Schwartz. New York: New York Review of Books.

Omry, Keren. 2013. "Israeli SF 101." *SFRA Review* 306 (Fall) 8–11.

Orwell, George. 1945. "Antisemitism in Britain." *Contemporary Jewish Record*, April 1945. https://www.orwellfoundation.com/the-orwell-foundation/orwell/ essays-and-other-works/antisemitism-in-britain.

———. 1971. *Collected Essays, Journalism and Letters of George Orwell.* Edited by Sonia Orwell and Ian Angus New York: Penguin.

Osherow, Michelle. 2000. "The Dawn of a New Lilith: Revisionary Mythmaking in Women's Science Fiction." *NWSA Journal* 12, no. 1 (Spring): 68–83.

Ozick, Cynthia. 1987. *The Messiah of Stockholm.* New York: Knopf.

Packer, Sharon. 2010. *Superheroes and Superegos: Analyzing the Minds behind the Masks.* Santa Barbara, CA: ABC-Clio.

Panizza, Oskar. (1893) 1980. "The Operated Jew." Translated by Jack Zipes. *New German Critique* No. 21, Special Issue 3: Germans and Jews (Autumn): 63–79. *Jstor.* https://www.jstor.org/stable/487997.

Pascal, Roy. 1980. "Kafka's Parables: Ways out of the Dead End." In *The World of Franz Kafka*, edited by J. P. Stern. 112–119. New York: Holt, Rinehart and Winston.

Pearse, Holly A. 2018. "Charlie Chaplin: Jewish Or Goyish?" *Jewish Quarterly*, October 19, 2018. https://www.jewishquarterly.org/2010/11/charlie-chaplin -jewish-or-goyish/.

Peretz, I. L. (1894) 1955. "Bontsha the Silent." Translated by Hilde Abel. In *A Treasury of Yiddish Stories*, edited by Irving Howe and Eliezer Greenberg. 223– 230. London: Andre Deutsch Ltd.

———. (1895) 2002. "The Dead Town." Translated by Hillel Hallan. In *The I. L. Peretz Reader*, edited by Ruth R. Wisse. Yale University Press: New Haven and London.

———. (1901) 1987. "The Three Wedding Canopies." In *The Great Works of Jewish Fantasy and Occult*, edited by Joseph Neugroschel. 60–104. New York: Overlook.

Peretz, I. L. and Hillel Halkin. "A Night in the Old Marketplace." *Prooftexts* 12, no. 1 (1992): 1–70. Jstor. http://www.jstor.org/stable/20689324.

Perl, Arnold. 1953. *The World of Sholom Aleichem.* New York: Dramatists Play Service.

Peterkiewicz, Jerzy. 1980. "A Triptych for the Jackdaw." In *The World of Franz Kafka*, edited by J. P. Stern. 218–219. New York: Holt, Rinehart and Winston.

Pierpont, Claudia Roth. 2013. *Roth Unbound: A Writer and his Books.* New York: Farrar, Straus and Giroux.

Pinsent, Pat. 2000. "After Fagin: Jewishness and Children's Literature." In *Christian-Jewish Relations Through the Centuries*, edited by Brook W. R. Pearson and Stanley E. Sheffield Porter. 311–328. Cambridge, MA: Academic Press.

Pinsky, Mark I. 2004. *The Gospel According to Disney*. Louisville, KY: Westminster John Knox Press.

Portelli, Alessandro. "The Three Laws of Robotics: Laws of the Text, Laws of Production, Laws of Society." *Science Fiction Studies* 7, no. 2 (1980): 150–156. Jstor. www.jstor.org/stable/4239326.

Pratchett, Terry. 2005. *Thud!* New York: HarperCollins.

Price, Roger. 2013. "Isaac Asimov, Two Foundations and the Jews." *Judaism and Science*, June 21, 2013. https://www.judaismandscience.com/isaac-asimov-two-foundations-and-the-jews.

Pynsent, Robert B. 2000. "Tolerance and the Karel Čapek Myth." *The Slavonic and East European Review* 78, no. 2: 331–353. Jstor. www.jstor.org/stable/4213057.

Rapaport, Lynn. 2006. "Hang Hitler—The Three Stooges Take Potshots at Nazis." In *American Judaism in Popular Culture*, edited by Leonard Jay Greenspoon and Ronald Simkins. 75–98. Omaha, NE: Creighton University Press.

Reitter, Paul. 2014. "Bambi's Jewish Roots." *Jewish Review of Books*, Winter 2014. https://jewishreviewofbooks.com/articles/618/bambis-jewish-roots.

Rey, H. A. 1941. *Curious George*. New York: Houghton Mifflin.

Rich, David Lowell, dir. (1959) 2014. *Have Rocket, Will Travel. The Three Stooges Collection*. Minnetonka, MN: Mill Creek Ent. DVD.

Rich, Mark. 2009. *C. M. Kornbluth: The Life and Works of a Science Fiction Visionary*. Jefferson, NC: McFarland.

Rosenberg, Warren. 2001. "A Heritage of Rage: Golems and Gimpels in Jewish Literature of the Early Twentieth Century." In *A Legacy of Rage: Jewish Masculinity, Violence, and Culture*, edited by Warren Rosenberg 69–114. Amherst, MA: University of Massachusetts Press.

Rosenhan, Claudia. 2003. "Aldous Huxley and Anti-Semitism." *Aldous Huxley Annual* 3: 217–237.

Roth, Philip. (1973) 2017. "'I Always Wanted You to Admire My Fasting'; or, Looking at Kafka." In *Why Write?* 5–24. New York: The Library of America.

———. 1975. "Conversation in New York with Isaac Bashevis Singer about Bruno Schulz." In *Why Write?* 246–254. New York: Literary Classics of the United States.

Rousseau, Victor. (1917) 1974. *The Messiah of the Cylinder*. Chicago: Hyperion.

Rovner, Adam. 2016. "What if the Jewish State Had Been Established in East Africa?" *What Ifs of Jewish History from Abraham to Zionism*, edited by Gavriel D. Rosenfeld. 165–186. Cambridge: Cambridge University Press.

Sacks, Esther. 2017. "What's So Jewish About Werewolves?" *Jewcy*, October 31, 2017. http://jewcy.com/jewish-arts-and-culture/whats-jewish-werewolves.

Saks, R. Jeffrey. 2013. "Tolkien and the Jews." *Torah Musings*, January 2013. https://www.torahmusings.com/2013/01/tolkien-and-the-jews.

Samberg, Joel. 2000. *Reel Jewish: A Century of Jewish Movies*. New York: Jonathan David Publishers.

Schachner, Nat. 1933a. "Ancestral Voices." *Astounding Stories*, December 1933.

————. 1933b. "The Eternal Dictator." *Wonder Stories*, February 1933.

————. 1935. "I Am Not God." *Astounding*, November 1935.

Schulz, Bruno. (1934) 2018a. "Cinnamon Shops." Translated by Madeline G. Levine. In *Bruno Schulz: Collected Stories*. 45–53. Evanston, IL: Northwestern University Press.

————. (1934) 2018b. "Mannequins." Translated by Madeline G. Levine. In *Bruno Schulz: Collected Stories*. 20–34. Evanston, IL: Northwestern University Press.

————. (1934) 2018c. "Pan." Translated by Madeline G. Levine. In *Bruno Schulz: Collected Stories*. 39–41. Evanston, IL: Northwestern University Press.

————. (1937) 2018a. "The Book." Translated by Madeline G. Levine. In *Bruno Schulz: Collected Stories*. 83–93. Evanston, IL: Northwestern University Press.

————. (1937) 2018b. "Sanatorium Under the Sign of the Hourglass." Translated by Madeline G. Levine. In *Bruno Schulz: Collected Stories*. 185–204. Evanston, IL: Northwestern University Press.

Schwadron, Hannah. 2017. *The Case of the Sexy Jewess*. Oxford: Oxford University Press.

Schwartz, Rabbi Barry. 2016. "One Earth." In *Touching the Face of the Cosmos: On the Intersection of Space Travel and Religion*, edited by Paul Levinson and Michael Waltemathe. 98–102. New Jersey: Connected Editions.

Schwartz, Howard, ed 1988a. "Introduction." In *Lilith's Cave: Jewish Tales of the Supernatural*. 1–19. New York: Harper & Row.

————. 1988b. "Lilith's Cave." In *Lilith's Cave: Jewish Tales of the Supernatural*. 128–130. New York: Harper & Row.

————. 2004a. "Demonic Doubles" In *Tree of Souls*. 230. Oxford: Oxford University Press.

————. 2004b. "The Tzohar." In *Tree of Souls*. 85–88. Oxford: Oxford University Press.

Schweitzer, Darrell. 2018. "The H. G. Wells Problem." *The New York Review of Science Fiction,* February 25, 2018. https://www.nyrsf.com/2018/02/darrell -schweitzer-the-hg-wells-problem.html.

"Science Fiction and Fantasy, Jewish." 2018. Encyclopaedia Judaica. *Encyclopedia.com.*

Scliar, Moacyr. (2000) 2011. *Kafka's Leopards*. Translated by Thomas O. BeeBee. Lubbock, TX: Texas Tech University Press.

Selvinsky, Ilya. (1920) 2007. "Bar Kokhba." Translated by Jaime Goodrich and Maxim D. Shrayer. In *An Anthology of Jewish-Russian Literature, Book One: Centuries of Dual Identity in Prose and Poetry*, edited by Maxim Shrayer. 228–236. Armonk, NY: Sharpe.

Seuss, Dr. (1937) 2013. *To Think that I Saw it on Mulberry Street*. New York: Random House.

————. (1939) 2016. *The King's Stilts*. New York: Random House.

————. (1940) 1968. *Horton Hatches the Egg*. New York: Random House.

————. (1949) 1976. *Bartholomew and the Oobleck*. New York: Random House.

————. (1950) 1986. *Yertle the Turtle and other Stories*. New York: Random House.

————. (1950) 2014. "How Officer Pat Saved the Whole Town." In *Horton and the Kwuggerbug and More Lost Stories*. 10–18. New York: Random House.

————. (1951) 2014. "Horton and the Kwuggerbug." In *Horton and the Kwuggerbug and More Lost Stories*. 10–18. New York: Random House.

———. (1954) 1982. *Horton Hears a Who!* New York: Random House.

———. (1961) 1989. *The Sneeches and other Stories.* New York: Random House.

Shechner, Mark. 1987. "Dear Mr. Einstein: Jewish Comedy and the Contradictions of Culture." In *Jewish Wry: Essays on Jewish Humor*, edited by Sarah Blacher Cohen. 141–157. Bloomington, IL: Indiana University Press.

Shiel, M. P. 1901. *The Lord of the Sea.* London: Grant Richards. *Gutenberg.net,* https://www.gutenberg.org/ebooks/6993.

Shullenberger, Geoffrey. 2013. "Borges's Jewish Uncanny and the Psychoanalytic Other: Uses of Paranoia in 'La Muerte Y la Brujula'" *Chasqui* 42, no. 2 (November): 59–72. Jstor, https://www.jstor.org/stable/43589563?seq=1#page_scan_tab_contents.

Siegel, Jerry (w) and Al Plastino (a). 1962. "One Minute of Doom." In *Superman* #150. New York: DC Comics.

Siegel, Jerry (w) and Joe Shuster (a). 2010. *Funnyman.* Edited by Thomas Andrae and Mel Gordon Port Townsend, WA: Feral House.

Simak, Clifford. 1931. "The World of the Red Sun." *Wonder Stories*, December 1931.

Simon, Joe (w) and Jack Kirby (a). 1941a. "Horror Hospital." In *Captain America* #4. New York: Timely.

———. 1941b. "The Strange Mystery of the Ruby of the Nile and Its Heritage of Horror." In *Captain America* #8. New York: Timely.

Singer, Isaac Bashevis. (1932) 1988. "The Jew from Babylon." In *The Death of Methuselah and Other Stories*, edited by Cynthia Krupat 3–13. New York: Farrar Straus, Giroux.

———. (1955) 1996. *Satan in Goray.* New York: Noonday Press.

———. (1957) 2004. "The Gentleman from Cracow." In *Isaac Bashevis Singer: Collected Stories*, edited by Ilan Stavans. 20–36. New York: Random House.

———. (1970) 1973. "The Lantuch." In *A Crown of Feathers and Other Stories.* 92–101. New York: Farrar, Strauss, and Giroux.

———. 1973. *The Fools of Chelm and their History.* Illustrated by Uri Shulevitz. New York: Farrar, Straus, and Giroux.

———. 1988. "The Death of Methuselah." In *The Death of Methuselah and Other Stories*, edited by Cynthia Krupat 233–244. New York: Farrar Straus, Giroux.

———. 1996. "The Lantuch." In *Stories for Children.* 231–236. New York: Farrar Straus Giroux.

Sokel, Walter H. 1986. "Language and Truth in the Two Worlds of Franz Kafka." In *Modern Critical Views: Franz Kafka*, edited by Harold Bloom. 169–182. New York: Chelsea House.

———. 1999. "Kafka as a Jew" *New Literary History* 30, no. 4, Case Studies (Autumn): 837–853. https://www.jstor.org/stable/20057574.

Spiegelman, Art. 2019. "Art Spiegelman: Golden Age Superheroes Were Shaped by the Rise of Fascism." *The Guardian*, August 17, 2019. https://www.theguardian .com/books/2019/aug/17/art-spiegelman-golden-age-superheroes-were-shaped-by -the-rise-of-fascism.

Stavans, Ilan. 2016a. "Borges's Philo-Semitism." *Jewish Book Council*, November 1, 2016. https://www.jewishbookcouncil.org/pb-daily/borgess-philo-semitism.

———. 2016b. *Borges, the Jew.* New York: State University of New York Press.

Steiner, George. 1992. "Introduction." In *The Trial*, edited by Franz Kafka, v–xviii. New York: Knopf.

Stern, J. P. 1980. "The Matljary Diary." In *The World of Franz Kafka*, edited by J. P. Stern. 238–250. New York: Holt, Rinehart and Winston.

Stoker, Bram. (1897) 2016. *Dracula.* London: Macmillan.

Stolzl, Christoph. 1989. "Kafka: Jew, Anti-Semite, Zionist." In *Reading Kafka*, edited by Mark Anderson. 53–79. New York: Schocken Books.

Stone, Leslie F. (1929a) 2010. "Men with Wings." *Femspec* 11, no. 1: 86–90.

———. 1929b. "Women with Wings." *Air Wonder Stories* 1 (July):58–87.

———. (1931) 2018. "The Conquest of Gola." In *The Future is Female*, edited by Lisa Yaszek. 24–43. New York: Library of America.

Tashlin, Frank and Walter Lang, dir. (1961) 2005. *Snow White and the Three Stooges.* Culver City, CA: 20th Century Fox.

Tenn, William. (1946) 2001. "Child's Play." In *Immodest Proposals*, edited by James A. Mann and Mary C. Tabasko, 251–272. Framingham, MA; NESFA Press.

———. (1966) 1991. "My Mother Was a Witch." In *Smart Dragons, Foolish Elves*, edited by Marty H. Greenberg and Alan Dean Foster. 215–222. New York: Ace.

Thiher, Allen. 1990. *Franz Kafka: A Study of the Short Fiction.* Woodbridges, CT: Twayne.

Thorlby, Anthony. 1980. "Kafka and Language." In *The World of Franz Kafka*, edited by J. P. Stern. 133–144. New York: Holt, Rinehart and Winston.

Tidhar, Lavie. 2013. *The Violent Century.* New York: St. Martin's Press.

Tolkien, Christopher, ed. 1996. *The Peoples of Middle-Earth.* Boston: Houghton Mifflin Co.

Tolkien, John Ronald Reuel. (1937) 1996. *The Hobbit.* New York: Ballantine.

———. (1954) 1994. *The Lord of the Rings.* New York: Houghton Mifflin.

———. (1965) 1979. Interview with Denys Gueroult. *Minas Tirith Evening-Star* 8, no.2 (January).

———. (1977) 2002. *The Silmarillion.* Edited by Christopher Tolkien. New York: Random House.

Tolkien, J. R. R. and John D. Rateliff. 2007. *The History of The Hobbit.* New York: Houghton Mifflin.

Trachtenberg, Joshua. 1939. *Jewish Magic and Superstition: A Study in Folk Religion.* Springfield, NJ: Behrman's Jewish Book House. *The Sacred Texts Archive.* http://www.sacred-texts.com/jud/jms/jms00.htm.

Troen, Saul B. 1994. "Science Fiction and the Reemergence of Jewish Mythology in a Contemporary Literary Genre." Diss. Department of Hebrew and Judaic Culture, New York University.

Tsenzor, Dmitri (1903) 2007. "The Old Ghetto." Translated by Alyssa Dinega Gillespe. In *An Anthology of Jewish-Russian Literature, Book One: Centuries of Dual Identity in Prose and Poetry*, edited by Maxim Shrayer. 144. Armonk, NY: Sharpe.

Urzidil, Johannes. "Two Recollections: Prague, June 11, 1924 and the Golem." In *The World of Franz Kafka*, edited by J. P. Stern. 56–68. New York: Holt, Rinehart and Winston.

Wagenbach, Klaus. 1980. "Kafka's Castle?" In *The World of Franz Kafka*, edited by J. P. Stern. 79–84. New York: Holt, Rinehart and Winston.

Waggner, George, dir. 1941. *The Wolf Man*. Universal City, CA: Universal.

Wagner, Hank, Christopher Golden and Stephen R. Bissette. 2008. *Prince of Stories: The Many Worlds of Neil Gaiman*. New York: St. Martins.

Watson, James Sibley and Melville Webber, dir. (1933) 2017. *Lot in Sodom*. CGiii Film. YouTube.

Wegener, Paul. (1915) 2002. *The Golem*. West Conshohocken, PA: Alpha Video. DVD.

Weilerstein, Sadie Rose. (1935) 1964. *The Adventures of K'tonton; A Little Jewish Tom Thumb*. Illustrated by Jeannette Berkowitz. New York: National Women's League of the United Synagogue.

———. 1942. *What the Moon Brought*. New York: Jewish Publication Society.

———. 1980. *The Best of K'tonton: The Greatest Adventures in the Life of the Jewish Thumbling*. Illustrated by Marilyn Hirsh. New York: Jewish Publication Society.

Weinbaum, Batya. 1998. "Leslie F. Stone's 'Men with Wings' and 'Women with Wings': A Woman's View of War Between the Wars." *Extrapolation* (Kent State University Press) 39, no. 4 (Winter): 299–313.

Weinbaum, Stanley G. (1920) 1969. *The New Adam*. New York: Avon.

———. (1934) 2003. "A Martian Odyssey." In *The Science Fiction Hall of Fame, Vol. 1 1929–1964*, edited by Robert Silverberg. 1–23. New York: Tor.

Weinreich, Beatrice Silverman, ed. 1988a. "The Beggar King and the Melamed." In *Yiddish Folktales*. 77–79. New York: Pantheon Books.

———. 1988b. "How Much Do You Love Me." In *Yiddish Folktales*. 85–88. New York: Pantheon Books.

———. 1988c. "Introduction." In *Yiddish Folktales*. xix–xxxii. New York: Pantheon Books.

———. 1988d. "Little Bean." In *Yiddish Folktales*. 47–49. New York: Pantheon Books.

———. 1988e. "Magic Rings, Feathers of Gold, Mountains of Glass: Wonder Tales." In *Yiddish Folktales*. 65–68. New York: Pantheon Books.

———. 1988f. "Stones and Bones Rattle in my Belly." In *Yiddish Folktales*. 44–45. New York: Pantheon Books.

———. 1988g. "Wisdom or Luck." In *Yiddish Folktales*. 15–18. New York: Pantheon Books.

Weinstein, Simcha. 2006. *Up Up and Oy Vey: How Jewish History, Culture and Values Shaped The Comic-Book Superhero*. Baltimore: Leviathan.

Weiss, Henry George. (Francis Flagg). 1921. "The Synthetic Monster." *Wonder Stories*, March 1921.

Wells, H. G. (1897) 2002. *The Invisible Man*. New York: Signet Classics.

———. (1898) 2018. *The War of the Worlds*. New York: Bantam.

———. (1922) 2000. *A Short History of the World*. Bartleby. https://www.bartleby.com/86.

Werfel, Franz. 1946. *Star of the Unborn*. New York: Viking Press.

Wiernik, Bertha. 1919. "The Menorah Spangled Ship." *Jewish Daily News*, April 23–28, 1919.

White, Jules, dir. 1940. "You Natzey Spy!" *Three Stooges: The Complete DVD Collection.* Culver City, CA: Sony: 2016. DVD.

———. 1941. "I'll Never Heil Again." In *Three Stooges: The Complete DVD Collection.* Culver City, CA: Sony: 2016. DVD.

———. 1943. "Back from the Front." In *Three Stooges: The Complete DVD Collection.* Culver City, CA: Sony: 2016. DVD.

Wilson, Emily. "The Story Behind Rube Goldberg's Complicated Contraptions." *SmithsonianMag.com,* May 1, 2018. https://www.smithsonianmag.com/history/story-behind-rube-goldbergs-complicated-contraptions-180968928/.

Winokur, Mark. 1985. "'Smile, Stranger': Aspects of Immigrant Humor in the Marx Brothers' Humor." *Literature/Film Quarterly* 13, no. 3 (1985): 161–171.

Wise, Irene. 2000. "Images of Anti-Semitism in Nineteenth- and Twentieth-Century Popular Culture." In *Christian-Jewish Relations Through the Centuries,* edited by Brook W. R. Pearson and Stanley E. Sheffield Porter. 329–350. Cambridge, MA: Academic Press.

Wisse, Ruth R. 2000. *The Modern Jewish Canon.* New York: The Free Press.

Wright, Melanie J. 2010. "Judaism." In *The Routledge Companion to Religion and Film,* edited by John Lynden. Philadelphia, PA: Routledge.

Van Der Naillen, Albert. 1925. *The Great Message.* San Francisco: California Press.

Verne, Jules. (1877) 2008. *Off on a Comet or Hector Servadac.* Edited by Charles F. Horne. London: F. Tyler Daniels Company, Inc. Project Gutenberg. https://www.gutenberg.org/files/1353/1353-h/1353-h.htm.

Verrill, A. Hyatt. 1930. "Beyond the Green Prism." *Amazing,* January–February 1930.

———. 1934. "Through the Andes." *Amazing,* September–November 1934.

Von Bernuth, Ruth. 2016. *How the Wise Men Got to Chelm: The Life and Times of a Yiddish Folk Tradition.* New York: New York University Press.

Yamazaki, Ema Ryan, dir. 2017. *Monkey Business: The Adventures of Curious George's Creators.* New York: Busy Monkey. DVD.

Zalmayev, Peter. 2016. "My Path to Bruno Schulz, The Messiah from Drohobych." *The Odessa Review,* August 18, 2016. http://odessareview.com/path-bruno-schulz-messiah-drohobych.

Zangwill, Israel. (1899) 2011. "Noah's Ark." In *Ghetto Tragedies.* Project Gutenberg. http://www.gutenberg.org/files/35076/35076-h/35076-h.htm.

Zipes, Jack. 1980. "Oskar Panizza: The Operated German as Operated Jew." *New German Critique* no. 21 (Autumn): 47–61. Jstor. https://www.jstor.org/stable/487996.

Index

Abraham (biblical), 132
Abraham ibn Ezra, 1, 4
Ackerman, Forrest J., 42, 44
Action Comics, 169
actors, 11, 119, 150, 153, 165
Adam (biblical), 27
Adam and Eve. *See* Eden; Genesis
Aderca, Felix, 102
Africa, 2, 138, 144
African, 21, 22, 83, 102, 153
afterlife, 10, 18, 28, 31, 99
Age of Wonder, 41
Agnon, S. Y., 24, 69, 70, 146, 147, 187
*The Airship or One Hundred Years
    Hence*, 149
Akiva, 62
alienation, 32, 40, 120
aliyah, 96, 188
Allen, Woody, 151, 162
alphabet, 4, 23–26, 28, 85, 97, 147
The Alphabet of Ben Sira, 2
alternate history, 1, 75, 143
Amazing Stories, 35, 39, 41, 169
amulets, 2. See also hamsa
Angel of Death, 20, 132
angels, 1, 2, 8, 19–21, 31, 32, 48, 51,
    62, 85, 92, 98, 99, 101, 124, 128,
    132, 145, 150
Animal Crackers, 152, 153

Ansky, S., 9–11, 17, 61, 101
anti-Fascism, 107, 168, 177
anti-Semitism, 16, 26, 34, 39, 44, 45,
    51, 63–68, 71–75, 80, 81, 83, 97,
    103, 106, 117, 118, 121, 130, 136,
    140, 142, 150, 156, 164, 170, 178,
    185. *See also* racism; Shylock;
    stereotypes
Arabs, 126, 135, 137
Arendt, Hannah, 123
Argentina, 21, 22, 24, 26, 138
Aryan, 54, 57, 67, 69, 83, 161, 178,
    183
Ashkenazi, 8, 13, 21, 35, 70, 145
Asimov, Isaac, 7, 33, 39, 42–58,
    74, 149; and Foundation, 47–48;
    "Nightfall," 49; parody, 49–50;
    Pebble in the Sky, 45–46; and robots,
    45, 47
assimilation, 10, 11, 15, 38, 46, 49, 57,
    65–68, 71, 95, 100, 102, 104–6, 120,
    125, 129, 133, 150, 168, 171, 173,
    177
Astounding Stories, 35, 38, 40, 50, 55
astronomy, 28, 52, 90
Atilla the Hun, 47
atom bomb, 32, 53, 60
Austria, 6, 64, 68, 70, 73, 100, 101, 104,
    105, 128, 161, 170

Baal, 108
Baal Shem Tov, 22, 24
Babel, Isaac, 95
Balaam (biblical), 63
Bambi, 104, 105, 133, 163
Bar Kokhba, 97, 106, 170, 172
Bar Mitzvah, 44, 94
Baron, Dvora, 145
Batman, 169, 170, 174, 177–79
Belgium, 113, 160, 184
Berlin, 72, 73, 155, 159, 182
Bester, Alfred, 41, 56
Betty Boop, 37, 162
bible, 1, 2, 4, 20, 21, 23, 27–37, 48–50,
　　53, 55, 57, 63, 68, 75–79, 85, 86,
　　90–93, 96, 97, 101, 104, 106, 112,
　　123, 136, 137, 147, 150, 168, 178
The Black Cat, 73
Blackhawk, 172
Blanc, Mel, 163
Borges, Jorge Luis, 23–28
Borsht Belt, 152
Brackett, Leigh, 42
Bradbury, Ray, 41, 44
Brazil, 13, 21, 35, 131, 180, 181
Broches, Rochel, 98
Brod, Max, 117, 123, 129, 130, 132
Bucharest, 102, 103
Bugs Bunny, 163
Bulgaria, 68
Bund, 164, 175
Burroughs, Edger Rice, 34

Cain (biblical), 19, 20, 32, 86
California, 105, 149. *See also*
　　Hollywood
Campbell, John W., 40, 42, 44, 190
Canada, 28
Čapek brothers, 7, 106–10
Captain America, 158, 167, 174–76, 189
Carmilla, 65
Catholic, 21, 22, 82, 104, 105, 129
Catskills, 152, 156, 189
Chaplin, Charlie, 97, 151, 156, 158–61
Chelm, 20, 21, 98

Chicago, 96
Chile, 96
China, 58, 109
Christian, 1, 6, 27, 31, 55, 61–65, 67,
　　69, 75–77, 79, 86, 94, 101, 108, 120,
　　122, 136, 172, 180
Cinderella, 61–62
Colonial America, 13
colonialism, 108, 136, 143, 179
comic books, 167, 168, 172, 174, 178,
　　179
Communism, 29, 34, 43, 58, 95, 104,
　　106, 141, 144, 160, 178
concentration camps, 27, 58, 60, 72,
　　103, 132, 143, 160, 161, 176
Curacao, 21
Curious George, 179–81
curses, 3, 14, 19, 52, 111
Czechoslovakia, 7, 100, 106, 108, 109,
　　117, 119, 122

Daniel, biblical, 76
Daredevil, 176
Davidson, Avram, 29, 42
DC Comics, 44, 168, 169
DeMille, Cecil B., 150
demons, 1–4, 8, 9, 14, 15, 18, 19, 21,
　　30, 31, 50, 62, 64, 94, 97, 98, 132
Diamant, Dora, 129, 132
diaspora, 24, 145
Dickens, Charles, 75, 133
dinosaurs, 90
Disney, 11, 104, 161, 163–65; creator,
　　164
Disraeli, Benjamin, 75
divination, 1
Donald Duck, 164
Donnelly, Ignatius, 77
Dracula, 60, 72, 79
Dr. Seuss, 167, 181–85
Duck Soup, 153–54
dwarves, 82–87
dybbuk, 3, 8, 9, 16, 18, 64, 170
dystopia, 33, 34, 77–81, 96, 97, 103,
　　104, 152, 153

Eden, 3, 7, 16, 27, 28, 32, 38, 51, 53, 54, 56, 86, 101, 106, 107, 122, 140, 146; story list, 56
Edison, Thomas, 56, 149
Egypt, 34, 80, 86, 106, 144, 176
Ehrenburg, Ilya, 96
Eichmann, Adolf, 143
Einstein, Albert, 20, 56, 174, 175
Eisner, Will, 40, 168, 172, 177, 178
Eleazar of Worms, 4
elf, 3, 30, 83, 85
Elijah, 29, 30, 36, 61, 62, 75, 98, 99
Elijah of Chelm, 5
epistolary writing, 90–91
Esau (biblical), 5
Esther (biblical), 99, 168
Euchel, Isaac, 90
Ewers, Hans Heinrich, 71–72
exorcism, 9–10

fairytales, 30, 68, 100, 178. *See also* Cinderella; Disney; folklore; The Jew Among Thorns; Snow White; Toads and Diamonds; Tom Thumb; The Wolf and the Seven Kids
false messiah, 19
Fantasy Magazine, 42
Fascism, 39, 57, 72
Feierberg, M. Z., 94
feminism, 8, 10, 18, 53, 89
Fiddler on the Roof, 98, 189
First Fandom, 41
The Flash, 33, 172, 174
Fleisher Studios, 161
folklore, 2, 3, 6–10, 14, 16, 17, 20, 21, 30, 43, 61–65, 73, 92, 93, 98, 99, 101, 123, 180; antisemitic, 64–65. *See also* curses; demons; dwarves; dybbuk; elf; fairytales; ghost; gilgul; goblins; golem; ibbur; jumping the road; kapelyushnikl; lamed vavniks; lantekh, letzim; Leviathan; Lilith; Lost Tribes; River Sambatyon; shretele; werewolf; witch; zmore

France, 38, 66, 73, 105, 143, 159, 160, 181
Frankenstein, 6, 7, 37
Frug, Simon, 94
Funnyman, 173
Futurians, 43, 44, 58

Gaiman, Neil, 82
Gaines, Max, 168
Galicia, 14, 146
Gallun, Raymond Z., 42
gargoyles, 100
gematria, 29. *See also* alphabet
Genesis, 5, 8, 26, 50, 55, 86, 124. *See also* Eden
Germany, 3, 20, 60, 65, 66, 72, 73, 81, 89, 100, 104, 105, 109, 138, 154, 156, 160, 169, 170, 172, 176, 178, 181, 182
Gernsback, Hugo, 41, 42, 73, 190
ghetto, 6, 70, 71, 98, 103, 112, 122, 139, 141, 151, 154, 159–61
ghost, 3, 8, 17–19, 22, 28, 31, 94, 99, 113, 121, 132
gilgul, 3, 98
Gillespie, Jack, 43, 44
Glasser, Allen, 17, 40, 41
goblins, 3, 4, 20, 21
Goebbels, Joseph, 104, 156, 159, 172
Goldberg, Rube, 167
Goldfaden, Avrom, 16
Gold, H. L., 39, 41–43, 52
golem, 4–8, 16, 27, 28, 30, 37, 45, 51, 54, 55, 71, 90, 99, 107, 116, 130, 133; female, 38, 54; and robots, 7; rules, 5; war metaphor, 7, 71
The Golem (film), 6
Goodman, Martin, 174
Göring, Hermann, 156, 159
gothic, 65, 66, 69, 70, 72, 130, 145, 146, 189
Grand Island, 138–39
Great Depression, 17, 151, 153, 168
The Great Dictator, 156, 159–60

Greek myth, 29, 30, 94, 157, 167
Green Lantern, 168, 172, 174, 177
Grifith, George, 77–78
Grimm Brothers, 61, 63, 64
Grossman, Vasily, 97

Haggadot, 167
Haggard, H. Rider, 34, 138, 177
hamsa, 2, 22
Hannukah, 30, 186
Haskalah, 18, 89, 90, 93
Hassidism, 91, 92, 141, 146, 149, 162,
    163
Have Rocket, Will Travel, 157
Hawkman, 168, 172
Hebrew, 4, 8, 14, 23, 30, 35, 36, 48, 59,
    68, 77, 79, 84–86, 89–94, 97, 117,
    135–39, 141–46, 168, 171, 186
Herzl, Theodor, 133, 135–39
Hitler, Adolf, 29, 33, 39, 52, 54, 58, 59,
    66, 73, 80, 81, 108, 109, 134, 143,
    149, 154–56, 159–64, 172, 175, 176,
    180–84; in comics, 174–76; parody,
    156, 159–61, 164, 170, 182–84
holidays. *See* Hannukah; Lag B'Omer;
    Passover; Purim; Shabbat; Shavuot;
    Shmini Atzeret; Sukkot; Tisha B'Av;
    Yom Kippur
Hollywood, 73, 104, 150, 151, 155, 156,
    164, 183
Holocaust, 11, 28, 29, 46, 47, 59, 69,
    96, 103, 110, 113–16, 129, 133, 134,
    137, 147, 163, 173, 176, 180, 189
Hugo Award, 44
Human Torch, 174
Huxley, Aldous, 75, 80–81

ibbur, 71
immigrants, 13–17, 36, 40, 41, 57, 91,
    101, 133, 137, 144, 150, 152, 155,
    164, 169, 170, 174, 178, 179, 186
Industrial Revolution, 39
Inquisition, 21, 79
Intolerance, 150
Isaac (biblical), 85, 128, 137

Israel, 24, 29, 46, 48, 76, 86, 91, 95,
    110, 130, 133–36, 177, 188; early
    literature, 144–45; founding, 29, 137

Jabotinsky, Vladimir, 97
The Jazz Singer, 150
Jesus, 31, 34, 38, 65, 66
The Jew Among Thorns, 64
Jewish Autonomous Region, 95
Jewish fantasy. *See* amulets; angels;
    curses; divination; dybbuk; ghost;
    gilgul; goblins; golem; ibbur;
    jumping the road; lamed vavniks;
    lantekh; letzim; Leviathan; Lilith;
    Lost Tribes; River Sambatyon;
    shretele; spellbooks; superstition;
    werewolf; witch; zmore
Jewish humor, 50, 151, 152, 155, 162,
    173
Jewish mother, 45, 48, 104, 162, 186
Jewish National Fund, 136, 188
Jonah (biblical), 21, 31, 32
Joshua (biblical), 104
Judea, 45, 46, 48
jumping the road, 92
Justice Society, 172, 177

Kabbalah, 22–26, 91, 120, 128
kabbalists, 2, 8, 25, 26, 48, 55, 71, 79
Kafka, Franz, 24, 96, 106, 115–33, 189;
    Amerika, 123, 124, 133; *The Castle*,
    123, 127–29; as fantasy subject,
    130–33; "Josephine the Singer," 119,
    132; "The Judgement, 37, 121, 125;
    "Metamorphosis," 106, 120; *The
    Trial*, 121–24, 128, 129, 133
kapelyushnikl, 3
Kiev, 98, 100
kindertransports, 173
Kipnis, Levin, 144–45
Kirby, Jack, 174–76, 178
Klein, Abraham Moses, 28–29
Knight, Daemon, 43
Ko-Ko the Clown, 162
Kornbluth, Cyril, 42–43, 55, 58–60

kosher, 59, 65, 69, 99, 152
Krakow, 62
Kraus, Karl, 104
Kreitman, Esther Singer, 18
K'tonton, 185–87
Kulisher, Ruvim, 94
Kuttner, Henry, 38, 41, 42, 52, 53

Ladino, 68
Lag B'Omer, 99, 140
lamed vavniks, 16, 63, 101, 106
Lang, Fritz, 104
lantekh, 3
Lasser, David, 41
Latin America, 21–24
Lazarus, Emma, 13
Lee, Stan, 172, 174, 176
Leivick, H., 7, 97, 98
Lenin, Vladimir, 38
letzim, 4
Leviathan, 4, 97
Levitsky Sees the Parade, 149
Levy, Amy, 78
Lilith, 2–4, 19, 22, 32, 53, 56, 57, 106
Linyetski, Y. Y., 92
Lithuania, 15, 92, 101, 141
Loew, Rabbi Judah, 5, 7, 28, 55
Lost Tribes, 2, 35, 36, 76, 91, 99, 139
lost world, 34–36, 114, 189
Lot in Sodom, 150
Lovecraft, H. P., 9, 23, 34, 41, 71
Lower East Side, 15, 153, 175
Lowndes, Robert, 43–44
Lugosi, Bela, 73

mad scientists, 37
Madagascar, 143
magazines, 33, 40, 42, 43, 169
magic. *See* amulets; curses; divination;
    exorcism; golem; jumping the road;
    possession; spellbooks; witch
magical creatures. *See* angels; demons;
    dwarves; dybbuk; elf; ghost; gilgul;
    goblin; golem; ibbur; lantekh; letzim;
    Leviathan; shretele; werewolf; zmore

magical realism, 23, 132
Manger, Itzik, 101
Marvel Comics, 174
Marx Brothers, 151–56
Maud, Zuni, 168
Mayakovsky, Vladimir, 96
Mayer, Sheldon, 172
medieval, 1, 2, 9, 39, 66, 68, 83
Meek, S. P., 35
melodrama, 16, 70, 150
Mendele Mokher Sefarim, 93, 99
Merril, Judith, 42, 43, 53
Messiah, 7, 19, 29, 36, 76, 78, 112–16,
    119, 139, 142, 147, 172
Metropolis, 73, 103
Mexico, 21–23, 71, 96
Meyrink, Gustav, 6, 70
Michel, John, 42–44
Mickey Mouse, 163
Middle Eastern, 2, 13. *See also*
    Muslim
midrashim, 86, 122
Minsk, 98, 100, 171
modernism, 29, 102, 147
Mohammad, 38
Moore, C. L., 38, 52, 53
Moroccan, 22
Moscow, 100
Moses (biblical), 106, 132, 170, 171
Moskowitz, Sam, 41–44
muscular Jews, 158, 170, 176
Muslim, 13, 101, 135
Mussolini, Benito, 38, 154, 156, 159

Nadir, Moyshe, 14
Namor the Sub-Mariner, 174
Nathan, Robert, 13, 30, 32
nationalism, 79, 102, 107, 109, 115,
    117, 154
Nazis, 24, 26, 29, 33, 39, 52, 54, 55,
    58, 69, 72, 73, 83, 97, 105, 107, 109,
    110, 113, 114, 133, 143, 144, 155,
    156, 159–61, 164, 170, 172–83
Nesbit, E., 79–80
New Christians, 21

New York, 17, 20, 40, 43, 44, 49–53,
55, 61, 100, 101, 130, 152, 157,
160–63, 167, 169, 175–78, 181, 186
A Night in Casablanca, 155
Noah (biblical), 19, 86, 89, 90, 124
Noah, Mordechai Manuel, 13, 138, 139
Nobel Prize, 17, 95, 134, 146
Norse myth, 83, 167
Nosferatu, 72

Olesha, Yuri, 97
Oliver Twist, 149
oral Torah, 47
Orwell, George, 75, 81

pagan, 2, 29, 47, 57, 110
Pale of Settlement, 92
Palestine, 37, 76, 77, 100, 126, 133–37,
140–42, 144, 146, 186
Passover, 29, 33, 59, 145, 187, 188
Perelman, Yakov, 95
Peretz, I. L., 99, 100, 123, 141
Perl, Joseph, 91
Peru, 35
picture books, 113, 144, 179, 181, 184,
188
Pines, Ned, 41
poems, 14–16, 32, 106, 131, 144
pogroms, 5, 10, 27, 36, 79, 80, 92–96,
98, 103, 138, 170, 187
Pohl, Fredrick, 40, 43, 44, 60
Poland, 10, 18–22, 60, 69, 74, 90, 92,
98–102, 110, 114, 143, 146, 170;
children's literature, 100
Popeye, 37, 162
portal fantasy, 2, 14, 146
Portugal, 13, 22, 24
possession, 8–10, 94, 128, 170
post-Holocaust, 17, 46, 98, 145, 147
post-modernism, 132
Prague, 5, 26, 70, 71, 115, 117–20, 123,
126, 129–34
Pratchett, Terry, 86–87
prayer, 4–6, 29, 59, 94, 119, 124, 125,
132, 147, 148, 150

propaganda, 46, 78, 83, 133, 156, 163,
172, 174, 183
Pulitzer Prize, 168
pulps, 34, 35, 37, 41–44, 58, 74
Purim, 17, 20, 69, 186

Questel, Mae, 162

racism, 33, 45–47, 59, 65–67, 76,
80–82, 101, 104, 106, 117, 120, 150,
151, 161, 164, 171, 179, 185, 190.
See also anti-Semitism; Shylock;
stereotypes
Ragnarök, 29
Rambam, 22
riddles, 63, 99
River Sambatyon, 15, 20, 36, 91, 93, 99
robots, 7, 45, 47, 55, 107, 190
Romania, 78, 79, 100, 102, 103
Romans, 1, 17, 38, 39, 45, 97
Rousseau, Victor, 78
R.U.R. (Rostrum's Universal Robots),
7, 107
Russia, 7, 9, 13, 16, 36, 41, 44, 49, 56,
58, 77, 79, 84, 92–97, 101, 104, 110,
131, 137, 140–42, 168, 174
Russian Revolution, 7, 13, 95

Salome, 38
Salten, Felix, 104, 105, 133, 163
Samson (biblical), 75, 78, 97, 170
Satan, 16, 19, 30, 73, 79, 94, 187
satire, 17, 19, 52, 54, 60, 67, 77, 91, 93,
94, 96, 101, 103, 107–9, 112, 118,
139, 154, 183, 189
scapegoating, 6, 81, 122, 147
Schachner, Nat, 42, 55, 57, 58
Schulz, Bruno, 102, 110–16
Schwartz, Julius, 40, 41, 106, 174
Scienceers, 40
Science Fiction League, 41, 43
Science Wonder Stories, 41
scientists, 28, 36, 37, 39, 48, 58, 59, 66,
103, 155, 157, 188
sea monster, 21

secret identity, 169
Sefer Yezirah, 4, 5, 26, 27
Selvinsky, Ilya, 97
Sephardic, 13, 30, 68, 138
sexism, 2, 8, 9, 55
Shabbat, 2, 10, 15, 59, 61, 91, 147, 186–88
Shabbtai Zvi, 19
The Shadow, 34
Shavuot, 187–88
Shazam, 177
Sheckley, Robert, 42
Sheena the Jungle Girl, 177
Shekhina, 19, 27
The Shield, 176
Shiel, M. P., 142
Sh'ma, 69, 139, 187
Shmini Atzeret, 187
shofar, 2, 30, 34, 99, 187
Sholem Aleichem, 98, 99, 123, 138, 189
shretele, 3, 4
Shteinberg, Ya'akov, 145
shtetl, 10, 16, 17, 21, 44, 69, 98, 114, 118, 127
Shuster, Joe, 169, 170, 173
Shylock, 37, 46, 75, 77, 92, 149
Siegel, Jerome, 169–73
Silberkleit, Louis, 41
silent films, 151
Simak, Clifford, 51–52
Simeon Bar Yochai, 188
Simon, Joe, 174, 175
Singer, Isaac Bashevis, 3, 4, 9, 17–21, 62, 102, 110, 112–14, 146
Singer, Israel Joshua, 7
Siodmak, Curt, 42, 73
Slonimski, Antoni, 102
Slonimski, Hayim, 90
Snow White, 62, 157
socialism, 20, 77, 79, 95, 103, 129, 135
Solomon (biblical), 15, 17, 34, 76, 86, 138, 140
Soviet Union, 95, 100, 141
space race, 95, 157
Spain, 13, 91
The Spectre, 172

spellbooks, 2
Spider-Man, 170
The Spirit, 178
Stalin, Joseph, 74, 81, 95, 170
stereotypes, 33–35, 38, 48, 51, 65–69, 72, 74, 75, 77–80, 83, 105–8, 118, 127, 142, 149–51, 153, 162, 163, 173, 186, 187
Stone, Leslie F., 54
The Story of Mankind, 155
Sukkot, 186–87
Supergirl, 173
Superman, 158, 167, 169–77, 189
superstition, 2, 8, 14, 16, 27, 93, 132
sword and sorcery, 34, 38
synagogue, 13, 16, 22, 23, 30, 31, 44, 70, 89, 94, 97, 126–30, 146

Talmud, 2, 4, 5, 16, 36, 45, 59, 61, 83, 86, 92, 100, 120, 122, 123, 130, 170, 187, 188
Tarzan, 33, 34, 144, 169, 170
Temple: First, 37, 86, 138; Second, 5, 36; Third, 37, 135
Temple Mount, 37, 82
Tenn, William, 14, 42, 50
Tesla, Nicola, 95
The Three Little Pigs, 163
The Three Stooges, 149, 152, 155–58, 163, 189
time travel, 38, 46, 57, 80, 102, 157
Tisha B'Av, 82, 146, 188
Toads and Diamonds, 62
Tolkien, J. R. R., 82–86
Tom Thumb, 62, 185, 187
Torah, 5, 8, 16, 22, 36, 55, 71, 90, 147, 186. *See also* bible
Tower of Babel, 124
travelogues, 2, 90, 91, 93, 123
tree of life, 97
Trilby, 79, 149
Tsenzor, Dmitri, 94
Turkey, 13
tzadik, 1, 2, 4–7, 11, 22, 28, 101
tzohar, 86

Uganda Plan, 138
Ukraine, 28, 92, 93, 110, 140, 141, 144, 146
utopia, 54, 58, 74, 76, 77, 90, 105, 106, 135–42, 144

vaudeville, 151, 152, 156, 162
Verne, Jules, 39, 74, 100
Vilna, 61, 100, 171
Vrchlický, J., 106

Wagner, Richard, 29, 82, 83
Wandering Jew, 29, 37, 38, 65, 66, 69, 79, 93, 101; fiction list, 65–66
Warner Brothers, 150, 163
Warsaw, 17, 21, 89, 100, 101, 143, 145, 171
wedding, 2, 10, 18, 19, 61, 67–70, 100, 105, 120, 132, 152
Wegener, Paul, 6, 71
Weilerstein, Sadie Rose, 186–88
Weinbaum, Stanley, 41, 42, 52, 56
Weinshall, Jacob, 143
weird fiction, 9, 23, 71, 189
Weird Tales, 34, 53, 169
Weisinger, Mort, 40, 41, 173
Weiss, Henry George, 37
Wells, H. G., 30, 39, 74, 75, 100, 102
werewolf, 17, 68, 73, 97, 98, 190; medieval Jewish, 68
Werfel, Franz, 105
Wertham, Fredrick, 178
Wiernik, Bertha, 141
Wirt, William, 37
witch, 14, 16, 18, 19, 30, 32, 63, 94
The Wolf and the Seven Kids, 63

The Wolf Man, 73
Wollheim, Donald A., 42–44
WorldCon, 43–44
World War I, 6, 7, 61, 73, 100, 104, 107, 144, 153, 154, 160, 176, 180, 181
World War II, 24, 28, 33, 40, 74, 86, 132, 153, 156, 161, 167, 172, 175

Yad v'Shem, 110
Yenne Velt, 9
Yeshiva, 40, 94, 123
Yhyoyesh, 15
Yiddish, 5, 11, 13, 15, 17, 21, 24, 26–30, 32, 34, 40, 42, 76, 90, 118, 120, 122, 144, 156, 164, 166, 168, 175, 177, 179, 181, 185; comics, 167–68; film, 101; literature, 17, 93, 99; news, 15–16, 95, 100, 159; novels, 15, 17, 189; radio, 16; schools, 100; science fiction, 17, 36; theater, 6, 15, 16, 20, 95, 100, 119, 123; Yiddishisms, 47, 52, 105
Yiddish Book Center, 17
The Yiddish Queen Lear, 101
YIVO Institute for Jewish Research, 61
Yom Kippur, 19, 33, 45, 97, 147, 187

Zangwill, Israel, 15, 78, 139, 140
Ziff, Bernard, 41
Zingman, Kalmen, 140–41
Zionism, 28, 59, 76, 77, 82, 91, 104, 120, 130, 133–44
zmore, 4
zombies, 100

About the Author

Valerie Estelle Frankel has won a Dream Realm Award, an Indie Excellence Award, and a *USA Book News* National Best Book Award for her Henry Potty parodies. Her *Chelm for the Holidays* was a PJ Library chapter book in 2019. She's the author of over eighty books on pop culture, including *Hunting for Meaning in The Mandalorian*; *Inside the Captain Marvel Film*; *Star Wars Meets the Eras of Feminism*; and *Who Tells Your Story? History, Pop Culture, and Hidden Meanings in Hamilton*. Many of her books focus on women's roles in fiction, from her heroine's journey guides *From Girl to Goddess* and *Buffy and the Heroine's Journey* to books like *Superheroines and the Epic Journey* and *The Many Faces of Katniss Everdeen*. Once a lecturer at San Jose State University, she now teaches at Mission College and San Jose City College and speaks often at conferences. Come explore her research at www.vefrankel.com